Literature as Moral Philosophy

ALSO AVAILABLE FROM BLOOMSBURY:

Iris Murdoch and the Ancient Quarrel, Lyra Ekström Lindbäck
Moral Matters, Mark Dooley
Undoing the Moral Empire, Lesley Chamberlain

Literature as Moral Philosophy

Edited by
Grace Whistler

BLOOMSBURY ACADEMIC
LONDON • NEW YORK • OXFORD • NEW DELHI • SYDNEY

BLOOMSBURY ACADEMIC
Bloomsbury Publishing Plc, 50 Bedford Square, London, WC1B 3DP, UK
Bloomsbury Publishing Inc, 1359 Broadway, New York, NY 10018, USA
Bloomsbury Publishing Ireland, 29 Earlsfort Terrace, Dublin 2, D02 AY28, Ireland

BLOOMSBURY, BLOOMSBURY ACADEMIC and the Diana logo are trademarks of Bloomsbury Publishing Plc

First published in Great Britain 2026

Cover design:
Cover image by DeAgostini via Getty Images

A catalogue record for this book is available from the British Library.

A catalog record for this book is available from the Library of Congress.

ISBN: HB: 978-1-3504-5614-3
PB: 978-1-3504-5613-6
ePDF: 978-1-3504-5615-0
eBook: 978-1-3504-5616-7

Typeset by Newgen KnowledgeWorks Pvt. Ltd., Chennai, India
Printed and bound in Great Britain

For product safety related questions contact productsafety@bloomsbury.com.

CONTENTS

Notes on Contributors vii
Preface xi

Editor's introduction 1
Grace Whistler

Part One: Literature as Argument

1 Reading as a way of seeing: Literature and the perception of place 11
Ghazouane Arslane

2 'My non-alibi in being': Bakhtinian ethics and the literary dynamics of subjectivity 33
Daphna Erdinast-Vulcan

3 Cows on the highroad: Making ethical literary criticism real 51
John Krapp

Part Two: Literature for Moral Growth

4 Community, self, trust and shared reality in Alice Munro's 'Fits' 77
Nora Hämäläinen

5 'A match in a dark wilderness': Philosophy, literature and morality 97
Christopher Hamilton

6 Ways of flourishing: Literature and moral philosophy 123
Anthony J. Cascardi

7 The ethics of narrative art: Philosophy in schools, compassion and learning from stories 137
Laura D'Olimpio and Andrew Peterson

Part Three: The Genres of Philosophy

8 The literary evolution of the philosophical metaphor of *theatrum mundi* 157
Sophie Bastien

9 The dream of reason: Giannina Braschi's ethics of in-betweenness 179
Grace Whistler

10 The sorrow of the lone one: Existential despair in Mary Shelley's *The Last Man* 195
Katalin Nun Stewart

11 'The salamander of the human soul': The melodrama of scepticism in Dostoevsky and Tarkovsky 217
Stephen Mulhall

Notes 239
Further reading 275
Index 277

NOTES ON CONTRIBUTORS

Ghazouane Arslane is an assistant professor of Arabic and Comparative Literature at Tulane University, US. He completed a PhD in Comparative Literature from Queen Mary University of London in 2020. His research focuses on the relationship between aesthetics, ethics and politics in modern and contemporary Arab literature and in world literature and cinema. He has contributed essays, articles and translations to *Journal of Arabic Literature*, *Life Writing*, *Philosophy East and West* and *Asymptote*. His first monograph is *Gibran Khalil Gibran as Arab World Literature* (2024).

Sophie Bastien is a full professor at the Royal Military College of Canada (in Kingston, Ontario), where she has worked for twenty-two years. Bastien edited the issue *La Scène surréaliste* of *L'Annuaire théâtral* (no. 59, 2016) and co-edited four collections of essays: *Postérité d'Albert Camus* (2024), *Camus l'artiste* (2015), *Le Surréalisme et les arts du spectacle* (2014) and *La Passion du théâtre: Camus à la scène* (2011). Her monograph *Caligula et Camus: Interférences transhistoriques* won the Canadian Association of University French Professors Award. She also has over sixty journal articles and book chapters to her credit.

Anthony J. Cascardi is Sidney and Margaret Ancker Distinguished Professor and former Dean of Arts and Humanities at the University of California, Berkeley. Among his numerous books are *Consequences of Enlightenment* (1999), *The Cambridge Introduction to Literature and Philosophy* (2014), *Cervantes, Literature, and the Discourse of Politics* (2012) and *Francisco de Goya and the Art of Critique* (2023). He currently serves as the general editor of the *Cambridge Studies in Literature and Philosophy*.

Laura D'Olimpio is Associate Professor of Philosophy of Education at the University of Birmingham, UK, and co-editor of the open access *Journal of Philosophy in Schools*. Her first book, *Media and Moral Education: A Philosophy of Critical Engagement* (2018) won the Philosophy of Education Society of Australasia's annual book prize. Her other publications include *Educating Character through the Arts* (2023, co-edited), a public philosophy book, *Short Cuts: Philosophy* (2023), and her second monograph, *The Necessity of Aesthetic Education: The Place of the Arts on the Curriculum* (2024). Laura regularly contributes to *The Conversation* and *Philosopher's Zone*.

Daphna Erdinast-Vulcan is Professor of English (emerita) at the University of Haifa, Israel, and the 2013 winner of the *Ian Watt Award* of the Joseph Conrad Society in America. Her publications include *Graham Greene's Childless Fathers* (1988), *Joseph Conrad and the Modern Temper* (1991), *The Strange Short Fiction of Joseph Conrad: Writing, Culture, and Subjectivity* (1999), *Between Philosophy and Literature: Bakhtin and the Question of the Subject* (2014) and *Joseph Conrad: The Short Fiction* (2004, co-edited). Her research interests include Conrad, Bakhtin, literary modernism, the intersections of literature and historiography, psychoanalysis, ethnography and, most recently, the theoretical concept of 'hetero-biography'.

Christopher Hamilton is Professor of Philosophy at King's College London. He works in philosophy mainly from an interdisciplinary perspective, exploring philosophical problems in the context of literature, autobiography, biography and film. He has published his work in ethics, aesthetics and philosophy of religion and on Nietzsche, Simone Weil, Walter Benjamin and other thinkers. His most recent books are *Philosophy and Autobiography: Reflections on Truth, Self-Knowledge and Knowledge of Others* (2021) and *Rapture* (2024). At present he is working on questions of human vulnerability and woundedness, taking the writings of Primo Levi as a starting point.

John Krapp is Associate Professor of Comparative Literature at Hofstra University. His primary interest is the conversation between art and philosophy, particularly the way literature dramatizes how human values are created, sustained, challenged and reconfigured. His articles have appeared in *Mosaic*, *Studies in Twentieth Century Literature*, *Texas Studies* *in Literature and Language*, *the minnesota review* and *The University of Toronto Quarterly*, among others. 'Apathy and the Politics of Identity' was included in *Modern Critical Interpretations: One Hundred Years of Solitude*. He is currently completing a book on the forms of evil.

Stephen Mulhall is Professor of Philosophy and the Russell H. Carpenter Fellow in Philosophy at New College, Oxford. His research interests include Wittgenstein, Heidegger and Nietzsche, the relation between philosophy and religion, and the relation between philosophy and the arts (especially literature and film). His most recent books are *The Ascetic Ideal: Genealogies of Life-Denial in Religion, Morality, Art, Science and Philosophy* (2021) and *In Other Words: Transpositions of Philosophy in J. M. Coetzee's* 'Jesus' *Trilogy* (2022).

Katalin Nun Stewart is a scholar, editor and graphic designer. She works at the Institute of Philosophy at the Slovak Academy of Sciences in Bratislava and received her PhD in German studies at the Goethe University in Frankfurt, Germany. Her publications include *Mädchenleben in Ost und West: DDR, Ungarn, Bundesrepublik Deutschland* (2001) and *Women of the Danish Golden Age: Literature and Theater and the Emancipation of Women* (2013). Her main areas of research include the history of women in Denmark in the nineteenth century and German and Hungarian youth literature in its social-political context from 1945 to 1989.

Andrew Peterson is Professor of character and citizenship education and is the Deputy Director of the Jubilee Centre for Character and Virtues, University of Birmingham. He is the editor of the *British Journal of Educational Studies* and co-editor of the *Journal of Philosophy in Schools*. His research concentrates on the connections between character and citizenship education, particularly on the nature of civic virtues and their education in schools. His books have covered educational ideas and themes covering compassion, civility and global citizenship among others.

Grace Whistler is an author, osteopath, researcher, editor and yoga teacher. She gained her PhD in Philosophy at the University of York. Her publications include the monograph *Camus' Literary Ethics: Between Form and Content* (2020) as well as numerous articles in academic journals, such as *Literature and Theology*, *Journal of Life Writing*, the *Journal of Camus*

Studies, *Clio*, and edited collections, including *Brill's Companion to Camus* (2019), for which she contributed the opening chapter on 'The Absurd'. Her research interests (both in arts and sciences) encompass narrative, ethics, mortality, pain and trauma.

PREFACE

It is hugely exciting for me as an editor to be bringing together this incredible group of authors on a topic close to my heart. The volume was dreamt up close to a decade ago, while I was writing my PhD thesis on Albert Camus, delineating what I saw to be his unique contribution to philosophical and ethical writing. Like many readers, I discovered Camus in my youth, but unlike many others, his writings stayed with me way beyond the angst of adolescence. I saw in Camus a defiant optimism – one that only comes across fully if we delve into the process of his writing. I aimed to show that Camus had distinct philosophical and ethical ideas which he believed could only be properly communicated by straying from the well-trodden path of the philosophical treatise. And so, I set about unpacking his inspiration, style and methodology as a means of bringing to light what I felt to be an oft-overlooked, yet fundamental, aspect to his work. The culmination of this research was my 2020 monograph, *Camus' Literary Ethics: Between Form and Content*, and what fun it was to immerse myself in the world and life of Albert Camus. I got to live in Paris, the city where he made his name, to trace his *pied noir* routes on Algerian soil, to drink tea in his study with his daughter Catherine and to give myself a headache trying to discern his terrible handwriting at the archives in Aix-en-Provence. But while I tried to remain faithful during this labour of love, like many researchers, I had a wandering eye for other projects, other authors. I knew that what I was claiming was special about Camus could also be said of many other authors.

It was during this period that I first approached Bloomsbury with the idea for this volume – and the idea has stayed with me throughout emergence of one global pandemic and two babies as well as numerous smaller hurdles to reaching the press at long last. I knew that so many esteemed researchers had 'had it out' over the possibility of reading literature for moral and philosophical content, and while, at the time, I was pretty determined about my own stance in this, I thought it would be wonderful to bring together other voices, both established and fresh, arguing for or against this practice, tracing its history or just hoping (as I had with Camus) to unearth some really exciting efforts of authors to tackle moral problems with creative writing. The final product is an eclectic and, by no means, exhaustive collection of essays from a truly wonderful selection of authors. And while I have mellowed somewhat in my claims about philosophy and literature since the publication of my previous book, it nevertheless brings me such excitement to present this volume to you, the reader, and I hope you will enjoy the journey of discovery reading these essays in situ as much as I have.

Editor's introduction

Grace Whistler

The present volume revolves around the central question of whether literature (however we may define it) is an appropriate medium for approaching moral philosophy and/or ethical problems – or more radically, whether one might successfully read literary texts *qua* philosophy. Readers of this volume will likely be aware that much has already been said about this topic within academic publishing (indeed I myself have written a monograph on the subject),[1] so rather than delve too deeply into what has been said before, I have chosen to begin with the following quote: 'Poetry is language against which you have no defences.'[2] These words come from contemporary poet-philosopher, David Whyte – a voice grounded in creative praxis, outside the echo chamber of academic philosophy. And while Whyte isn't specifically talking about ethics or even philosophy here, I believe he is communicating an idea which will echo throughout many of the following chapters – that there is something special about the way we are present when we engage with literary works.

That is not to say that the contributors to what follows are in agreement on the matter – in fact, they precisely aren't, which makes for much better reading. Some follow Martha Nussbaum, who argued that the reading of literary texts 'develops moral capacities without which citizens will not succeed in making reality out of the normative conclusions of any moral or political theory, however excellent'.[3] Others are indeed more closely aligned with Richard Posner, who famously claimed quite the converse: 'Cultured people are not on the whole morally superior to philistines. Immersion in literature and art can breed rancorous and destructive feelings of personal superiority, alienation, and resentment.'[4] Nevertheless, the authors who have come together here to discuss this topic take seriously the unique role that literature specifically, and the arts more generally, play in helping us to understand and cope with what it means to be human. Whether or not they conclude that we should seek out the moral content of works of art we engage with, and attempt to better ourselves by it, the attention, insight and care the enclosed essays pay to the topic and the works studied herein are testament to the centrality of the arts in human experience and development.

One of my hopes for this volume, as its editor, was that, not only would it *be about* different genres and styles of philosophical writing, it would also, to some extent, *consist of* different genres and styles of philosophical writing – addressing its focus in form as well as content. As such, what follows is a delightfully eclectic mix of approaches – from scholarly case studies of works and motifs to conversational and exploratory reflections on encounters with texts, and even theories of teaching praxis. The volume also brings together perspectives from backgrounds just as diverse, including specialists well established in the field, young scholars breaking new ground, contributions from adjacent disciplines and contemporary voices from the Middle East, Europe, North Africa and the Americas.

It should also be noted that many chapters, rather than focussing explicitly on the relationship between moral philosophy and literature as such, focus on issues which they take to be intrinsically relevant to literature's value as a vehicle for moral philosophy (e.g. the fundamentality of moral discourse within communities for Hämäläinen, moral personhood as always in formation for D'Olimpio and Peterson, the importance of confronting alterity in Erdinast-Vulcan's essay, or performativity in Bastien's). This highlights a central uncertainty within the very practice of reading literature for moral content – that certain themes in literature will be incontrovertibly morally salient to some readers, while other readers may be more receptive to direct modes of addressing philosophical content. This inherent conflict will perhaps never be resolved, but the chapters that follow will certainly provide much food for thought to those readers concerned with doing so.

Part One of this volume is entitled 'Literature as Argument', and while it would be reductive to interpret such a title too literally, this section does look at literature's potential to critique, argue and persuade – whether explicitly or implicitly. The authors in this section provide evidence that literary writers devise their own ways of 'doing' philosophy. Ghazouane Arslane argues that the capacity of literature to see, with language, what is experienced in lived reality but remains unarticulated is what makes it, among other things, ethically engaging and unique. Arslane's essay illustrates this argument by focusing on the representation of place in novels as diverse as Virginia Woolf's *Mrs Dalloway*, Tahar Wattar's *The Earthquake* and Mourid Barghouti's *I Saw Ramallah*, in addition to Abdelfattah Kilito's story 'A Season in the Hammam'. Arslane suggests that to read is to see in a novel or different way, to experience place in an intimate manner. According to Arslane, this may enable a more sensitive and thoughtful – more ethical – connection to place, in that we see the places we live in and those we discover with the conscious or subconscious effects that the reading leaves behind, with a poetic mode of perception. That is, this essay argues, how literature can produce an ethics of place.

Daphna Erdinast-Vulcan's contribution offers a discussion of the architectonics of subjectivity, distilled from the philosophical work of Mikhail Bakhtin. It sets out from the distinction between 'moral philosophy' as a normative code, abstracted, illustrated or thematized in and through literary texts, and Bakhtin's conception of ethics as a reading of oneself in relation to alterity, best exemplified in his reading of Dostoevsky's 'small-scale Copernican revolution'. Erdinast-Vulcan shows how Bakhtin's conception of ethical subjectivity as singular, embodied and historically contextualized may be read both as an early precursor of the 'narrative identity' thesis and as a modified rendering of the Formalist conceptions of 'habituation' and 'defamiliarization'. Its relevance in the present context calls for a shift from *thematics* to *poetics*, and a focus on the discursive strategies which galvanize the reader's mode of ethical engagement. Erdinast-Vulcan highlights the significance of this shift in some concluding comments on Achebe's critique of Conrad's *Heart of Darkness*.

Referencing literature of antiquity and Arthur Miller's *The Crucible*, John Krapp compares monistic and dualistic moral landscapes to commend the contemporary value of ethical literary criticism. Krapp does this by exploring how forms of community are disrupted when certainty is thrown into doubt, and by discussing the ethically instructive dimension of the deliberations and negotiations required to re-establish form.

Part Two revolves around the topic of 'Literature for Moral Growth'. Arguably, all great novels contain moral content – but whether or not reading them can make us better people is the question at the foundation of this section. Here Nora Hämäläinen offers a refreshingly reflective reading of Alice Munro's short story, 'Fits', based on her experiences of teaching the text to MA students who predominantly had little background in either literature or philosophy. Here, Hämäläinen candidly addresses the key characters in this short story as people with inner lives, histories, significant relations, emotional temperaments and intellectual hang-ups: people whose 'lives' we can talk about in order to get clearer about some points of moral life or philosophy. Drawing on examples from the text, she identifies three constitutive relations in ethical life: between the self to the other, the self to oneself, and the self to the larger collective; its shared language, norms, shared habits and forms of meaning-making.

Conversely, Christopher Hamilton argues that there is little plausibility in the claim that literature can educate us morally. He suggests that, if there is any truth in the claim in question, it is merely a matter of hope, not assurance, and one likely, generally speaking, to remain unfulfilled. Hamilton goes on to argue that philosophy, despite its claims to the contrary, cannot solve the fundamental questions it poses and that, when it deals with literature, it should accept the latter's willingness to acknowledge our incapacity to answer those questions, rather than seeking to press it into its own image. Hamilton suggests that philosophy would do well to learn from this acknowledgement on literature's part and goes on to sketch briefly what such a philosophy might look like.

Anthony J. Cascardi also addresses the claim that reading literature might make us better human beings, suggesting that most efforts to substantiate this claim flounder, and for several reasons. Cascardi argues that there is no empirical evidence to suggest that such claims are true, and that indeed there is some non-trivial evidence to the contrary. When it comes to sheer matters of content, Cascardi claims, there is so much literature that is other than 'exemplary' that we would be hard-pressed to claim that we are made better because of the models that literature presents. This leaves us, according to him, to appeal with the more plausible idea that literature makes us better human beings by developing some of the capacities that make us truly human. This is the claim that Cascardi develops in this essay, suggesting that there is a fundamental, indeed, *necessary*, circularity in the argument that the capacities literature cultivates are the ones that make us most human.

Following neo-Aristotelians Alasdair MacIntyre and Martha Nussbaum, Laura D'Olimpio and Andrew Peterson claim in their chapter that humans are storytelling animals who learn from the stories of diverse others. They suggest that moral agents use rational emotions, such as compassion, to imaginatively reconstruct others' thoughts, feelings and goals, and that in turn, this imaginative reconstruction plays a crucial role in deliberating and discerning how to act. In this chapter, taking compassion as an illustrative focus, D'Olimpio and Peterson examine the ways that students' moral education might usefully develop from engaging with narrative artworks. They argue that narrative artworks provide useful stimulus material to engage students, generate student questions, and motivate philosophical dialogue and the formation of good habits, which, in turn, supports the argument for philosophy to be taught in schools.

Part Three takes a look at some of the possible 'Genres of Philosophy'. Inviting diversity into philosophical writing opens a world of possibility, and the writers in this section explore how works as diverse as poetry, theatre and film can do the work of philosophizing. In her enclosed chapter, Sophie Bastien demonstrates how the metaphor of *theatrum mundi* represents a conception of existence with great versatility. This chapter studies its multiple functions (metaphysical, theological, political, historiographical, literary, dramaturgical), the ideologies it serves (paganist, Christian, agnostic) and its various tones (cynical, detached, anguished). It is divided into three parts. The first one traces the philosophical origins of *theatrum mundi*, highlighting its cognitive utility. Using a diachronic approach, it begins in Antiquity and concludes in the Middle Ages. The second part focuses on the Renaissance and the seventeenth century using a synchronic method, as the theatre metaphor is found throughout the many disciplines of the period, but for the first time in History, it is prevalent within the theatre itself. The final part of the chapter resumes the metaphor's chronological trajectory, laying emphasis on the twentieth century and culminating in the twenty-first century. It examines the unprecedented features of the contemporary reappropriations of the *topos*.

Puerto Rican poet, essayist, novelist and academic, writing in Spanish, English and Spanglish, Giannina Braschi is a unique voice in the literary world, and it is to her work that Whistler's chapter is dedicated. Not only are her writings full of fiery political critique and visceral realism – she also writes with a magnification and distance comparable to Joyce. What is of most interest to this essay, however, is how she crosses borders with her writing – between genres, between languages, between consciousnesses. Drawing on the work of Goya and critique by Nehamas, Whistler's contribution to this volume aims to demonstrate Braschi's quest for that fruitful and dreamlike state between imagination and reason, where artistic creation takes place, and the human can reach her full capacity as an ethical animal.

Mary Shelley, the daughter of the feminist writer Mary Wollstonecraft and the wife of the poet Percy Bysshe Shelley, was an accomplished writer in her own right. And Katalin Nun Stewart argues that, although Shelley wrote highly thought-provoking novels filled with philosophical questions, the philosophical value of her writings has not yet been recognized. This chapter focusses on Mary Shelley's novel *The Last Man* (1826), which presents an apocalyptic vision of Europe of the late twenty-first century. Nun Stewart suggests that the novel is primarily autobiographical and that the first-person narrator, in spite of being a male character, represents Mary Shelley herself. Moreover, Nun Stewart argues that the work can be regarded as a forerunner of the existentialist novel inasmuch as it deals with existential pain and suffering on the individual level, while also exploring more general philosophical questions about the meaning of life and the human condition.

In the final chapter of this volume, Stephen Mulhall looks at melodrama in Dostoevsky and Tarkovsky, showing that it's not just the written word which has the power to do philosophy. In *Tolstoy or Dostoevsky: An Essay in Contrast*, George Steiner assigns a central role to the concept of melodrama in its characterization of Dostoevsky's achievement. Mulhall suggests that, in part, this indicates an important continuity between Dostoevsky's body of work and a central strand of the literary and theatrical culture of his time, for which Peter Brooks's more recent book, *The Melodramatic Imagination: Balzac, Henry James, Melodrama and the Mode of Excess* is intended to supply an interpretation. In this essay, Mulhall proposes to use Stanley Cavell's critical engagement with Brooks's interpretative schema, and the alternative interpretation of melodrama in film, psychoanalysis and philosophy upon which it draws, to develop a reading of Dostoevsky that brings out points of contrast (and so of comparison) with the cinematic achievement of Tarkovsky that might otherwise be overlooked.

PART ONE

Literature as Argument

1

Reading as a way of seeing: Literature and the perception of place

Ghazouane Arslane

Literature's capacity to render the complexity of human behaviour and psychology, of human relationships and of our connection to place is enormous and arguably unique. This capacity is enabled by a creative use of language that transforms – rather than simply reflects – the multiple manifestations and impressions of reality into language. To render is not to explain, interpret or simply mimic. To render a place in a novel, a short story or even a poem is to capture and transform its intricate details in language. The choice of those details and the connection or correlation between them depend on the perception of the writer. What matters is that this rendition of actual or imagined reality in language is regulated by style and form: the very act of writing produces a style, and that style renders particular and poetic that linguistic expression of reality. Writing, thus, is a way of reading reality, which means that reading becomes a way of seeing that very reality. Contrary to the idea that aesthetic pleasure is separate from moral content, the poetic here is precisely what allows for the ethical, more precisely, for a different or alternative manner of perceiving and connecting to place. By focusing on the representation of place in novels as diverse as Virginia Woolf's *Mrs Dalloway* (1925), Tahir Wattar's *The Earthquake* (1974) and Mourid Barghouti's *I Saw Ramallah*

(1997), in addition to Abdelfattah Kilito's story 'A Season in the Hammam' (1995), I demonstrate that the capacity of literature to see with language what is experienced – seen, heard, touched, felt and imagined – in lived reality but remains unarticulated is what makes it, among other things, ethically engaging and unique. To read is to see in a novel or different way, to experience place, whether one has been in it or not, in an *intimate* manner. This, crucially, may enable a more sensitive and thoughtful connection to place, in that we see the places we live in and those we discover with the conscious or subconscious effects that the reading leaves behind, that is, with a poetic mode of perception.

One limitation to this argument, however, is that representation is problematic, and this is especially the case in the colonial or imperial novel. Yet even in such novels as Joseph Conrad's *Heart of Darkness* (1899) or Rudyard Kipling's *Kim* (1901), the novel's formal devices, as Edward Said has shown in *Culture and Imperialism* (1993), may undermine or question the ideological matrix within which the novel exists even as it reproduces or embodies imperial ideas and interests. The unreliable narrator in *Heart of Darkness*, for instance, may indicate a crisis of truth in European, imperial imagination in the late nineteenth century, despite the novel's 'politicized, ideologically saturated Africa'.[1] The novel's representation of the other, of the other's place, produces an internal conflict, an ambivalence, a crisis within the space of the novel, because 'those many [imperial] interests and ideas [are] furiously at work in it, not just a photographic literary "reflection" of it'.[2] Only by paying close attention to how the novel's form and style are related to its cultural and historical world do we gain a more complex understanding of its mode of representation. What remains crucial is that literature creates the captured or imagined reality in a poetic language, in a singular style that at once draws attention to itself and to what it represents. This can produce a heightened sense of spatial perception and/or may alert us to the limitations of our attempt to see the other – for acts of seeing can also be acts of blinding. In both cases, however, poetics remains indissociable from ethics.

We may therefore speak of a topographical mode of reading, one that accentuates the experience of the subject as inextricably bound to place, that attends to the geographies of literature, to the places it depicts and transforms and, more importantly, to how they are seen and how we see them. But despite the fact that 'place is indeed an inextricable element in human life and being', as Jeff Malpas points out, it 'also has the potential to be ethically and politically destructive'.[3] Malpas nevertheless observes that 'it is precisely the centrality of place that allows it to be drawn on in such destructive ways'.[4] We shall see how this tension is illustrated in Tahir Wattar's novel *The Earthquake*, a classic of post-independence Algerian literature in Arabic, and Mourid Barghouti's celebrated autobiography *I Saw Ramallah*. My reading of these novels will demonstrate how an ethics of place, following Malpas, attends to 'the singular, the concrete, the particular'.[5] This ethics concerns the human experience of place: how people are attached to, and engage with, certain places; how places change *over* time and are reflections or invocations *of* time; and how that attachment manifests itself and is conditioned by political, historical and economic forces. It is crucial to emphasize, in this respect, what in humanistic geography is called the 'sense of place'[6] or, in the words of Irish poet Seamus Heaney, the 'assenting, equable marriage between the geographical country and the country of the mind', a marriage 'that constitutes the sense of place in its richest possible manifestation'.[7] This will be manifest in remarkable ways in Barghouti's *I Saw Ramallah* and, in a more problematic fashion, in Wattar's *The Earthquake*.

An essential component of my argument in this essay lies in stressing the role of language and form in literature – the role of its poetics – in enabling this ethics of place, one that does not obscure but intervenes, via poetics, in the politics of place; that is to say, of inclusion and exclusion in certain places, of who lives in them, who claims them, who sees them, who senses them, who imagines them, who remembers them. The major aim of this essay is to demonstrate that our experience of place itself can be deepened and rendered more attentive or careful thanks to literature, to its aesthetic capacity to describe and capture the details, the mood, the atmosphere, the character, the concreteness – what is or remains unseen in its obviousness – of certain places, what those places mean and how they are experienced individually and collectively. This will be shown in my reading of the sense of place and the sense of self in Virginia Woolf's *Mrs Dalloway*; of the city that is torn between postcolonial ruination and progressive forces in Tahir Wattar's *The Earthquake*; of Palestine under occupation as seen by the returning exile in Mourid Barghouti's *I saw Ramallah*; and of the hammam as a locus of universal reflections in Abdelfattah Kilito's 'A Season in the Hammam'.

If we are attentive to the topographical aspect when we read, literature may allow us to see, in ways unique to it, how places shape us as individuals and groups, how they affect our lives in various ways, and how they are deeply individual *and* political at the same time. In *A Small Place* (1988), for instance, Jamica Kincaid powerfully describes how Antigua is *seen* by the Euro-American tourist and how it is experienced by the native Antiguan. She reveals the ways in which Antigua as a place is constituted by the dark history of colonial violence and slavery and by its postcolonial aftermath of corruption and ruination, a history and a present invisible to Euro-American tourists. These tourists see *their* Antigua, the one that concerns them as tourists, not the Antigua that Kincaid grew up in, that she can see and has always seen: the beautiful, small place that has been shaped by an ugly history, that is being shaped by an ugly present.[8] Her essay is therefore a remarkable example of the inseparability of the ethics and politics of place, and of the necessity of literature in revealing and underscoring that inseparability and its internal relationship, that is, what we (can) see and sense and do when it comes to place.

'Life; London; this moment in June': The sense of place and the sense of self in Virginia Woolf's *Mrs Dalloway*

In *Mrs Dalloway*, London is a place in which the characters' movements across it are, to a large extent, inseparable from their feelings, interactions, ruminations and remembrances. London shapes the characters' minds and lives; without it, one cannot imagine the identity and personality of Clarissa Dalloway, for instance. London is central to the manner in which she leads her life as an upper middle-class woman. This is visible in the very beginning of the novel:

> For having lived in Westminster – how many years now? over twenty – one feels even in the midst of the traffic, or waking at night, Clarissa was positive, a particular hush, or solemnity;

> an indescribable pause; a suspense (but that might be her heart, affected, they said, by influenza) before Big Ben strikes. There! Out it boomed. First a warning, musical; then the hour, irrevocable. The leaden circles dissolved in the air. Such fools we are, she thought, crossing Victoria Street. For heaven only knows why one loves it so, how one sees it so, making it up, building up, building it around one, tumbling it, creating it every moment afresh; but the variest frumps, the most dejected of miseries sitting on doorstep (drink their downfall) do the same; can't be dealt with, she felt positive, by Acts of Parliament for that very reason: they love life. In people's eyes, in the swing, tramp, and trudge; in the bellow and uproar; the carriages, motor cars, omnibuses, vans, sandwich men shuffling and swinging; brass bands, barrel organs; in the triumph and the jingle and the strange high singing of some aeroplane overhead was what she loved; life; London; this moment in June.[9]

The relationship between Mrs Dalloway and London is established in this passage, which illustrates and condenses the novel's narrative mode. Place, time and subjectivity are intimately wedded. London here is not just subjective; it is that which allows the subject to live in a particular way, to perceive reality and oneself in a particular way. One can go as far as claiming that the place at once contains and constrains the subject: Mrs Dalloway's London is that of the middle classes; it is London seen through and by the prism of that class (the novel as an expression of bourgeois society). But this does not account for the psychological complexity of that way of seeing, precisely because place is the arena of social and psychological realities – which are interrelated but not, strictly speaking, the same – yet not their producer. That is to say, one can speak of an existential relationship with place that can be illuminated by socio-economic reality but is not reducible to it, even though socio-economic conditions play an enormous role in shaping the psychological lives of individuals.

What this shows us as readers, however, is that place and experience are connected in ways that are not necessarily visible or readily discernible to us. It is the novel as a narrative, and more specifically its own mode of narration – the free indirect speech, the smooth, almost musical alternation between the narrator and the characters' minds, between objectivity and subjectivity – that enables us to see how place and human experience are interdependent, how 'place is not founded *on* subjectivity but is that *on which* subjectivity itself is founded',[10] to follow Malpas's argument. Woolf's narrative style is one that moves in accordance with the tempo of the characters' internal lives, so to speak, but this interiority for her is embedded in, and triggered by, external reality: the city, the hustle-bustle of London, its absorbing peculiarities, its (in)visible details, its sheer energy, so that the internal and the external are interactive, interpenetrative.[11] The place becomes not an object of perception but that which shapes and is shaped in multiple ways by our changing perception; it becomes at once subjective – one can speak of Mrs Dalloway's London, *her* London – and objective, that is, as the place that exists simultaneously there *and* here, around and inside people's lives. The narrative poetics is precisely what reveals this interdependence of place and human experience, of the sense of place and the sense of self.

A few pages later, as Clarissa is walking across London, an intense passage shows a specific mode of experiencing the city, a way of seeing place as an overriding presence at once annihilating the self and subsisting in it, to use the language of Sufism:

> What she loved was this, here, now, in front of her; the fat lady in the cab. Did it matter then, she asked herself, walking towards Bond Street, did it matter that she must inevitably cease completely; all this must go on without her; did she resent it; or did it not become consoling to believe that death ended absolutely? but that somehow in the streets of London, on the ebb and flow of things, here, there, she survived.[12]

Such powerful moments are epiphanic not just in the sense of revealing penetrating insights about the self, but in the sense of allowing the reader to perceive the extent to which place, the modern metropolitan city, exerts a profound effect on us. To read such a passage is to see both Clarissa and London as inextricably linked, to realize, that is, that one's experience of place is collective but can be very intimately subjective, that one *can* have a deeply personal relationship with a place – the city, in this case, perhaps *the* most important character of the modern novel.

But the novel is not just about Clarissa. Other characters – less wealthy and fortunate than Clarissa, particularly Septimus and his

Italian wife Rezia, as well as Peter Walsh – also experience London in fascinating ways. Rezia, the outsider, cries in the presence of her husband, 'I am alone; I am alone! … by the fountain in Regents Park (staring at the Indian and his cross), as perhaps at midnight, when all boundaries are lost, the country reverts to its ancient shape, as the Romans saw it, lying cloudy, when they landed, and the hills had no names and rivers wound they know not where – such was her darkness'.[13] The city simply disappears, for she is an outsider, and an outsider can make a city disappear; for she never realized, furthermore, 'that he [Septimus] was mad'.[14] It is as though Septimus himself embodied the madness of a city in which one remained an outsider, as though (because of Septimus) Rezia has erased the whole history of London, and sees it as it was before it became 'British' – before it made her an outsider.

Septimus himself, at one point in Regent's Park, lost in thoughts and reveries,

> had only to open his eyes; but a weight was on them; a fear. He strained; he pushed; he looked; he saw Regent's Park before him. Long streamers of light fawned at his feet. The trees waved, brandished. We welcome, the world seemed to say; we accept; we create. Beauty, the world seemed to say. And as if to prove (scientifically) wherever he looked, at the houses, the railings, at the antelopes stretching over the palings, beauty sprang instantly. To watch a leaf quivering in the rush of air was an exquisite joy. Up in the sky swallows swooping, swerving, flinging themselves in and out, round and round, yet always with perfect control as if elastics held them; and the flies rising and falling; and the sun spotting now this leaf, now that, in mockery, dazzling it with soft gold in pure good temper; and now and again some chime (it might be a motor horn) tinkling divinely on the grass stalks – all of this, calm and reasonable as it was, made out of ordinary things as it was, was the truth now; beauty, that was the truth now. Beauty was everywhere.[15]

The weight on the eyes was lifted by the entrancing and immersive beauty of the place, as though the place had a quality of lightness to it, as though it welcomed without conditions. But is this Septimus speaking, the narrator, or both? Is this London as he saw it then, his impression of Regent's Park, or Regent's Park from the narrator's perspective? The ambiguity is deliberate, and is made deliberate, thanks to Woolf's hypnotic narrative style. Through Septimus, one sees Regent's Park from a poetic point of view, that is, to use the formalist term, from an 'enstranging'[16] or defamiliarizing perspective. As Victor Shklovsky famously wrote: 'Art exists in order to restore the sensation of life, in order to make us feel things, in order to make a stone stony. The goal of art is to create the sensation of seeing, and not merely recognizing, things.'[17] This is all too known, but this 'enstrangement' is particularly relevant when it comes to the seeing, and not just recognizing, of familiar or unknown places. Shklovsky contends that 'the process of perception, in art, is an end in itself and must be prolonged',[18] but I should add that the process can be both an end in itself at the moment of seeing, of reading – the form that renders the place anew, that recreates it, that expresses its 'poeticity' with words[19] – and, at the same time, a mode of perception which, by virtue of this process, sees *all* places, *all* things, from a poetic perspective. I am here speaking about the process of reading, what it can do, rather than what it actually does or does not. This relationship between places and individuals as seen in *Mrs Dalloway* renders London itself a major character; isn't London the novel's node of gravity, the space from and through which we can see the characters' thoughts and, through those thoughts, the city itself?

The city in flux: Ruination and change in Tahir Wattar's *The Earthquake*

I wish to move, now, to another novel, a novel from the South, Tahir Wattar's *The Earthquake*. A classic of post-independence Algerian literature in Arabic, Wattar's novel is set in Constantine, also known as the city of the hanging bridges, one of the oldest cities in the east of Algeria and one of the biggest cities in the country. But contrary to imperial London, Constantine in the novel emerges as a post-imperial city threatened by overpopulation and chaos, at least as seen through the eyes of its anti-socialist protagonist Sheikh Boularwah. Boularwah, who used to live in Constantine before independence, returns to it on a visit in the hope of finding a distant relative who could inherit his lands, in fear that the 'socialist' government will confiscate those lands for agricultural purposes in case he has no inheritor. The novel follows his movement in the now overcrowded city, along seven chapters, each chapter bearing the name of one of the seven bridges in Constantine. This is a city-novel par excellence, as there are almost no interior spaces except the self, the mind and heart of Boularwah himself, through whose eyes, thoughts, visceral reactions, dark memories and hallucinations – of an inevitable earthquake in the city, like the one occurring in the Judgement Day as described in *Surat al-Hajj* (the chapter of 'The Pilgrimage') in the Koran – we see the city itself, its inhabitants and, of course, Boularwah himself.

The novel, which is self-consciously deemed part of 'socialist' literature, creates an anti-socialist old man as its protagonist. Boularwah is now (after independence) the headmaster of a school in Algiers. He was educated in the famous al-Zaituna Mosque in Tunisia during colonial rule. His great-grandfather, as we discover later in the novel, was a collaborator with the French during the nineteenth century; he helped thwart a local rebellion in exchange for land and high status. What we see therefore is the perception of a man who is (unconsciously) gripped by nostalgia to colonial Constantine, now that the city houses far more people than before, half a million as he says, its fabric and topography drastically transformed after independence. Before delving into how Constantine is seen and experienced in the novel, it is worth noting that seeing it through the eyes and movements of such a character can be read as both an endorsement and critique of government policies: an endorsement of its socialist stance and a subtle critique of the way those polices – and others – are implemented; Boularwah, for instance, overhears two young men one of whom points out the irony of a socialist government silencing its socialist critics and putting them in jail.[20] And this is the case because Wattar's novelistic skill and narrative choices – mastery of free indirect speech, interior dialogue, narrative flow, and Koran intertextuality – allow for such a reading.

My interest here is with the ways in which the novel creates a tension, through its narrative poetics, between the politics and ethics of place. In the novel, you can see, smell, sense, feel and almost experience the city. The opening paragraph of the novel is a case in point: 'The sense of smell overwhelms all other senses in Constantine. You are assaulted by one odour or another with every step, every glance and every breath you take. It's usually an obnoxious odour that grates on your nerves and weighs heavily on your heart.'[21] The narrator tells us in the next paragraph that that was what Boularwah was thinking about 'as he opened his car door, after parking in a tight space which had taken him a long time to find'.[22] What the novel registers is the transformation of a city in the aftermath of independence, the physical changes that occur to a city like Constantine in a country torn between postcolonial ruination and progressive change. From a certain angle, however, 'everything seemed to him as it always had, the greenness of the trees and all the different buildings he could identify'.[23] Yet what attracts attention is 'the suspension bridge', as his 'heart fluttered' upon noticing it.

> Doesn't it [Constantine] look cleaner than it used to, he wondered, brighter, more colourful? Hasn't the dull, drab European colour faded? Also, doesn't it seem to tilt more as if it wanted to look out over the depth of the vast ravine? I have no idea whatever possessed the Rhumel Valley to open itself up to the heart of a city so preoccupied with itself.[24]

But as he walks across the city, Boularwah notes, frustratingly, that Constantine 'has turned upside down', now that it looks more diverse than ever: 'The faces are all different in Constantine ... At the time of French, people looked either European or Arab, but not now.'[25] To read this is to see postcolonial history unfolding before your very eyes: when the colonizers leave, people are liberated from colonialism, but that liberation comes at a cost – an avoidable one according to Frantz Fanon – which some people inside the country cannot bear, those used to the colonial, Manichean world eloquently described in *The Wretched of the Earth* (1963), those who might oppose colonialism but not the logic and mindset of colonial authorities. As Fanon presciently observed, one also sees the failure of the postcolonial state to think outside the European framework that privileges the capital city, for social and political consciousness, according to Fanon, must begin in the rural areas, in the countryside, outside the city:

> In an underdeveloped country the creation of dynamic regional bureaus halts the process of urban macrocephaly and the chaotic exodus of the rural masses toward the towns. The establishment,

> during the very first days of independence, of regional bureaus with the power to stimulate, revive, and accelerate the citizens' consciousness is an inevitable prerequisite for any country that wants to progress.[26]

In *The Earthquake*, we see that the city was 'invaded' by people living outside it, in the villages and deserts, who had suffered from unemployment and inattention. 'In an underdeveloped country the leading party members should flee the capital like the plague', writes Fanon. 'With the exception of a few', he adds, 'they should reside in the rural areas ... No administrative pretext can justify the bustle of the capital already overpopulated and overdeveloped compared with nine tenths of the territory. This is the only way to revive the regions that are dead, the regions that have not yet woken up to life.'[27] Failure to heed this advice led, as it were, to the hallucinatory 'earthquake' we observe in post-independence Constantine, a regional capital in Algeria.

Wattar's brilliant novel, however, renders 'this city of contradictions' as both attractive and repulsive. Its enduring significance, its appealing aura, its fascinating topography are nevertheless emphasized even as it is rapidly changing. But perhaps that is where the power of the novel stems from. It registers the postcolonial city in flux, it captures an obvious universal fact in a very local context: places change and the perceiver of change sees both what is constant and what is changing. The nature of that perception, however, depends on the background and interest of the perceiver. And Wattar deliberately creates his protagonist as someone opposed to that change, someone who would exaggerate the politics of place and thereby allow us to see what an endorser of that change – even a reserved one – would or could not see. The 'real heartland of the Constantinian', for instance, 'is as it always was. The prickly pear vendors are still at their stalls and the other vendors are in theirs selling the same goods they always did. And then there are the same old songs.'[28] The narration then emphasizes that this place is 'where he [the Constantinian] watches his own history pass him by, where he protects himself with his handicrafts against every intruder. It is the place where he launches his attack all the way east as far as the Sahara, with his skills and copper, his perfumes and incense, his embroidered slippers and *kuffiyyas*, even his candle and bridal kits.'[29] This is one of the essential attributes of

Constantine then: a city whose identity partly rests on its exported handicrafts, but also on its being on a rock, so to speak, overlooking green mountains and fertile hills by which Boularwah's eyes, as he 'hid beneath the shade of a passageway', are captivated:

> The views of the mountain tops of endless shapes and sizes sometimes lose themselves in the whiteness of the clouds, and sometimes in the dark shadow of trees. Range of hills crawl behind them towards the depression. Some are in full view, while others are totally stripped of any herbage save a few patches of green. At the foot of the mountain range, the green vegetation extends all along the right side and encircles the twists and turns of the river with its brackish waters and gleaming white rocks. All the way down below, there is a pier that stretches from the foot of the mountain and cuts across the river. This is the Sidi M'sid Bridge.[30]

The juxtaposition between the city and the mountains, the city and the natural landscape, is in full display here. And the bridge is the human construction that creates both the urban landscape and the illusion that this urban landscape is part – or an extension – of the natural one. What about the Sidi M'sid quarter? It 'looks like the Garabi' quarter in Najib Mahfouz's novel, *The Children of the Alley*'.[31] It looks like it *in literature* – literature is the necessary mediation here. Without it, both places would remain unwritten, unread, non-literary – that is to say, neglected, forgotten. Places acquire, in literature, another life, a written life, a literary life, a life of their own.

The Sidi Rashid Bridge will even survive the pending earthquake that Boularwah is hallucinating about and obsessed with; his turbulent mind pictures an image of survival by mythologizing the bridge:

> Over yonder you can see a part of the Sidi Rashid Bridge, sitting on top of arches fortified by rocks and cement. It valiantly resists the heavy carts and enormous trucks that trample on it. However awesome the earthquake may be, however strong and mighty, this bridge will never collapse. It will surely remain a bridge, even if the river below ceases to flow or all of its foundations crumble. It's a bastion of men's insistence on being defiant and arrogant.

> More than that, it is a symbol of their ardent desire to participate in creation. Whoever finds himself on top of the bridge when the rock shakes and the city melts will have the best chance to be saved.[32]

This subjective image of the Bridge is precisely what partakes in mythologizing it, even if one does not subscribe to Boularwah's vision. The bridge 'makes one forget that awesome chasm that lies between us and the earth'[33] – the bridge as mediator, protector and inspirer. The bridge as reality and myth. For 'it has the shape of a crescent moon', but 'the great ravine fades in comparison to its splendour',[34] even though 'they [the bridge and the ravine] are engaged in a constant struggle where the ravine tries to bring itself together but the bridge prevents it from succeeding'.[35] The novel is teeming with such humanized descriptions of geography. But it also paints – through Boularwah – an eschatological picture of a city that has become an arena where postcolonial ruination and difficult progressive change drag each other incessantly. Yet only by virtue of a specific kind of novelistic narrativization that we can see this conflict, this struggle between dialectical, complex forces taking place inside place. The politics of place is in full view here thanks largely to the poetics of narrative writing, which makes it difficult to make any facile judgement on the place itself. Reading such a novel complicates the rigid binaries – either ruination or progress – through which we see place in history; it might even encourage us to look beyond the novel in order to comprehend its complexity.

Place under occupation: Acts of seeing in Mourid Barghouti's *I Saw Ramallah*

If Boularwah returns to Constantine only to see its dilapidation, chaos and abiding attractiveness, to see it as city of contradictions reflecting his own and his time, in *I Saw Ramallah* Mourid Barghouti recounts the agonizing and deeply transformative experience of returning to Ramallah after thirty years in exile. Here, the politics of place, of geography, of colonial domination determines Barghouti's relationship with his homeland. But Barghouti is not concerned with politics per se or straightforwardly. As the title indicates, it is the experience of seeing Ramallah, of seeing Palestine – or what he is allowed to see of Palestine – in time that concerns him, that he narrates with remarkable and insightful sensitivity: the time of the exile, of the displaced, for whom the place is at once profoundly entrenched in memory but also, after a long exile, evasive and disturbingly dissimilar. As he writes, 'My relationship with place is in truth a relationship with time. I move in patches of time, some I have lost and some I possess for a while and then I lose because I am always without a place.'[36]

The ethical power of the autobiography stems, fundamentally, from its poetic power, its capacity to articulate the complex emotional and experiential subtleties of the exile's field of vision, of physical connections and disconnections, of lived confrontation with the place – and everything it represents and invokes – as he returns to it. Politics is there, *all over the place*, but we see politics in a different way because we see it through poetics, through the eyes of a poet who is acutely and painfully aware of the importance of sense experience when it comes to the perception of place, homeland, belonging and memory. As he is about to cross the famous bridge that connects the West Bank and Jordan, for instance, he sees that 'there is no topological difference between this Jordanian land I stand on and that Palestinian land on the other side of the Bridge', realizing that this is the 'Occupied Territory' and remembering a visit with a group of writers to the city of Quneitra in Syria in 1979. He narrates:

> A convoy of cars took us on a short journey and we saw the destruction visited by the Israelis on the city. We stood by the barbed wire behind which flew the Israeli flag. I stretched my hand across the wire and took hold of a shrub growing wild on the occupied side of the Golan. I shook the shrub and said to Hussein Muruwwa, who stood next to me: 'Here is the Occupied Territory, Abu Nizar, I can hold it with my hand!'
>
> When you hear on the radio and read in newspapers and magazines and books and speeches the words 'the Occupied Territories' year after year, and festival and after festival, and summit conference after summit conference, you think it's somewhere at the end of the earth. You think there is absolutely no way you can get to it. Do you see how close it is? How touchable? How real? I can hold it in my hand, like a handkerchief.

> ...
> Who would dare make it into an abstraction now that it has declared its physical self to the senses?[37]

This movement from abstraction to concreteness is precisely how literature *as* literature intervenes in politics – and Barghouti restores to the 'Occupied Territories' what politics has veiled and obscured, namely its being a perceivable and touchable place. Place is first and foremost an experience of the senses; it is alive because our being in it makes it so, but its aliveness and realness are all the more acute when we are aware – or made aware – of how our senses experience it, beneath or around the abstraction that mediates our relationship with it. After crossing the Jordan Bridge and being finally granted entry by the Israeli officer, he writes: 'Palestine at this moment is not the golden map hanging on a golden chain adorning the throats of women in exile. I used to wonder – every time I saw that map encircling their necks – if Canadian women, or Norwegians, or Chinese carried their maps around their necks as our women do.'[38]

The bridge itself, which as Barghouti tells us has been given many names, becomes a locus of intense existential experience, which is essentially the effect of military and political domination. 'The whole story is about place',[39] Barghouti tells us, adding later that 'all eyes these days look at geography more than they look at history'.[40] Which is why his autobiography can be read as a deeply personal and – because he represents the fate of millions of Palestinian refugees – historical account of how we experience place and geography, of how they affect who we are and the way we see the world and how we, in turn, shape the way we perceive and imagine them, of how 'symbolic geography' is maintained or altered beyond our will and freedom, for 'the others are still the masters of the place'.[41]

Almost all the places that Barghouti returns to and speaks about are seen anew, are reinvented in a sense, not just because the exile has returned to his homeland – 'our homeland is the shape of time we spent in it'[42] – but because he sees it, in a way, through writing. Writing is an embodiment of a singular way of seeing. It displaces place from documents and slogans to a lived and sensible experience, which is by its very nature singular; his long exile is the measure of the distance, as it were, between what is said and what is lived. The juxtaposition of documentation and reality is key to the way

Barghouti senses place; as he is about to enter Deir Ghassanah, for instance, the village of his childhood, he notes that it 'is no longer an idea or an entry in a file',[43] no longer on the map of administration and bureaucracy. The place is almost humanized, is alive, is real: 'She [Deir Ghassanah] is about to open huge parentheses in which thirty years of life will be placed; my displacement will be contained in parenthesis.'[44] Why is Barghouti almost obsessed with concreteness and detail? What does this have to do with poetry and the poetic? And what can poetry and literature do in this context?

> The long Occupation has succeeded in changing us from children of Palestine to children of the idea of Palestine. I only started to believe in myself as a poet when I discovered how faded all abstracts and absolutes were. When I discovered the accuracy of the concrete detail and the truthfulness of the five senses, and *the great gift, in particular, of sight*. When I discovered the justice and genius of *the language of the camera*, which presents its view in an amazing whisper, however noisy this view was in fact or in history.[45] [emphasis added]

But to see Ramallah and the West Bank after thirty years of exile is to see geography disfigured and reshaped. And we, as readers, along with him, see that. Barghouti discovers, for the first time, the Israeli settlements in the West bank. 'The weave of the carpet is the settlements', he writes. 'Some scattered figures here and there are all that is left of Palestine.'[46] He is not even allowed to enter Jerusalem now, for the road from Ramallah to Jerusalem 'changed via a complex of winding roads so that we may not see the city even from the car window'.[47] Occupation determines what you can and cannot see; it occupies your field of sense and vision; it occupies and therefore redistributes the sensible. As Jacques Rancière conceives of it in relation to aesthetics, politics is, indeed, 'the distribution of the sensible'.[48] Politics determines what you can and cannot say about certain places: 'Perhaps the worst thing about occupied cities is that their children cannot make fun of them. Who could make fun of Jerusalem!'[49]

On the other hand, Barghouti notes that it is not change per se that matters so much as change that is forced, the ruination, the effect of the occupation which 'forced us to remain with the old .... It did not deprive us of the clay ovens of yesterday, but of the mystery of what we would invent tomorrow.'[50] Here, we can see that place exists in time and time is subject to the changes we (can) effect in it, which in turn affect how we perceive and inhabit place itself. In other words, time, and not just place, is political. For if one's place is occupied so is one's time, the right to inhabit time as something changeable and not fixed, the right to shape your homeland with the form of time you wish to lend to it, to use Barghouti's metaphor, not the one you are forced to attribute to it. Occupation fixates one in the past. Thus, 'it is in the interests of an occupation, any occupation, that the homeland should be transformed in the memory of its people into a bouquet of "symbols." Merely symbols'.[51] Hence Barghouti's adamant insistence on restoring the palpability and concreteness of places, and on emphasizing the varied connections between place and time, place and the ordinary, which his writing never tires of making visible, of expressing.[52] Nowhere is this more powerful perhaps than when he speaks about Jerusalem:

> All that the world knows of Jerusalem is the power of the symbol. The Dome of the Rock is what the eye sees, and so it sees Jerusalem and is satisfied. The Jerusalem of religions, the Jerusalem of politics, the Jerusalem of conflict is the Jerusalem of the world. But the world does not care for our Jerusalem, the Jerusalem of the people. The Jerusalem of houses and cobbled streets and spice markets, the Jerusalem of the Arab College, the Rashidiya School, and Omariya school. The Jerusalem of the porters and the tourist guides who know just enough of languages to guarantee them three reasonable meals a day. The oil market and the sellers of antiques and mother-of-pearl and sesame cakes ... The Jerusalem of white cheese, of oil and olives and thyme, of baskets of figs and necklaces and leather and Salah al-Din Street ... *This is the city of our senses, our bodies and our childhood.* The Jerusalem that we walk in without much noticing its 'sacredness', because we are in it, because it is us.[53] [emphasis added]

Sometimes to see a place is, in a sense, to demythologize it, or to show what its mythology has obfuscated, namely the lives of ordinary people who grew up in it, the lives of Palestinians that go unnoticed because our ways of seeing can be ways of blinding. Where else can we find this 'ordinary Jerusalem', this Jerusalem of the senses, of Palestinian senses? To read is therefore to see beyond mythology, beneath it to be more precise; for 'the Jerusalem of the sky will live forever, but our life in it is threatened with extinction'.[54] To see the ordinary – that is, to acknowledge and celebrate it – is to resist the politics of the extraordinary, the small things that cannot be accommodated in the big picture but must stand, must be shown, as they are: small but essential, creating a form of life which, because of power, runs the risk of extinction. It is here where the memory of small things resists – or can resist – the history of warfare and domination.

Seeing the universal in the particular: Living and reading in Abdelfattah Kilito's 'A Season in the Hammam'

Acts of seeing of course differ, depending on the context and purpose of writing. Places themselves differ. I am not speaking of place in the abstract sense, but of particular places whose existence in reality and memory is inseparable from those who have inhabited or visited them. In this respect, it is not just the homeland, the city or the village that matters. Specific public places, like the library, the mosque or – as the following example evinces – the hammam, also matter, particularly when they acquire a new life because they are read, and not just represented, with creative originality. This is the case with Abdelfattah Kilito's story 'A Season in the Hammam', published in his fascinating collection of stories *The Clash of Images* (2010), originally written in French (1995). By virtue of seeing the extraordinary in the ordinary, the universal in the particular, the strange in the familiar, Kilito narrates the experience of going to the hammam in his childhood in Rabat with rare and graceful insight, giving a specific form to that experience in a manner analogous to how John Berger describes the act of storytelling: 'The act of approaching a given moment of experience involves both scrutiny (closeness) and the capacity to connect (distance).'[55] Closeness: because Kilito takes us with him, like a good host, to the hammam. And distance: because Kilito connects that experience with human existence as imagined by religion:

> [L]et's enter the hammam. Our steps lead us slowly but surely toward the overheated third chamber. On the way we can see, amidst the humid chiaroscuro, silhouettes that stand or sit or lounge on their sides. We'll dip out some water from the streaming fountain, scrub ourselves briskly, then walk back out into the daylight, clean and comfortable in our bodies. All true enough, but we should also remark that in the meantime we've lived through the crucial moments of human existence as they have been imagined by religion: life and death, submission and revolt, merits and demerits, grace and punishment, hope and despair, the mundane and the transcendent, the appeal to God and the answer – never unambiguous – that falls from the sky.[56]

Really? How exactly? First, the hammam is an egalitarian space, in that it imposes 'absolute uniformity' on its 'many indistinct, interchangeable, naked bodies',[57] reminding one, specifically because one *descends and never ascends* into its hellish atmosphere, of the Day of Judgement. The bathers are directed towards the third chamber, the hot basin, the heart and soul of the hammam, which can be seen either as a *mihrab* (because everyone, as in a mosque, is oriented towards it) or as hell (because as one ladles buckets of water from it one is attracted, tempted by its abyss). The hammam is an underworld, 'a dark place, starless and sunless, far from the day and the night, outside all calendars and chronologies'.[58] The hammam is a ritualistic space of resurrection, where your body and soul are rejuvenated. The hammam is a living embodiment of the world of the dead, of the invisible – in its dimness, you strip of everything that socially identifies you, becoming almost like a ghost. The most dramatic scene in the hammam occurs when water runs out, but what matters here is not just what happens but how it is narrated:

> What are all these shades doing in this hellish place [the third chamber]? They're waiting. They wait for the divine manifestation, the sign of epiphany, the oft-doubted announcement of deliverance. You know, of course, that the most precious substance in the hammam is water, hot water, which sometimes gushes forth but is very often scarce, parsimonious, and so gives rise to the most dramatic and terrible of scenes. Having scarped the bottom of the basin, the bathers crouch and wait for the

> providential waters to run once more. The great test begins, which is at first a test of language: one must communicate with the giver of the water, that invisible being situated on the other side of the wall, the other side of the rock. His intentions are unfathomable yet everything depends on his good will. He might provide the water willingly, just as he might hold it back. Master of water and fire, his behaviour is, to all appearances, utterly arbitrary.[59]

This invisible being acts, obviously, like a god. As the bathers are unanswered, feeling abandoned, desperate, their cries become increasingly violent. But the invisible being remains silent. As a result, 'the tone of their appeal (and of their hammering on the rock) changes, passing from beseechment and supplication to protestation and indignation, and even threats and insults'.[60] Helpless, they turn to the hammam's watchman, this mediator between 'the world of clothing and the world of nudity, the world of the living and the world of the dead',[61] the direct link with 'the master of water and fire'. But as nothing happens after the message is delivered to the invisible being, the bathers scapegoat the watchman, venting their rage on him. 'And then, abruptly, the miracle occurs: a think trickle of water begins to flow. The rock has at last softened, releasing liquid! The shades rejoice.'[62]

Kilito's picture of the hammam is not just allegorical; it enacts, it performs that allegory, because the hammam itself is read – and lived – as its theatre. The experience of the hammam is by its very nature theatrical, and that theatricality invites comparison with familiar (or familiarly strange) scenes drawn from religion, producing the effect of 'enstrangement'. It is the narrator who reads, who discovers, this theatre, this rehearsal of the Day of Judgement, in the hammam. Kilito's brilliance lies also in his unassuming, elegant prose, which counterpoises the movement of proximity with that of distance, the here and the beyond, the experienced and the read, dramatizing what occurs in the hammam by virtue of a narrator who simultaneously lives and reads. The narrator is therefore not just a storyteller; he is a particular reader of what he narrates. He narrates his experience by reading it, by seeing it, in a certain way. But he does so because the hammam has changed, the experience has changed, the theatricality is gone; the basin has been replaced by faucets, the wood by coal and so on: 'The hammam is no longer a hammam; it's a public bath, a place of hygiene, nothing more ... A great fragment of our childhood crumbles away.'[63] One shouldn't just read this as simply an act of nostalgia. The desire for convenience entailed the end of the hammam as the narrator lived it, the end of its theatrical experience. Writing therefore not only recollects that lived but now unavailable experience; in a way peculiar to literature, it reveals its universal dimension as a human experience. For the place here has become more than a place, because it was perhaps more than that from the very beginning. To read it, to narrate it, to see its familiar strangeness is to retrieve its peculiarity and perpetuate it beyond its locality, its time. This perceptive and creative reading of the hammam's experience is, hence, at once a celebration of cultural particularity (closeness) and an illumination of its unseen and universal meanings (distance).

The creative ways of connecting place and experience discussed in this essay attest to the elasticity of literature to capture, detect, depict, express and reveal what habit, forgetfulness and politics may blind us to, namely the complex nature and specificity of place, of all places. Reading literature – and the works selected here are only illustrative – can cultivate in us a way of seeing and a mode of perception which can be called, therefore, poetic, that is, attentive, slow, self-aware, intimate, immersive. It is in this sense that poetics can forge an ethics of place. Yet one should foreground and encourage, and not take for granted, this mode of reading literature, reading that attends to how places are transformed in and by virtue of literary language, which has the potential to transform our experience of place in general. One might call attention, however, to the fact that cinematic language can produce a similar effect; one can only think of the films of masters such as Andrei Tarkovsky or Theodoros Angelopoulos to realize the power of 'the language of the camera' as Barghouti calls it. But this cinematic language does draw inspiration from literary language, and I am not speaking about adaptation here. In *Sculpting in Time* (1985), Tarkovsky emphasizes the difference between the language of cinema on the one hand, and that of literature and theatre on the other, but when he speaks about the nature of cinema, the way in which time appears in it in the form of fact, that fact itself 'is given in the form of simple, direct observation'.[64] How exactly does he explain this? By quoting, after Sergei Eisenstein, traditional examples from haiku poetry, I will mention two:

Coldly shining moon;
Near the ancient monastery
A wolf is howling

As it passes by
The full moon barely touches
Fishhooks in the waves.[65]

Tarkovsky notes that 'this is pure observation' whose 'aptness and precision will make anyone, however crude his receptivity, feel the power of poetry',[66] going on to assert that 'this particular example seems to me close to the truth of cinema'.[67] Here, it is literary language that inspires cinematic language, however different one is from the other. This overlap means that one sees with words first before seeing with the camera; the words observe and condense while the camera translates the movement of language. To what extent can reading change or sharpen the prism through which we look at place, at the world? One has to read in order to have an answer, for the answer is the experience, and experience – however shared it is – is singular and cumulative. My attempt in this essay is simply an emphasis on how that experience can cultivate a way of seeing place that we can call ethical.

2

'My non-alibi in being': Bakhtinian ethics and the literary dynamics of subjectivity

Daphna Erdinast-Vulcan

The inclusion of this essay in a collection titled *New Readings in Literature as Moral Philosophy* requires a brief introductory comment. The following discussion engages with the philosophical work of M. M. Bakhtin (1895–1975), a corpus of writing accomplished under conditions of brutal state terrorism and ruthless censorship, dire material poverty, poor health and enforced exile. Given the circumstances of its genesis and the temperamental nonchalance of its author, this body of work does not seem to offer a systematic and coherent theory of moral philosophy, inasmuch as none of these texts (or fragments) explicitly refers to the earlier texts, and each of them seems to stand on its own, so that any sense of conceptual cohesiveness must necessarily be constructed by the reader. I believe, however, that Bakhtin's work – fragmented, truncated and incomplete as it is – can be synthesized and distilled into a complex but coherent philosophical theoretical position as to the dynamics of subjectivity, and may well offer some valuable insights on the relation of ethics and narrativity. Having engaged with this project of synthesis and distillation for the best part of the past thirty years or so, I would draw on some of my earlier work on Bakhtin's philosophical contribution in order to address some of the questions raised by the present volume,[1] and conclude with some commentary on the reception of Conrad's *Heart of Darkness* following the critique of Chinua Achebe.[2]

Following Bakhtin's own distinction, this essay would use the term 'ethics' rather than 'moral philosophy' throughout. To clarify this preference, we should refer to one of the earliest surviving fragments of Bakhtin's work, titled by its editors *Toward a Philosophy of the Act.*[3] The fragment reads like the beginning of what could have been a monumental philosophical project, whose tenor is a sense of profound disenchantment with formal Kantian ethics. Bakhtin objects to what he calls the 'fatal theoreticism' of Kantian ethics inasmuch as it is based upon abstraction, generalization, systematization and disembodiment. This theory, he writes, cannot account for the ethical moment, the concrete and singular event of ethical choice made by an individual at a specific point in time and space: 'The theoretical world is obtained through an essential and fundamental abstraction from the fact of my unique being and from the moral sense of that fact – "as if I did not exist"'.[4]
Against the construction of categorical imperatives, laws and propositions, Bakhtin argues that 'the ought is ... a certain attitude of consciousness. ... There *are* no moral norms that are determinate and valid in themselves as *moral* norms, but there is a moral subiectum with a determinate structure ... and it is upon him that we have to rely.'[5]

As we can see, Bakhtin does not subscribe to the equation of ethics with a moral or social code or with any formal and universal system of values. For him, the question of ethics concerns not the code, but the particular act, or 'signature' of a concrete and singular individual, the 'moral subiectum' facing the moment of ethical choice.[6] As I have previously suggested, our concrete and specific historicity, the singularity and unrepeatability of every human act, situated in a particular time and place as the act of an embodied individual, cannot be abstracted or translated into a system of abstract laws. It is this singularity which makes us fully accountable for our choices, inasmuch as 'that which can be done by me can never be done by any one else'. This is why we have no 'alibi in Being'.[7] Being positioned at a singular point in time and space, we cannot be 'elsewhere' (which is the literal translation of *alibi*), and it is this very experiential and irreducible singularity which makes the future truly open-ended and allows us to assume both agency and responsibility for our acts.[8]

This preliminary distinction between abstract 'theoreticism' and the singular ethical choice of a particular individual at a particular moment highlights the first and perhaps the most important point of the present essay: I suggest that what triggers the reader's ethical engagement with a literary work is not necessarily the moral *content* of the text and its overt or covert *thematic* messages but rather the way the text *works*, or as Bakhtin might put it, the 'poetics' of the text; its deployment of discursive strategies and modes of characterization; and the ways in which these aspects may impact the reader's modes of engagements.

Bakhtin's work was relayed to the West by Julia Kristeva in the mid-1970s,[9] and its enthusiastic reception as a forerunner of postmodernist thought, based mostly on his writings from the 1930s onwards, generated numerous essays embellished by ostensibly 'Bakhtinian' terminology – dialogism, polyponony, heteroglossia and the carnivalesque – which became common currency in academic publications both in the humanities and in the social sciences. But this all-too-easy assimilation came at a cost. In the early 1990s, when Bakhtin's earlier works (most notably 'Toward a Philosophy of the Act' and 'Author and Hero in Aesthetic Activity') were translated into English and published, it was difficult to reconcile them with the view of his better-known, later texts or to attend to his terminology and conceptualization in a more nuanced manner. And thus, by the mid-1990s, the 'Bakhtin industry' of the earlier two decades seemed to exhaust itself and gave way to newer academic fashions. To offer some correction of this partial view, the present discussion would focus mostly on the earlier texts and fragments which, I suggest, lay the philosophical foundations for much of the subsequent writings. While much of Bakhtin's middle and late work is broadly read as reflections on literature, literary discourse and culture, I would argue that these ostensibly literary discussions were, in fact, a more congenial mode of philosophizing or articulating his conception of the dynamics of human subjectivity. Needless to say, the focus on literature might well have resulted from considerations of expediency, in view of the need to deflect any suspicion of ideological subversion, which would have been extremely dangerous in an overtly philosophical text. Be that as it may, however, I believe that given Bakhtin's disillusionment with philosophy and his pronounced aversion to theoretical abstractions, his choice of literature as the arena for his nascent theory of subjectivity was not only a mode of 'writing under a mask', or 'Aesopean writing' (as it was known in the Soviet Union at the time), but a genuine and profound engagement with the dynamics of literature.

The focus of this engagement, which follows from Bakhtin's insistence that our conception of ethics should focus not on an abstract moral system or a code but on the 'moral subiectum' is, then, the Bakhtinian conception of the dynamics of subjectivity, as articulated at some length in 'Author and Hero in Aesthetic Activity'.[10] Using Bakhtin's own rather idiosyncratic vocabulary, this conception of subjectivity may be dubbed 'architectonic' in that it is premised on the tensile relations between two simultaneous and equally powerful psychic 'movements' (vectors or forces), which structure the experience of the subject. This is, in other words, a relational process, a 'meeting of two movements on the surface of a human being that consolidates or gives body to his axiological boundaries'.[11] Putting it in a nutshell, before we unpack this formulation and follow its trajectory through Bakhtin's work, the first of these 'movements' is the need to perceive oneself as an integral whole and to be securely anchored and framed within recognizable boundaries. It is a 'centripetal' desire for an emplotment of one's life story, for a sense of significant self-coherence, for clearly defined contours of identity, which Bakhtin will tag as the 'aesthetic' mode of being. The second 'movement', conversely, is an equally compelling 'centrifugal' need to break out and away from any and all modes of external framing, to transcend and transgress externally imposed boundaries and definitions, which Bakhtin will significantly denote as an 'ethical' need.

'Author and Hero' (1990) was almost certainly written at about the same time as the fragment 'Toward a Philosophy of the Act' (1993), but seems to turn from philosophy to literature in that it focuses on the dynamics of omniscient authoring in fictional work, and appears to be curiously conservative in its implicit analogy between the human author (invariably referenced in the masculine gender) and the divine *Auctor Mundi*. Bakhtin writes of the position of the omniscient author as being benevolently 'transgredient' to that of the characters, positioned outside and above them, having a complete view of their acts and their innermost thoughts as well as their past, present and future. The author's 'outsideness' allows him [*sic*] a 'surplus of vision' in relation to his characters; he can see each of them as a 'whole'; he can frame (or, as Bakhtin puts it 'consummate') their entire existence, including their birth and their death, and like the divine author of the world – the Auctor Mundi – he can bestow understanding and forgiveness, that is, the 'gift of grace' upon their very existence.

However, this ostensible literary treatise is, in fact, philosophically charged and may well be read as an essay on subjectivity. The essay is premised at the outset on phenomenological observations regarding the lived experience and self-perception of the embodied human subject, and there is a persistent slippage between the concept of the literary 'hero' and the human subject, to whom Bakhtin refers as 'I-for-myself'. Like the 'hero' in a work of fiction, says Bakhtin, 'I-for-myself' cannot perceive myself as a whole. In terms of spatial perception, I am unable to see either the top of my head, or my back; in terms of temporal perception, I am unable to witness the moment of my own birth or my death. I cannot, in fact, write my own full autobiography, and 'my own word about myself is in principle incapable of being the last word'[12] inasmuch as I cannot encompass the moment of my beginning and that of my end. Notably, however, Bakhtin extrapolates these spatial and temporal experiential limitations, projecting them into the axiological dimension of one's life as well: again, like a hero in a work of fiction, 'I-for-myself' cannot evaluate or understand the meaning and value of my own life, either:

> In this sense one can speak of a human being's absolute need for the other, for the other's seeing, remembering, gathering, and unifying self-activity – the only self-activity capable of producing his outwardly finished personality. This outward personality could not exist, if the other did not create it.[13]

Just like a fictional character who needs the author to represent him or her as a whole, represent the context, the background, the 'before' and 'after' of his or her actions and the implications of these actions, the embodied human subject needs the other who is situated outside her for a complete axiological perspective or, as Bakhtin calls it, for 'the unity of consummation'. The limited and partial self-perception of 'I-for-myself', that is, the living subject, like that of a character in a work of fiction, can thus only be complemented and made whole through the external, encompassing eyes of another (or an author) who can frame my existence from an external and superior vantage point. The perceptual and axiological limitations of 'I-for-myself' thus generate the second mode of subjectivity, dubbed 'I-for-the-other', which allows the subject to perceive herself or himself through the eyes of an authorial other, who can evaluate and understand the meaning of my life in its broader spatial, temporal and axiological context, grant its coherence and see it as a meaningful whole. 'A whole, integral human being is the product of the aesthetic, creative point of view and of that point of view alone ... A whole, integral human being presupposes an aesthetically active subiectum situated outside him (we are abstracting from man's religious experience in the present context).'[14] For the early Bakhtin, then, 'aesthetic culture is a culture of boundaries', and the hero in the fictional work is, or should be, framed and contained within set boundary-lines (or 'consummated', to use the Bakhtinian idiom again) under a benevolent authorial and authoritative gaze. It is the author who is 'the living bearer and sustainer of the unity of consummation': his outsideness or 'transgredience', as Bakhtin calls it, enables him 'to collect the hero and his life and to complete him to the point where he forms a whole by supplying all those moments which are inaccessible to the hero himself from within himself'.[15]

As we can see, the 'aesthetic', for Bakhtin, is not confined to literary texts alone: it is a powerful psychic modality, a mode of being, or a 'movement' within the architectonics of subjectivity.

> It is only in a life perceived in the category of the *other* that my body can become aesthetically valid, and not in the context of my own life as lived for myself, that is, not in the context of my self-consciousness.[16]
>
> My own axiological relationship to myself is completely unproductive aesthetically: for myself, I am aesthetically unreal.[17]

Being 'aesthetically real' or 'valid' for Bakhtin entails a sense of form and clear-cut boundary-lines, which can only be produced through the transgredient perspective of an other, that is, the third-person perspective which enables the narrative configuration of one's life.

Bakhtin's recognition of the psychological need for the transgredient perspective of an authorial other seems to position him neatly as early precursor of the 'narrative identity' thesis, whose ubiquity in the broad arena of humanities and the social sciences is rarely challenged today. Indeed, over the past five decades or so, it has become a truth, (almost) universally acknowledged (to misquote Jane Austen), that humans are fundamentally storytelling beings, and that our self-perceptions are generated by and embedded in communal or personal narratives. Versions of the narrative identity thesis have been expounded and developed at length and in great depth by prominent theorists, most notably Alasdair MacIntyre[18] and Paul Ricoeur,[19] straddling both the arena of literature and that of philosophy, and the diverse interpretative positions as to the implications of this thesis conception for both psychology and philosophy are, apparently, here to stay. I would suggest, however, that Bakhtin's work, though clearly an early forerunner of this approach, may offer some nuanced and complex insights as to the relation of ethics and narrativity.[20]

Unlike many Western thinkers, Bakhtin did not enjoy a sheltered life. His own bitter experience and the fate of many of his associates and friends under Stalinist autocracy may well have taught him that the containment of one's life within a set narrative authored from without by a 'transgredient' being – be it religious, national, ethnic or ideological – entails a profound loss of individual freedom and ethical choice, and the 'authorial other' of our lives is often far less benevolent than his portrayal in the metaphysically inspired aesthetics of 'Author and Hero'. More crucially still, being entirely contained within a communal, religious or ideological narrative which is not of one's own making suggests a degree of external determinism that does not allow for free will and choice, that is, the very fundamentals of ethical agency. Bakhtin is well aware of these issues at the outset. Even in 'Author and Hero', with its religiously inflected conception of omniscience, he makes a clear distinction between the *aesthetic* mode of being, wherein the subject is fully enframed, and the *ethical* mode of subjectivity:

> The ethical subiectum is present to itself as a task, the task of actualizing himself as a value, and is in principle incapable of being given, of being present-on-hand, of being contemplated: it is I-for-myself.[21]

> Ethical freedom ('freedom of the will') is not only freedom from cognitive necessity (causal necessity), but also freedom from aesthetic necessity.[22]

Unlike the hero in a work of fiction, who can be made to 'coincide with himself' through authorial framing, the living subject cannot be aesthetically consummated and framed, and 'will always transgress its own boundaries, as a state of self-coincidence or equilibrium is tantamount to death'.[23] The distinction is explicitly predicated on the possibility of ethical agency:

> If I am consummated and my life is consummated, I am no longer capable of living and acting. For in order to live and act, I need to be unconsummated, I need to be open for myself – at least in all the essential moments constituting my life; I have to be, for myself, someone who is axiologically yet-to-be, someone who does not coincide with his already existing makeup. [24]
>
> [The ethical moment] is a moment where that which *is* in me must overcome itself for the sake of that which *ought* to be; where being and obligation meet in conflict with me; where is and ought mutually exclude each other. It is a moment of fundamental and essential dissonance, inasmuch as what-is and what-ought-to-be, what-is-given and what-is-imposed-as-a-task, are incapable of being rhythmically bound within me myself from within me myself, i.e. they are incapable of being perceived on one and the same plane.[25]

And thus, counter-intuitively perhaps (if we tend to think of ethics in terms of a moral code positing of set boundary-lines between 'right' and 'wrong'), the *ethical* vector of subjectivity is associated by Bakhtin *not* with codes or set imperatives but with the *transgression* of aesthetic boundary-lines and narrative frames. The ethical subject – 'I-for-myself' – must perceive and experience his or her own actions as open and incomplete, always yet-to-be, for it is only this diachronic openness into the future, the loophole out of all form-giving boundaries and narratives that allows for the making of choices. Axiological boundaries are thus never given once and for all, and they are certainly not given to the subject's own experience of ethical choices. To make these choices in life as in literature, one must feel free to become 'other than one is' in the context of any and all framing narratives.

In 'Author and Hero' Bakhtin makes several passing remarks about Dostoevsky, who features as a case of 'aesthetic failure' in the context of aesthetics. Dostoevsky, Bakhtin writes, has abdicated the authorial prerogative of benign 'outsideness', and has failed to 'consummate' his characters and subsume their voices under his own. This failure of 'transgredience' in relation to his characters is presented in the essay as an inability on Dosteovsky's part 'to find any convincing and stable axiological point of support outside the hero'.[26] Only five years later, however, Bakhtin would publish the first edition of his monograph on Dostoevsky's poetics, engaging with boundless admiration with what he dubs 'Dostoevsky's small-scale Copernican revolution' in literature.[27] If, in terms of the 'aesthetic' relation outlined in the earlier text, Dostoevsky is portrayed as a maverick who has not attained the 'transgredience' which would allow him to frame, contain and 'consummate' his characters, he is now celebrated as a forerunner of a whole new era, and his abdication of the omniscient 'transgredient' authorial position is now conceived as a strategic and revolutionary move.

Dostoevsky, as read by Bakhtin, has indeed abdicated the aesthetic authorial prerogative of transgredience, the all-comprehending gaze which would have allowed him to frame and contain his characters, and turned himself into yet another voice among the equally authoritative living voices of his characters. But in terms of ethics, this is not an authorial failure but a revolutionary position, inasmuch as it does not attempt to subsume or assimilate the characters; it respects and allows for their alterity, and enables them to outgrow any and all authorial definitions. The Dostoevskean hero, according to Bakhtin, 'is not an objectified image'[28] or a 'voiceless object',[29] but an 'autonomous discourse, pure voice',[30] which is not subsumed under any authorial voice or discourse. Having abdicated the authorial position, Dostoevsky has allowed his characters the fullest measure of freedom and choice, even at the expense of aesthetic closure. It is arguable, then, that the 'small-scale Copernican revolution', attributed to Dostoevsky (whether it is Dostoevskian or Bakhtinian is irrelevant for our purposes), consists in the move from an aesthetic to an ethical relation to his characters.

This apparent turnabout in Bakhtin's evaluation of Dostoevsky marks a shift not only from aesthetics to ethics but also a move away from 'thematic' or 'representative' reading of the nexus of literature and ethics to what might be conceived as a 'perfomative reading' on Bakhtin's part.[31] Unlike other readers of Dostoevsky, Bakhtin does not engage with the explicit positions of Dostoevsky's characters, the moral dilemmas they face, the values they specifically endorse or reject, the decisions they make or, indeed, their very actions. Rather than relate to these characters as representatives of diverse moral positions or theses, Bakhtin writes almost exclusively about their discursive interactions, their intonations, their voices and their complex speech acts. In other words, Dostoevsky becomes Bakhtin's hero not because of the values endorsed by the characters in his novels but because he has granted each character the freedom to transgress the authorial boundary-lines, to break free of any and all 'second hand definitions'. Dostoevsky's characters, then, are unfinished, always in the process of becoming, incomplete. But rather than a flaw of composition, or an 'aesthetic failure' (as suggested in 'Author and Hero'), this very incompleteness is now conceived as a gift of freedom, which is the first condition of ethical agency.

Rather than a failure, then, the Dostoevskean abdication of the authorial prerogative is precisely that which enables his characters 'to outgrow, as it were, from within and to render untrue any externalizing and finalizing definition of them. Has in life, as long as a person is alive he lives by the fact that he is not yet finalized, that he has not yet uttered his ultimate word', and Dostoevsky's work allows the genuine life of the personality to take place at the point of non-coincidence between a man and himself, at this point of departure beyond the limits of all that he is as a material being, a being that can be spied on, defined, predicted apart from its own will, 'at second hand'.[32] The linkage of these authorial dynamics with the 'ethical' modality of subjectivity is further reinforced in Bakhtin's later, fragmented notes 'Toward a Re-working of the Dostoevsky Book' (written in 1961). Self-consciousness, Bakhtin writes, is

> not that which takes place *within*, but that which takes place on the *boundary* between one's own and someone else's consciousness, on the *threshold*. And everything internal gravitates not toward itself but is turned to the outside and dialogized, every internal

> experience ends up *on the boundary*, encounters another, and in this tension-filled encounter lies its entire essence. [33]

Bakhtin's conception of 'dialogicity' is, then, rather more complex than a mere conversation between two people. It is, in fact, turned inwards as well, relating not only to inter-subjectivity but to intra-subjectivity as well. Ethics, on this reading, is premised on the subject's encounter with 'something else', but it is not just the alterity of another person. It is, rather, that alterity which inheres in the very concept of the subject: 'A man never coincides with himself. One cannot apply to him the formula of identity A=A.'[34] Inter-subjectivity and intra-subjectivity are difficult to tell apart, as the human subject is an entity which lives on its own borderlines. This, for Bakhtin, is both the Dostoevkian space and the liminal space of human subjectivity itself: the ubiquity of physically liminal spaces – the threshold, the staircase, the corridor – in Dostoevsky's work is, then, a trope which is also clearly related to the ethical subject's encounter with an inherent and irreducible alterity within herself. Once again, this recognition of heteronomy and the encounter with alterity, both within and without the subject, is further reinforced in Bakhtin's later notes for the reworking of Dostoevsky's *Poetics*: 'A person has no internal sovereign territory, he is wholly and always on the boundary; looking inside himself, he looks into the eyes of another or with the eyes of another ... I receive my name from others, and it exists for others (self-nomination is imposture).'[35] Bakhtin will go on to extend his literary insights first from Dostoevsky's work to the novel in general, and then from the novel to discourse, aiming to go far beyond a theory of aesthetics or of literary production. Prompted by the sense of philosophical disillusionment articulated in 'Toward a Philosophy of the Act', his literary work is, from the very outset, a conceptualization of subjectivity designed to address the epistemological and the ethical need for a new philosophical idiom. Far from a system of norms, values or codes, ethics, according to his conception, is a mode of being, an abdication of the territorial enclosure of selfhood and sameness, an acknowledgement that 'my own word about myself is in principle incapable of being the last word',[36] and that human subjectivity cannot stake out but must live on its own boundary-lines.

Getting back to Bakhtin's 'architectonics' of subjectivity, we can now see how the two movements whose tensile relation underlies the dynamics of subjectivity may be rendered in terms of the aesthetic and the ethical modalities: the aesthetic, in a very broad sense, is a 'centripetal' movement, or 'I-for-the-other' as Bakhtin calls it, which – by consolidating boundary-lines, by framing and containing the subject under the gaze of the 'transgredient' authorial other – offers the subject some grounding and definition within a whole larger than the self. It is, in other words, the *aesthetic* vector which generates that narrative coherence we call the self. Against that 'whole, integral human being' who is 'aesthetically' framed by the transgredient other, Bakhtin positions the 'ethical subiecum' who is 'nonunitary in principle' as it lives in the gap between 'is' and 'ought',[37] where the only sense of its own wholeness is no more than a 'unity yet-to-be'.[38] The counter-movement is the 'centrifugal', ethical movement, which marks the experience of selfhood as 'I-for-myself', the subject who lives on its own boundary-lines, who can transcend any and all external definition of herself, who is invariably open into the future, capable of change and free to act.

Unlike the fictional hero who is eventually aesthetically framed and subsumed by the omniscient author, the ethical subject must always be 'unconsummated', must transgress the narratives which frame its life in order to be free to choose and to act. Bakhtin is explicit on this point: 'Ethical freedom ("freedom of the will") is not only freedom from cognitive necessity (causal necessity), but also freedom from aesthetic necessity':[39]

> If I am consummated and my life is consummated, I am no longer capable of living and acting. For in order to live and act, I need to be unconsummated, I need to be open for myself – at least in all the essential moments constituting my life; I have to be, for myself, someone who is axiologically yet-to-be, someone who does not coincide with his already existing makeup.[40]
>
> The ethical *subiectum* is present to itself as a task, the task of actualizing himself as a value, and is in principle incapable of being given, of being present-on-hand, of being contemplated: it is I-for-myself.[41]

Bakhtin's conception of subjectivity is, then, premised on the encounter of the subject with alterity. In the 'aesthetic' modality it is the alterity of the other – a community or an ideology – who is either the author or transmitter of the narrative frame within which the subject inheres. In the 'ethical' modality, the alterity is internal, inasmuch as it is the encounter of the subject with an 'other' within him or herself. At the moment of ethical choice and action, the subject who has 'no alibi in being' must face his or her own singularity and – if necessary – venture outside the narrative frame in order to act.[42]

Human subjectivity, according to Bakhtin, thus emerges architectonically in and from the tensile relation of the centripetal and the centrifugal vectors, the 'aesthetic' and the 'ethical' modes of being, both essential for our psychic makeup, which, though mutually complementary, are constantly at odds with each other. Notably, Bakhtin sometimes refers to these two movements under the respective headings of 'rhythm' and 'loophole', and we should pause for a moment to consider the significance of these synonyms. The concept of 'rhythm' as deployed in 'Author and Hero' refers to the 'plot-bearing significance'[43] of our life, our embeddedness in the infrastructure of commonality, our self-definition in and through a narrative of grounding, continuity and coherence, which can be established and ratified only from outside, through the containing, aestheticizing eyes of an authorial other.[44]

But while this pattern, or 'rhythm', affords a much-needed sense of grounding, cohesion and wholeness, it also 'presupposes a certain *predeterminedness* of striving, experiencing, action (a certain hopelessness with respect to meaning)'.[45] Translated into our own terms, this 'predeterminedness' means that there is an inverse relation between the degree of narrative coherence (rhythm) in our self-perception and our freedom of choice and action. In order to live, to make choices and to act, the ethical subject, 'I-for-myself' must always slip out through a 'loophole', transgressing the boundaries of the narrative frame.

The Bakhtinian conception of the 'loophole' marks the moment of ethical choice and action. It is a moment which

> does not submit to rhythm – it is in principle extrarhythmic, nonadequate to rhythm. Here rhythm becomes a distortion and a lie. It is a moment where … being and obligation meet in conflict within me; where *is* and *ought* mutually exclude each other … Free will and self-activity are incompatible with rhythm. A life (lived experience, striving, performed action, though) that

> is lived and experienced in the categories of moral freedom and of self-activity cannot be rhythmicized.[46]

'I myself as *subiectum* never coincide with me myself; I – the *subiectum* of the act of self-consciousness – exceed the bounds of this act's content. [It is a matter of] an intuitively experienced loophole out of time, out of everything given, everything finitely present-on-hand.'[47]

The Bakhtinian subject is thus 'poetic' through and through in that, while thoroughly embedded in the infrastructure of commonality, the narrative 'rhythm' of continuity and coherence, it will always attempt to transcend and exceed it through 'loopholes' of its own making. Rendered through these terms, Bakhtin's conception of subjectivity seems to be quite close to the definition of 'literariness', formulated by Viktor Shklovsky, Bakhtin's contemporary and one of the pioneers of formalist theory.[48] The complexity of Bakhtin's relation to the formalists is obviously beyond the scope of this essay, but we should note that his juxtaposition of the terms 'rhythm' and 'loophole' is very similar to Shklovky's juxtaposition of 'habituation' and 'defamiliarization'. Indeed, for Shklovsky, the very definition and *raison d'être* of art is to awaken us into a renewed experience of our everyday, habitual reality through strategies of 'defamiliarization', of making the familiar strange again.[49] This recognition of heteronomy, let us recall, is further reinforced in Bakhtin's later insistence that the subject is 'wholly and always on the boundary', having no sovereign internal territory, inasmuch as one receives one's name 'from others'.[50]

To conclude this discussion, we may now turn to the nexus of literature and moral philosophy, as refracted through a Bakhtinian prism. Bakhtin does not deal with the relation of reader and text, but when we extrapolate his conception of ethics into the process of reading, it becomes clear that the underlying principle of this process should be *performative* rather than thematic. As any reader of literature would recognize, the distinctive trait of good literature is the impossibility of separating form and contents and the manifest insufficiency of resorting to paraphrase as a substitute for the actual experience of the literary text. As Bakhtin's reading of Dostoevsky suggests, the ethical impact of literature cannot be found in any explicit theses or arguments which seem to emerge from the literary text. It does not emerge from anything that a text has to 'say *about* ethics', but from the way it *acts*, generating its truth in and through the encounter of self and other and the recognition of an otherness within oneself. To use the categories favoured by Levinas, it is not in the 'said' but in the 'saying' that the dynamics of ethical subjectivity take place, and when it comes to literature it is impossible to disentangle them. Dialogism, to recall our earlier formulation, is not only an *inter-subjective* phenomenon but an *intra-subjective* articulation of non-self-coincidence.

The 'ethical turn' of literary studies over the past twenty years has taken different forms, ranging from various conceptions of literature as a mode of moral philosophy to discussions of the ethics of reading, canonicity and ideology. Their diversity notwithstanding, many of these discussions take a primarily thematic approach, relating to literary works as test cases, illustrations, sublimations or concrete representations of norms, values and attitudes. The insistence on the ethical import of literature is thus sometimes translated rather reductively into ideological pieties and polemics, and even – in extreme, but not very rare instances – demands to strike some allegedly offensive classics off the canon. But good literature, as we well know, is all-too-often resistant to political, ideological and even moral correctness. A good story does not always have a good moral; evil characters are often more real, attractive and memorable than virtuous ones; good authors are often far from exemplary figures in their private lives and histories; and the best literary works tend to leave us with more questions than answers. The representational or thematic approach is clearly not adequate to the complexity of the relation between literature and ethics. This is certainly not to say that literature can be disassociated from the question of value, but it does suggest that the limitations of the representational or thematic approach should be seriously probed when we consider the nexus of literature and ethics.

The best case in point is probably Conrad's *Heart of Darkness*,[51] which had been read since publication as a vehement condemnation of colonial practices, ideology and rhetoric until, seventy odd years after its publication, it was strongly critiqued by Chinua Achebe, for the apparent racism of its author. Achebe's article[52] generated a huge amount of discussion, and the debate is by now amply evident in academic syllabi, making it familiar to most readers (and far too complex and prolonged for inclusion in the present discussion). So, rather than engage with Achebe's claims and with the subsequent discussions that followed in his footsteps, I would point out that Achebe focuses mainly on some of Marlow's expressions, identifying the character with his author, failing to recognize the irony in some of these comments and – most problematically – dismissing the framing narrative and the temporal and spatial distancing it generates. Putting it briefly, Achebe's thematic or 'representational' approach and his summary judgement of Conrad as a 'thoroughgoing racist' are self-defeating reading strategies, which fail to do full justice to the issues involved. I believe that this debate may be better conceived – following Bakhtin – through a *performative* rather than a *representational* or thematic perspective.

The performativity of this text is generated precisely by its relative opacity and the various instances which trigger unease on the part of both Marlow's listeners and the readers of the narrative. Thus, for instance, the difficulty of determining Marlow's stance when he prefaces his narrative with the comment 'and this also ... has been one of the dark places of the earth',[53] and then proceeds with an imaginary reconstruction of the experience of a Roman commander of a trireme during the conquest of Britain.[54] Is the analogy meant ironically? The answer to this question would depend on the stance of the listener, who serves as the frame narrator and somewhat impatiently refers to 'Marlow's inconclusive experiences',[55] and that of the reader, which may well go through some modification in the course of his or her engagement with the text. This opacity is further reinforced when Marlow refers to British imperialism, its 'efficiency' and the redeeming 'idea' behind the conquest of the earth which 'mostly means the taking it away from those who have a different complexion or slightly flatter noses than ourselves, [and] is not a pretty thing when you look into it too much'.[56] There are many more instances of these triggering points, where the degree of Marlow's complicity, or indeed, his awareness of complicity either at the time of his journey into the darkness or later, in the course of the narration, is left for the reader to determine.

Having taught this novella time and again throughout decades of academic work mostly in a politically troubled and conflicted setting, I have realized that most mature readers, confronted with the question of Marlow's (or Conrad's) alleged racism, or his position vis-à-vis the horrors of European colonial practices in Africa and the brutal dehumanization of the Africans, which is at the core of Achebe's condemnation, would not only fail to remain personally uninvolved but would also be impelled precisely due to these and many more instances of opacity to ask themselves how they would act or feel in Marlow's place. The question is simple enough, but it does involve a consideration of the historical and the biographical context of the writing, the distancing of Marlow's narration through the introduction of a frame narrative, the unresolved issues of whether Marlow's retrospective account, or some of it, is rendered ironically, the significance of the time gap between the journey to Africa and the belated narration of what happened during this journey and Marlow's return to Europe, as well as the relevant question of Conrad's own position as an author addressing a readership of many whose livelihoods and careers were interlinked with the fortunes of the British empire. For most readers, in my experience, the answer to the question 'what would I do in Marlow's place?' is never easy, glib or uniform, of course.

I suggest, then, that regardless of their ultimate ideological positions, what happens to readers in the process of engagement with this text is in itself highly significant: to put it briefly, it is precisely the urge to ask the question, to look at oneself as an unknown 'other', and to experience some bafflement as to the answer, which makes *Heart of Darkness* such a fine example of performative literary ethics, and it is the very challenge of reading one's hypothetical self in quotation marks, as it were, and seeing it as potentially refracted in and through Marlow's narrative which makes this text so ethically compelling. Reading this novella with its challenging ambiguities and its refusal of a neat closure is in itself a performative process, an ethical mode of communication, inasmuch as it underscores the borderline position of the reading subject and triggers a constant modification of one's self-definition in the contact with the otherness of the text. To follow Bakhtin's conception of subjectivity, the discovery that we are never identical to ourselves and can never know ourselves in our entirety, the response into which we are impelled in the process of confronting the alterity of the text along with our own strangeness to ourselves (to paraphrase Kristeva) amounts to living on our own borderlines, that is, the first step towards an ethical mode of being. The admission of alterity – 'admission' both in the sense of 'acknowledgement' and in the sense of 'letting in' – is what causes the ethical to stir underneath the surface of textual aesthetics.

3

Cows on the highroad: Making ethical literary criticism real

John Krapp

It is hard to believe that the field of literary study ever passed through a decades long period in the second half of the twentieth century when the legitimacy of ethical literary criticism was either diminished or dismissed outright. There is no need to rehearse the arguments for these criticisms here.[1] I note instead that the institutional suspicion of, and antagonism towards, exploring literature for its ethical value is rather clearly in the past.[2] I do not imagine things could have really gone any other way. If we can agree that human beings exist in time, then we must concomitantly permit that human beings are constantly exposed to change. Change is prompted by conflict, by tension, by whatever interrupts stasis. The existential reality of time assures that conflict and tension are inescapable in the material world. Thus, then, are ethics. In their most fundamentally pragmatic expression, ethics provide the vocabulary by which human beings negotiate scenes of conflict, of tension, that are framed by language and concepts clarifying a difference between good and bad, right and wrong, however these categories may be defined. Ethics are an operational tool with which human beings may try to establish some form of certainty when confronted by choices of a very specific kind. Because it is such a natural medium for representing the conflicts and tensions in the subjective interpretation of various ideological claims, literature has always been among the most ideal vehicles for elucidating and refining the methods by which, the standards on which, we make choices.[3] There was never a compelling reason to believe that one's reading choices could be entirely divested of ethical considerations. Depreciating the ethically instructive potential of literature was fated to be proven little more than fashionably short-sighted.[4]

Commending the ethical value of literature is not, however, without its problems. One of the limitations that any ethical study of literature has always confronted involves audience.[5] So much literary theory and criticism has inevitably been a conversation among professionals who have chosen one or another similar niche for their academic labour; it is in many instances an isolated, insular enterprise. This is not to detract from the value of this intellectual work, so much of it outstanding. It is just to say that the impact of much excellent ethical literary criticism has predictably and unfortunately been limited to members of the scholarly community.[6] What has always interested me is a way to write about the ethically instructive potential of literature as it is embedded in textual moments that can easily be translated into much more general experiential practice, a practice so substantively and linguistically accessible that any curious individual may use it to address the ethical complexities that life presents each day.[7] On this view, literature may be read for its broad capacity to encourage readers to reflect on how and why they think about ethics the way they do. It may help readers develop an appreciation of the nuances inhering in the process of ethical decision making even as they may incline towards authorizing one ethical position over another.[8]

To explore how literature may encourage intellectual activity invested in practical ethical concerns, I wish here to focus on how literature can help human beings negotiate a need for certainty in order to create and maintain community.[9] Literature can achieve this goal by demonstrating how forms of community are disrupted when certainty is thrown into doubt, and by representing the ethically instructive dimension of the deliberations required to re-establish form. The literary options to explore these dynamics are limited only by imagination. I will narrow my argument to the disruption catalysed by a literary character appearing frequently throughout the chronicle of western art – the devil – as he appears in Arthur Miller's *The Crucible*. The devil is a particularly felicitous site to explore the human inclination towards certainty because of his evolving role in intellectual history. Some features are, however, consistent. The devil upsets the calm of stasis. He is characteristically a source of uncertainty. He may be viewed as an irrepressible agent of chaos, causing dislocation, disorientation, distress, disease. Simultaneously, the devil is just as often characteristically and apodictically represented with authoritative certainty as the distillation and apotheosis of evil. Few, if any, literary characters have such causal impact that demands some kind of reactive engagement. My route through the reflections that follow begins with some general claims about the ethical dimension of literature in ancient world communities with a monistic understanding of its most foundational values. This will allow me to draw comparison to the search for certainty in the rigidly dualistic ideological environment of Miller's play.

Elaborating the negotiation of ethical tension in moments of formal disruption suggestive of nefarious influence may also prove to have real-world significance of enduring value. It can open a way to understand and to address a complex phenomenon that has become nearly inescapable in a variety of discourses in early twentieth-century western culture; that is, the way communities are fractured when the desire for certainty prompts some people to demonize those that they identify as other. In the United States alone, to which I will restrict my concluding summary comments, the price we pay for the demonization of others is immediate, clear and real. Perhaps ethical literary criticism can play a role in reconfiguring how we understand certainty in the service of repairing community. Even if this goal proves too ambitious, my hope in the end is to share impressions and observations convincing enough to warrant a response that may challenge or even defeat them, an outcome that will, if ironically, continue to endorse the vital importance of ethical literary study while simultaneously demonstrating the ethically instructive potential of literature.[10]

From its classical roots in Antiquity, a primary goal of western philosophy and theology has been the search for certainty that, at least until the middle of the second millennium CE, was typically defined by a conception of truth that is objective and absolute, qualities assured by its origin, which is metaphysical. Within ancient world communities, some form of divine authority or privileged spokesperson, typically clergy or royalty, often expresses the community's values. The access to absolute truth, meaning and value gives a figure of authority extraordinary power, because power, as I will define it throughout the reflections that follow, is the ability to represent reality. The Hebrew Bible puts this expression of power on display in the story of the Special Creation recounted in the opening of Genesis, where Yahweh quite literally speaks the truth of things, and their essential value, into existence in the act of incarnationist signification and judges them good. Once truth and value are understood to exist objectively, human beings are tasked to try to be as precise as possible in using words to correspond to these concepts and categories. The closer people get to accurate correspondence, the closer they get to understanding the mind of God and the more accurately and authoritatively they can speak for God. Priests and kings, especially when the latter rule either by the will of the gods or are reflections of divinity, get closer than anyone else. Their insight into the truth and value of things seems to transcend the ideological and to exist as a reflection of the natural order of things, which is free of human bias, prejudice and error.

One of the effects of the certainty underpinning ancient world cultures is that it theoretically shuts down *conversation* about ethics because conversation requires at least the possibility of intellectual error, of a change of thought or opinion. Ethics are simply legislated. Nevertheless, in many of these ancient cultures, most obviously those traditionally designated as humanistic, we see literature that problematizes the ontological and epistemological qualities of value. This literature makes a critical contribution to our understanding of the difference between the theoretical and the practical by illustrating the ambivalences and ambiguities that underpin the production of knowledge when uncritical capitulation to authority is presumed to be the norm. At the same time that absolute values that issue from divine sources are being put into tension with more relativistic ones that issue from human beings, there is often a reciprocal sense that the absolute cannot be so easily refused as a foundation for knowledge. This literature thus presents the reader with the ethical possibility of what might paradoxically be called a contingent absolute. To appreciate such a philosophical circumstance requires intellectual flexibility and adaptability willing to entertain the idea of certainty in uncertainty, which, as *The Crucible* will dramatize, can be a forbidding habit of thought.

In *The Devil: Perceptions of Evil from Antiquity to Primitive Christianity*, which is the first part of his four-book study of the evolution of the mythology of the devil throughout intellectual history, Jeffrey Burton Russell offers an explanation for why ancient world communities may have been well-practised in accepting ambiguity and ambivalence in their foundational values. It begins with the idea of monism as it applies to aspects of the divine in the ancient world. On its most basic definition, monism is any of several theories holding that reality is only one basic substance or principle, that all processes, structures, concepts may be reduced to a single governing principle. Of the impact of monism on the ancient world's conception of the divine, Russell notes:

> The Gods of the Greeks, like those of Egypt and Mesopotamia, were ambivalent manifestations of the one God. The apparently contradictory ethical and ontological qualities of the gods indicate confusion less than they do the coincidence of opposites. In Homer, little distinction is made between *theos* and *daimon*, and the characteristics of both are ambiguous ... Both good and evil are seen to proceed from the one God, of whom the individual gods are manifestations. Thus the gods as a class, and each god or goddess independently, possess both good and evil qualities. This ethical ambivalence is underscored by another. Almost every god shows signs of both an ouranic (heavenly) and a chthonic (underworld) character, the chthonic being more often assimilated to the concept of evil. All these ambiguities result in part from the fact that the figure of each god as known in the classical period is a synthesis of many diverse elements derived from local cults, some as old as the Minoan period and some even derived from Near Eastern origins.[11]

Monism of the kind Russell describes demands acceptance of ambiguity and ambivalence, of inconsistency and contradiction, in any effort towards apprehending stable knowledge of phenomena. Conceptually, monism presents an irreducible complexity that pre-empts easy evaluation of the categories captured by it. It problematizes ethical judgement, blurs the lines between right and wrong, good and evil, which one might expect to be clear in a culture constructed on absolute values. The ideological tensions monism inexorably engenders can only really be conclusively resolved through an act of faith.[12]

A salient example of ambiguity and ambivalence inhering in a monistic concept lies at the heart of Socrates' conversation with Euthyphro on the value of piety in the *Dialogue* titled *Euthyphro*. Euthyphro begins his argument with a claim to the insight to absolute knowledge of the meaning (Form or *eidos*) of piety, defining it as 'what is dear to the gods is pious, what is not is impious'.[13] Socrates methodically erodes this certainty until he literally puts Euthyphro on his heels. At the centre of the debate is whether it is good for Kronos to have castrated Ouranus, and it becomes clear that what is dear to one god might not be dear to another. How might the dialogue have gone if Euthyphro had responded to Socrates' relentless questions about the gods' intent with a statement like, 'yes, the gods contradict themselves, and who are we to try to understand that? They are gods. We are not.' In a way, Euthyphro's mistake is that he does not simply profess a faith. He tries to make a reasonable argument for his position, and, in so doing, he directly demonstrates a facet of ethical literary criticism I find compelling. It is not to authoritatively define 'piety' in terms that exclude others. It is to explore whether such authority exists and why it is desirable in the first place. Socrates contends that the gods are beyond human understanding; their monistic character makes it virtually impossible to consistently predict them. So, it's a fool's game to try. Instead, we need to stop bending our knee to an authority we cannot comprehend and focus our efforts on understanding truth and meaning and value in the human community. Imagine the tension such a conflict between the truth of absolute and relative values might cause in a community not quite prepared for it. Imagine, too, the tension it might cause the individual mind thinking it.[14] Literary texts illustrating ways in which ethically consequential encounters with monistic concepts impact the search for certainty in creating and maintaining community abound in the ancient world.[15] For its graphic mapping of the Roman underworld, Vergil's *The Aeneid* best accommodates my discussion of how a literary text might inspire readers to negotiate the pluralistic meanings of monistic concepts as they consider their own community's foundational values. It is a model of how literary criticism can be translated into ethically informed, existential practice.

The Aeneid was written from approximately 30 to 19 BCE. It was commissioned by Octavian, or Caesar Augustus, who ruled from 31 BCE until his death in 14 CE. Octavian was Julius Caesar's great nephew and chosen heir, a relationship he was not unwilling to exploit. In 42 BCE, two years after his death, Julius Caesar became the first Roman citizen to be deified. He was named in death 'The Divine Julius'. Octavian used this as an opportunity to claim divine paternity and to promote the idea that he was the son of a god. Octavian's rise to power was, however, freighted with ambiguity and ambivalence within the Roman community. Octavian had consolidated Roman rule under his authority, which effectively rendered Rome a democratic republic in name only. He still maintained the pretence of elections, but the Senate essentially capitulated to his sovereignty and, in 27 BCE awarded Octavian the name 'Augustus', 'the Illustrious One'. It's not hard to imagine Octavian surveying the nation to which he had brought the *Pax Romana* and wondering why Rome did not have a national epic to celebrate the history of its birth, its status as first among nations, and the values of the mighty Roman people culminating in his leadership. *The Aeneid* would be this epic. It would solidify the Roman community after a period of discord. As Shadi Bartsch notes in the introduction to her translation: 'Here, then, was a Roman poem which ... told the story of a nation as much as of an individual.'[16] Vergil was tasked with composing a story that could explain the founding of Rome in a way that would celebrate a man who, by all appearance and understanding, ruled as a king in a community that had proscribed such an office and that made calling oneself king a treasonable offence punishable by death.[17] So there was clearly some ambiguity in the way language signified meaning when referring to what exactly Augustus was. Moreover, Vergil was describing the Trojan War, which is usually dated to the twelfth century BCE, as it was stylized by Homer in the eighth century BCE, in the first century BCE in order to concretize his contemporary community's values in a way that would provide clarity and instruction for future generations of Romans.

In its dramatization of the concept of piety, *The Aeneid* reflects the unstable inflection point of interrogation into a critical value upon which many ancient communities sought certainty. Bartsch writes:

> The Latin term pius has a broader compass than the English word 'pious' and refers to at least three simultaneous kinds of piety: piety towards the Olympian and household gods, as manifested in prayer, obedience, and offerings; piety towards one's family and ancestors, in particular the male line; and piety toward one's country, which demands a willingness to die fighting for it. Aeneas is characterized as pious in over twenty places in the epic.

He concludes that '*the Aeneid's* hero models many of the Romans' own beliefs about themselves – piety, self-sacrifice, endurance. In the episodes where Aeneas seems less heroic and more confused than his Homeric predecessors, the critics credit precisely his piety, maintaining that it is a difficult quality in an epic warrior.'[18] But, Bartsch argues, these critics miss the point, which is that piety itself is being held up to scrutiny because there is no way to understand a value that prompts its aspirant to contradictory behaviour. Bartsch is implying that Vergil is in a way playing Socrates, here. Vergil is writing a text that celebrates absolute authority at the same time that it undermines it as a pretence. As such, it forces any reader of it to confront the idea that truth and meaning and value are fluid, mutable, and that any claim to the opposite is ultimately unsupportable, any belief in the opposite an act of faith.

The Aeneid reveals the monistic ambiguity upsetting conceptual determinacy at the very beginning of Book 1, when Venus comes to her father Jupiter and reminds him that the founding of Rome by her son Aeneas was her promised return when she 'weighed one fate against the other'[19] and allowed Troy to be sacked by the Mycenean Greeks. With Venus's comment, Vergil immediately throws down the gauntlet. How can there be two fates? Fate is fate. It is one thing. If fate is so far beyond human comprehension, can we, *should* we, really invest it with such authority? If any attempt to make sense of it is likely to be wrong, why pretend that a single 'right' is ever within reach? Perhaps it is time to think differently and to confront the notion of the absolute unknown for what it is: unknowable. The notion of fate, so fundamental to a conventional understanding of the Greco-Roman world at this time, is consistently questioned when it appears in Vergil's text.

Vergil further problematizes the value of piety as it makes demands upon empathy. While the rhetoric of violent atrocities committed even against women and children may not actually have been reflective of univocal material practice in the ancient world, it was nevertheless understood that you sometimes had to treat those who did not share your values with ruthless violence.[20] Yet, when Aeneas first arrives in Carthage, which has been primed by Mercury to be receptive towards a community outside its own, a difficult and potentially dangerous attitude in the ancient world, a mist protects him as he observes his new surroundings and comes to a temple that Dido is building in gratitude to Juno and sees 'the stages of the Trojan War, the battles blazoned / by their fame across the world'.[21] This act of Dido's piety is also an act of affiliation as it shows Aeneas that Dido values his fallen community and begins to build a sense of empathy between the two even while Aeneas reflects on the values of war. In *The Aeneid*, Vergil is reconfiguring a thousand-year-old attitude towards empathy in war at a time when Augustus seems to be betraying republican ideals and walking a tightrope over a world that he is trying to define as it is changing beneath him.

Sinon, the Mycenean Greek who gains the Trojans' confidence and dupes them into bringing the Trojan horse into the walls of the citadel, plays on the quality of empathy as he works to convince the enemy that he can be trusted. On the counsel of his mother Venus, Aeneas demonstrates empathy towards Helen when he has an opportunity to kill her for bringing so much death to his community; Venus reminds him of his larger purpose. Examples of empathy abound in the epic and, at nodal moments, suggest the possibility that one can express empathy even towards another who should be identified as undeserving of it. In a scene revealing Vergil's profound artistic gift at connecting his Roman epic with its Greek predecessors, Aeneas and his crew come across a Mycenean Greek left behind by Odysseus in the land of the Cyclops. He begs for help even as he admits to his role in the Trojan War and knows that, as a member of the wrong community, he is not entitled to it. Recognizing their common humanity in their shared enemy the Cyclops, Aeneas rescues him. This is an act of empathy. Is it an act of piety? It does not seem to meet any of the three criteria delineated by Bartsch. Could Vergil be redefining piety again as something more relative to human practice, more contingent to circumstance that recognizes a conception of human community more expansive than one based in national identity? How many competing meanings can a word have, how many competing demands can a concept make, before the options become paralyzing? Vergil refuses to release the pressure on his characters because he sees the pedagogic value of such uncertain ethical rumination.

One of the two most famous sequences in *The Aeneid* occurs in Book 4, when Dido and Aeneas (steered by the goddesses Juno and Venus) consummate, he leaves, and she takes her life. At stake is whether Dido and Aeneas are married. She says yes. He says no. How can anything so concretely defined and authoritatively ordained as marriage be a matter of disagreement? I again recall *Euthyphro* because, besides being a crucial moment of ambiguity and uncertainty, Aeneas's piety hangs in the balance. If Dido is his wife, then Aeneas owes her piety at the same time he owes it to the community of Trojans he represents to found them a new nation. How does one choose? How does one overcome this ambiguity? The most practical way is to remove it so that no choice has to be made, to flatten the depth of an overdetermined monistic concept to arrive at certainty, which is what Dido's curse on Aeneas in the underworld attempts to accomplish.

Like the gods of the ancient Greeks and Romans, their underworlds were also monistic. The landscapes varied depending on one's eternal fate, but there was no separate heaven for those who lived and died virtuously. The shades in *The Aeneid*'s underworld are dispersed into their eternal fates based primarily on their devotion to piety as defined by Bartsch in the introduction: piety to gods, to country and to family. This had to have been instructive to the Roman reading public of the time because such a concrete distinction between virtue and vice and the eternal fate that corresponded to it would have provided some certainty about a concept that may have seemed wobbly while on earth. Book 6 is a place in the epic where indeterminacy and doubt, ambiguity and ambivalence do not appear to confront the reader the way they might when considering concepts like piety or any other values debated among the living. We can now understand why Anchises' speech to Aeneas when father and son meet in Elysium is so important in any conversation about values in the ancient world in general and in Octavian's Rome in particular.

Anchises is telling his son Aeneas what values the latter must exhibit in war and peace in order to set the example that will inform the Roman community and its future leaders so that Rome can realize its destiny as a great nation, advice that culminates in the exhortation, 'Remember, Roman, it is for you to rule the nations with your power, / that will be your skill, to crown peace with law, / to spare the conquered, and subdue the proud'[22] and proves exceptionally Delphic. The remaining books of the epic show Aeneas carving his way up the western coast of Italy to found Rome, and in the final scene of Book 12, in the very last moment of the action, Aeneas is given a crucial opportunity to display the values on which his father instructs him when he has to choose whether to spare the life of Turnus, his once ferocious, arrogant enemy who essentially surrenders and requests mercy in defeat so that he may see his father again. Aeneas considers granting Turnus's plea until he is reminded that Turnus murdered his dear friend, succumbs to anger and kills him. The ending is the text's most profound moment of ambiguity, and it has prompted unresolved critical discussion as readers have tried to decide what it signifies. There does seem to be some agreement that the ending is meant to speak to Octavian and the direction in which the Roman community was heading as it was leaving the last remnants of republican values behind in its move towards empire. Beyond that, the ending defies univocal interpretation. Is this intentional? In the end of a text whose goal was to create certainty regarding the character of a people and its national identity, is Vergil endorsing the idea that uncertainty is more desirable than the wrong certainty because it prolongs debate through which values may be refined? Is he trying to warn his readers not to get complacent in their beliefs? Is Aeneas's final choice in battle a way to promote the value that a healthy community requires scepticism, critical inquiry and analysis so that ethical understanding may be adapted to a life lived in real, material time?

Fewer than one hundred years after the publication of *The Aeneid*, Christianities begin to take shape in the Roman Empire, and from the start, the various ideologies joined by a belief in personal salvation through Jesus Christ have a profoundly complex relationship to monism.[23] Again, my source is Russell for his exhaustive research on the inescapable, irreconcilable ideological conflicts devolving on the discord between Christianity's monistic and dualistic qualities, a phenomenon that is already present in Ancient Hebrew theology:

> The Hebrews early insisted that Yahweh was the only manifestation of the divine principle: their god became the God. They wanted their one god to be all good as well, however, and so they implicitly and unconsciously separated the evil side of the God from the good side, calling the good side the Lord and the evil side the Devil. But as the essential principle of their religion was monotheism … they had to stop short of positing two separate principles. That left the evil spirit, the Devil, in an anomalous position. On the one hand he was the author of evil, and his existence relieved the Lord of direct responsibility for many of the evils of the world. On the other hand, he was not an independent principle but the creature and even the servant of the Lord. This anomaly led to an implicit tension between monism and dualism.[24]

Christianity has no easier time articulating absolute certainty on this fundamental structural dilemma: 'Christianity is in fact a *semi-dualist* religion. On the one hand it rejects the full dualism that asserts the opposition of two eternal cosmic principles. But it has also generally rejected the monistic complacency of the hidden harmony. The tension between monism and dualism has led to inconsistencies in Christian theodicy.'[25] Russell further observes, 'Some writers still insist simplistically that religions are either dualist or not and that Christianity is therefore not a dualist religion. In fact a spectrum stretches between strongly monist religions and strongly dualist religions, and Christianity is somewhere in the middle of the spectrum, its exact position varying with the individual Christian thinker.'[26] While early Christian thinkers laboured to pinpoint exactly where the religion fell on the monistic-dualistic spectrum and to define with exactness the relationship between God and the devil, the ambiguity and ambivalence attending the role of the latter in all of this remained an intractable practical problem for people seeking certainty on matters of good and evil as they tried to work out their salvation with diligence within Christian communities. With stakes as high as these, error could be eternally catastrophic.

In November 1877, the American philosopher Charles Sanders Peirce contributed a short essay entitled 'The Fixation of Belief' to *The Popular Science Monthly*. Essentially a defence of the scientific method as the most authoritative way to epistemological certainty,

Peirce's essay observed the role that feeling plays in human cognition:[27]

> There is a dissimilarity between the sensation of doubting and that of believing ... But this is not all which distinguishes doubt from belief. There is a practical difference. Our beliefs guide our desires and shape our actions ... The feeling of believing is a more or less sure indication of there being established in our nature some habit which will determine our actions. Doubt never has such an effect ... Doubt is an uneasy and dissatisfied state from which we struggle to free ourselves and pass into the state of belief; while the latter is a calm and satisfactory state which we do not wish to avoid, or to change to a belief in anything else. On the contrary, we cling tenaciously, not merely to believing, but to believing just what we do believe ... Belief does not make us act at once, but puts us into such a condition that we shall behave in some certain way, when the occasion arises. Doubt has not the least such active effect, but stimulates us to inquiry until it is destroyed.[28]

Peirce's speculations support Russell's explanation for why, faced with the uncertainties attending a monistic view of the devil, some might incline towards Christian theology's more dualistic expression to avoid potential ethical misstep. After all,

> dualism wrenches from the unity of the God a portion of his power in order to preserve his perfect goodness ... In addition, dualism does seem to offer an explanation of the world as we really observe it, a world in which the mixing of impulses to good and impulses to evil is not readily explicable. Much would in fact become understandable if there were a force drawing us to evil as well as one beckoning us to good ... In any event, dualism insists upon the existence of an absolute and radical evil.[29]

Impressed by conceptual coordinates both monistic and dualistic, the devil comes to occupy a liminal position in the evolution of western literature, which is inextricably entangled with Christian ideologies that inform the cultural context for western artistic expression from the late Empire even to the twenty-first century. This is how the devil is simultaneously a site of certainty and uncertainty for people trying to establish practical ethical bearings to maintain community and their place in it. Framed in this manner, Arthur Miller's *The Crucible* reveals the way literary characters in the devil's disruptive presence seek ethical certainty that is undermined by the literary landscape into which their authors have situated them. This disjunction between characters' ethical agenda and the logic of their environments provides insight to the dynamics of concretizing practical ethical judgement; it also illuminates the mechanism of specific cultural behaviour that is so deleterious to community building in the twenty-first century.

At the start of Act 4 of *The Crucible*, the magistrates Reverend Danforth and Reverend Hathorne, who have been deputed to Salem to rid the village of the Devil, are speaking with Ezekiel Cheever, a Salem tailor now serving the court's official proceedings, when the following conversation about Reverend Parris, Salem's minister, occurs:

HATHORNE: I met him yesterday coming out of his house, and I bid him good morning – and he wept and went his way. I think it is not well the village sees him so unsteady.
DANFORTH: Perhaps he have some sorrow.
CHEEVER, *stamping his feet against the cold*: I think it be the cows, sir.
DANFORTH: Cows?
CHEEVER: There be so many cows wanderin' the highroads, now their masters are in the jails, and much disagreement who they will belong to now. I know Mr. Parris be arguin' with farmers all yesterday – there is great contention, sir, about the cows.[30]

The description is easy to glide over, but in his introductory essay to the volume, Bigsby notes that, in the screenplay for the film adaptation, 'Miller has the camera observe the depredations of the countryside: unharvested crops, untended animals, houses in disrepair. But, more fundamentally than this, Miller is concerned with the breaking of the social contract that binds a community together.'[31] The Devil is mentioned in *The Crucible* over eighty times by a wide range of the characters, and nearly every evocation of the name is clearly literal. Whether as the ideological projection of psychological ideations or as an ontological reality moving within the village, the Devil *is* in Salem, and the evidence of his presence is precisely the disruption he effects in the community, the uncertainty that leads family, friends and neighbours to 'break charity' with one another.[32]

During the witch trials of 1692, Salem was a Puritan Christian theocracy that functioned on the twin principles that Absolute Truth existed and was the manifestation of a God that designated privileged human beings to express it: 'Their universe was absolute, lacking in ambivalence ... the church ... provides the defining language within which all social, political, and moral debate is conducted.'[33] Consequentially, 'in Salem, Massachusetts, there was to be a single text, a single language, a single reality. Authority invoked demons from whose grasp it offered to liberate its citizens if they would only surrender their consciences to others and acquiesce in the silencing of those who appeared to threaten order.'[34] Salem's theology, then, might appear to be a living manifestation of ancient world monistic complexity, most famously (and, perhaps, inadvertently) articulated when Reverend Hale tells John Proctor, 'Man, remember, until an hour before the Devil fell, God thought him beautiful in Heaven'[35] when, in Act 2, he visits the Proctors to 'put some questions as to the Christian character of [their] house'.[36] Hale's pronouncement, made in a moment of passion, stands, however, as an outlier in a community that otherwise has no place for theological nuance. Thus, in the same act, he is obliged to remind John Proctor that 'your house is not a church; your theology must tell you that',[37] and Hale's language grows sharper when he detects laxity in John Proctor's religious commitment: 'Theology, sir, is a fortress; no crack in a fortress may be accounted small.'[38] Danforth erases any possibility of ethical ambiguity in Puritan theology in Act 3, when he addresses the growing ambivalence about the court's charge to eradicate Satan from the village: 'This is a sharp time, now, a precise time – we live no longer in the dusky afternoon when evil mixed itself with good and befuddled the world.'[39] Danforth's assurance notwithstanding, the relentlessly dualistic depiction of the Devil as the embodiment and apotheosis of evil forced the Salemites into cascading ethical dilemmas that reveal the risk of asserting certainty where it may not exist. From the start, *The Crucible*'s dramatic tension is plotted on the oscillation between moments of ambiguity that interrupt the formal rhythm of the community and the attempt to erase doubt with clarity underwritten by divine authority conveyed primarily by Hale and Danforth. Their presumption of certainty leads directly to the communal tragedy of the trials; however, the path each is taking by the end of the play presents the reader with an opportunity to reflect on ethical presumption.

Betty Parris's stupor catalyses the play's action, and the problem is not so much that she is 'desperate'[40] but that no one in the village is immediately able to explain the cause of her condition. Unexplained is not inexplicable, but explanation often requires time, and time is something that the Salemites cannot afford if the cause of Betty's ailment leads towards the chthonic. They require fast answers of the kind a more studied exorcist can provide, and Hale arrives in Act 1 with books 'weighted with authority'.[41] The first impression he makes disarms those assembled in Parris's house because, as Hale insists, 'We cannot look to superstition in this. The Devil is precise; the marks of his presence are definite as stone, and I must tell you all that I shall not proceed unless you are prepared to believe me if I should find no bruise of Hell upon her.'[42] While this open-mindedness is not insincere, Hale leaves little doubt about his ability to arrive at truth because, contained in his books 'is all the invisible world, caught, defined, *calculated*'.[43] Hale's default setting is inevitably authority of mathematic certainty. His confidence is perhaps best conveyed in his assurance to Tituba, whom he is trying to bring back to Jesus, that 'the Devil can never overcome a minister'.[44] No falter attends Hale's conviction that his finite mind can comprehend the Infinite, nor should it in Salem's Puritan theocracy; as Hale will soon enough remind John Proctor when the latter expresses his doubts about Parris's sanctity, 'that is not for you to decide. The man's ordained, therefore the light of God is in him.'[45] Tragically, Hale's confidence that he has broken the Devil's hold over Tituba, Abigail and the rest of the afflicted girls becomes an endorsement of what was initially pretence and gives cover to the accusers now able to sustain the momentum of the witch trials.

Hale's conversation with the Proctors in Act 2 further solidifies the landscape of ethical dualism. Every time either John or Elizabeth acknowledges the possibility of ethical ambiguity regarding accusations of witchcraft or the work of the court, Hale snaps the conversation back to the absolute certainty that dualism provides. As John Proctor reflects on Rebecca Nurse that 'it's hard to think so pious a woman be secretly a Devil's bitch after seventy year of such good prayer', Hale reminds that 'the Devil is a wily one, you cannot deny it'.[46] Hale's response to John Proctor's aforementioned doubt of Parris's ministry is followed by his request that John Proctor recites the Ten Commandments, which are, of course, literally written in stone. When John Proctor asks if Hale has considered that the girls may be lying to avoid hanging, Hale momentarily demurs but recovers and shifts to ask John Proctor whether he believes in witches. John Proctor's honest moment of uncertainty before declaring 'the Bible speaks of witches, and I will not deny them'[47] leads to Elizabeth Proctor's own profession of faith: 'I cannot think the Devil may own a woman's soul, Mr. Hale, when she keeps an upright way, as I have. I am a good woman, I know it; and if you believe I may do only good work in the world, and yet be secretly bound to Satan, then I must tell you, sir, I do not believe it.'[48] Elizabeth Proctor's certainty is not Hale's certainty, and someone has to yield. Having realized that Elizabeth Proctor has 'bewilder[ed]'[49] Hale with something as natural as doubt, John Proctor puts an end to the developing strain of dissention when he assures Hale that Elizabeth Proctor does indeed 'believe in the Gospel, every word!'[50] The practical limits of Hale's dualistic ethical sensibility begin to appear at the end of Act 2. As Elizabeth Proctor is being arrested for witchcraft, Hale confesses that he cannot judge her guilty or innocent and deflects to a sermon on how the Salemites have evidently provoked God somehow, a claim that is theoretically unfalsifiable because it rests on a faith that every Puritan is expected to hold.

Hale may introduce the play's formal scaffolding that sees characters depend on the authority of theological dualism to eradicate ethical disequilibrium in the face of what they understand as absolute evil, but, in Act 3, Danforth shows that he has perfected it. As Deputy Governor of the Massachusetts Bay Colony sent to Salem to direct the proceedings of 'the highest court of the supreme government of th[e] province',[51] Reverand Danforth speaks with authority inspired by God and privileged above even his ministerial colleagues. Thus he is able to assert that 'the entire contention of the state in these trials is that the voice of Heaven is speaking through the children',[52] and that no one may question that 'there is a moving plot to topple Christ in the country'.[53] Both Danforth's role and his reputation depend on an unimpeachable belief in his probity, a probity requiring unyielding belief in ethical dualism. Yet Danforth faces a nearly impossible ethical paradox. Salem's spiritual future depends on his judgement, but he has no clear path forward to decide which of the girls' contradictory claims is morally sound. Does he believe the egregious sinner, Abigail, whose return to God signals His forgiveness of her because He has recognized a conscience and character powerful enough to have overcome the temptation of Satan himself? Or does he believe Mary Warren, a common liar whose earlier misrepresentation of the truth seems to have been prompted by a kind of passive moral cowardice in the face of pressure both from her friends and from the Puritan community to which she belongs? Either girl could be considered more virtuous, Abigail because of her successful striving against the ultimate force of evil in the Christian world, or Mary because she never succumbed to this force in the first place. Danforth's dilemma is one faced by any human mind obliged to comprehend the divine. Danforth must choose if he is to execute the responsibility for which he has been deputed to Salem and redirect the village towards God, but the proceeding 'is growing into a nightmare',[54] and he has no solid foundation for choice.

Abigail nearly offers Danforth a way past ambiguity by pretending to feel the Devil's presence after realizing she may have overstepped her own power when she threateningly asks him, 'think you to be so mighty that the power of Hell may not turn your wits'.[55] Whatever clarity Danforth may gain in this moment is dispelled when John Proctor immediately thereafter reveals his affair with Abigail. It is fair to say that, at this point in the play, Danforth is lost. He has no authoritative way to plot an ethically sound path forward. Facing nothing but uncertainty, and with both the spiritual welfare of the Salem community and his own reputation in the balance, he finds his solution not in God, or scripture, or dogma, or any other absolute differentiation between good and evil, right and wrong, truth and falsehood. He finds it in the testimony of Elizabeth Proctor's judgement of her husband's moral character because he has been told earlier by John Proctor that 'in her life, sir, she have [*sic*] never lied. There are them that cannot sing, and them that cannot weep – my wife cannot lie. I have paid much to learn it, sir.'[56] The inescapable need to meet the theological demands of ethical dualism has pushed Danforth to depend on what is confirmed in his theology to be entirely fallible.

No character's ethical sensibility in *The Crucible* is tossed about more than Mary Warren's. Mary knows the truth of what happened in the forest, and the subsequent misrepresentations of the girls' behaviour, but she is pressured by them, by John Proctor, by her own terrified conscience, to express competing ethical values until the conflict is too great to bear; anxious that her own salvation may be imperilled by her lies, facing banishment from her cohort of friends, she denounces John Proctor at the end of Act 3 as 'the Devil's man!'[57] There will always be debate on why Danforth takes Mary Warren's pronouncement in this moment as truth; his motivations – vanity, conviction, confirmation bias – are many. What is not in question is that he rests his judgement to condemn John Proctor on the word of some human beings over others for the apparent reason that the community requires an absolute judgement to cleanse itself of the Satanic influence by which they believe it is being destroyed. John Proctor's 'God is dead'[58] says as much about the way the pretence of ethical dualism can shatter community as it does about any theological scenario.

Danforth's triumphant ethical authority at the end of Act 3 bespeaks Parris's claim that the stress caused by doubt occasions the need for belief; the more conclusive the belief, the more efficiently it banishes stress. Nor does his authority waver in Act 4 as he commands his fellow clergy after Parris and Hale suggest postponing executions, 'While I speak God's law, I will not crack its voice with whimpering ... Now draw yourselves up like men and help me, as you are bound by heaven to do.'[59] What then might a reader make of Hale's very different ethical position in the play's final scenes. His doubt of the girls' veracity having grown since Elizabeth Proctor's arrest, having quit the court at the end of Act 3 because he is by then convinced they are lying, and avowing in Act 4 that he has returned to Salem 'to do the Devil's work' because there is 'blood on his head',[60] he explains to Elizabeth Proctor as he pleads with her to save John Proctor's life,

> Let you not mistake your duty as I mistook my own. I came into this village like a bridegroom to his beloved, bearing gifts of high religion; the very crowns of holy law I brought, and what I touched with my bright confidence, it died; and where I turned the eye of my great faith, blood flowed up. Beware,

> Goody Proctor – cleave to no faith when faith brings blood. It is mistaken law that leads you to sacrifice. Life, woman, life is God's most precious gift; no principle, however glorious, may justify the taking of it. I beg you, woman, prevail upon your husband to confess. Let him give his lie. Quail not before God's judgment in this, for it may well be God damns a liar less than he that throws his life away for pride.[61]

Embedded in Hale's exhortation is recognition, carried on the simple phrase 'for it may well be', of the impossibility of Danforth's absolute ethical certainty. For the ethical literary criticism that I am proposing, the abiding question is, what motivates the difference between Hale's ethical landing place and Danforth's as dawn approaches on John Proctor's hanging? It goes too far to assert that Hale is renouncing ethical dualism, but he has quite clearly embraced its limitations after witnessing the tragedy to which he has contributed. Why is he able to extend doubt about the sincerity of the girls' claims, of the justice of the executions, indeed, of the very will of God once Danforth has abolished his temporary ambivalences and accepted all of the death his judgement will bring to Salem? The distinction between the reverends' respective ethical positions as the drama concludes is informed by the ethical architecture of Miller's play and forces open a dialogue about values that dualism works to pre-empt. It encourages the reader to reflect on why people seek certainty the way they do, about what counts as evidence for belief, about whom they select as the spokesperson for truth. This is to say that *The Crucible* models the upset of habits of thought on which the mind tends to incline over time in order to maintain the desired forms of things, forms that impact the way we conceive of, and maintain, community.

No one even casually aware of the sociopolitical climate in the first quarter of the twenty-first century is unfamiliar with the way some represent it as a hellscape of devils, witch hunts and other Satanic influences pushing towards a cosmic war. The US political discourse itself can make it seem as though we have never moved beyond the 'demon-haunted world' that Carl Sagan described in his 1995 discussion of how science could serve to illuminate understanding of things once thought to be beyond human comprehension. Evidence does not require academic research or scholarship, though this is growing more abundant and also recalls the long history of conjuring the forces of evil as part of an ideological agenda.[62] Consumers of mainstream media are constantly confronted by ideas and images of nefarious powers that would have been comfortably at home in Salem in 1692.[63] On 31 May 2024, fewer than twenty-four hours after his conviction on thirty-four felony counts of falsifying business records to influence the 2016 American presidential election, the former US president Donald Trump spoke outside of Trump Tower in New York and described Juan Merchan, the New York County Supreme Court Justice presiding over the proceedings, as 'this man who looks like an angel, but he's really a devil'. Following the unsuccessful attempt on Trump's life at a 13 July 2024 political rally in Butler, Pennsylvania, Colorado state representative Steven Woodrow posted on X that 'the last thing America needed was sympathy for the devil but here we are'. The devil, then, is not particularly partisan. He is essentially a cipher first deployed to signify disruption before being pressed into the service of judgement in the expectation of ethical certainty in a landscape whose very language of left wing and right wing neatly aligns with theological descriptions of good and evil that collectively express a bedrock dualism in American values. The demonization of others most typically follows a form of disruption – a truth claim, a belief, a cultural difference, a lifestyle – that throws someone's comfortable way of thinking into disequilibrium; as in Salem, the goal is a conclusive return to cognitively assuring certainty that only an idea like an unequivocally conceptualized devil can affect. What might happen if that idea were not so clearly defined, or if so defined, not accepted on the terms dictated by another so that mention of it did not elicit an uncritically reflexive response? What if concepts like the devil, demons, hell, scattered through contemporary American discourse and wielded for the power of their absolute connotative value, were interpreted less dualistically, were instead a repository of ambiguity, of ambivalence, of nuance?

The possibility of problematizing the significance of superficially accepted language is not without precedent even in the current political moment. The images of the US Capitol building on the afternoon of 6 January 2021 have been widely enough circulated to evoke as example. The rioters, many wearing dark clothing, swarming around the white neoclassical façade upset the building's typically calm symmetrical form. It is not difficult for the human mind to move from 'that's different' to 'that's bad' when confronted with phenomena that interrupt routines of thought. Returning to Peirce, the different incites doubt, which incites stress, which teases us into action coterminous with deliberation on value. The Capitol looked different that afternoon. For many, it looked wrong; others revelled in what they were watching. The same event provoked contrary ethical responses.[64] Instructively, the dualism of visual effect was complicated by the monistic quality of the word 'patriot', whose meaning proved as fluid as 'piety' in the ancient world. Both 'sides' of the commentary on the 6 July riot constructed their arguments on their competing claims of patriotism. On one view, the rioters were patriotically exclaiming their commitment to the ideal of free, fair elections by interrupting what they identified as fraudulent governance similar to England's interference in the American colonists' efforts at political independence. On another, the rioters were thought to have engaged in behaviour that a patriot could only represent as treasonous. Had this scenario been contrived in a work of fiction, we could say that, deferring questions of right or wrong, it presents an opportunity for ethical reflection on what defines a patriot, on what terms the definition is based, on who is authorized to inscribe the definition and by whom, and, perhaps most important, why a person or community makes the ethical choices it does.

Moving beyond the internal dialogue on ethical value that literature so easily encourages is a challenge, due not least to the elemental human need for certainty, a need that increases based on the severity of the manifold consequences of its opposite. Moreover, individuals dependably demonstrate that they will prioritize self over community when uncertainty becomes too troubling. It would profit future ethical literary criticism to investigate ways human beings might become more comfortable with doubt, ambivalence, ambiguity in order to open the time and space to contend with a plurality of values. Emphasis on the form of ethical thinking rather than any specific ethical position does not have to mean surrender of the latter. But it has the potential to hold the rush to judgement in abeyance a bit longer than might otherwise be the case; much can change in the time needed to fill space that inevitably remains static in space's absence. No time, no ethics. One very practical means of combatting a reflexive desire for certainty is a rejection of slogans that saturate so many significant facets of contemporary discourse. By characteristically oversimplifying often profoundly complex ideas, slogans quickly lead to complacent, predictable rhythms of lazy, even sloppy, thinking. On perhaps the most apt comparison to conclude this essay, I return to *The Crucible*.

When he accepted his party's nomination for president at the Republican National Convention on 21 July 2016, candidate Trump represented America as a modern hellscape and declared 'I alone can fix it', invoking the absolute authority that underpinned Danforth's inflated sense of judicial acuity and that brought great suffering to the Salem community. During both his first presidency and since, Trump has faced consistent legal trouble for various acts that run contrary to established law. He has just as consistently labelled the detractions against him a 'witch hunt'. Whatever might be said for the historical accuracy of this reference, there is nothing ambiguous about Trump's intention in using it: he is signalling total, uncritical condemnation of those he perceives as upsetting form: of his self-image, of the way he wishes to live his life, of the way he imagines government is supposed to function. Trump is depending on the phrase to eliminate doubt about his behaviour before doubt is granted time to do the work of inquiry. If Peirce is correct on the anxiety engendered by doubt, it is not surprising that Trump's language elicits the reactions it does from both his supporters and his critics alike. The call of and response to the slogan immediately reinforces ethical habit. Put very simply: in different ways, it makes people invested in ethical judgement feel good. With the devil loose in the Massachusetts Bay Colony, Miller shows his readers that the desire to feel the good of certainty must be weighed against the collective harm that certainty may cause. The work is hard. It takes time. It is unrelenting. It may also be all that distinguishes future communities from the suffering experienced in Salem in 1692.

PART TWO

Literature for Moral Growth

4

Community, self, trust and shared reality in Alice Munro's 'Fits'

Nora Hämäläinen

Sometimes a very short narrative can bring us to the heart of central ethical issues, not only relevant for us as moral beings, but also as moral philosophers. For me Alice Munro's short story, 'Fits' is a case of this.[1] I used it in teaching once, some years ago, inspired by what I thought of as its capacity to spur ethically engaged literary discussion in a group of MA students, many of whom had little background in either literature or philosophy. When preparing for class it surprised me, however, with its inherent complexity of ethical significance. This chapter is an attempt to spell out some of what I find and – at the same time, leaning on the story – to say something about what could be called three constitutive relations in ethical life: between the self to the other, the self to oneself and the self to the larger collective; its shared language, norms, shared habits and forms of meaning-making.[2]

The story

The story revolves around two couples. The older couple of the story, the Weebles, are in their sixties, reasonably handsome, well off and fashionable, and have bought their house in the small town of Gilmore to enjoy an early retirement. The man of the younger couple, Robert, is in his forties and is described as stocky, athletic looking, with curly greying hair, large brown eyes and an affable air. A stranger to small town life, he is a civil engineer who after his father's death left an unsatisfactory job in Toronto moved to Gilmore to manage three stores in the area that his grandfather purchased as an investment after the war. Robert came to look for a simpler life and seems to fit in very well:

> His friendliness and obligingness are often emphatic, so that people get the feeling of being buffeted from all sides. This is a manner that serves him well in Gilmore, where assurances are supposed to be repeated, and in fact much of conversation is repetition, a sort of dance of good intentions, without surprises.[3]

For the past five years he has been married to Peg who works in one of the stores: a small slim woman with a 'youthful scrubbed look' sporting pleated skirts with neat blouses and sweaters. Her two sons from a previous early marriage are now in their teens. We learn that 'for a Gilmore person, Peg is reserved'. In one of the first scenes where we meet her, she smiles 'as she would smile in the store when she gave you your change – a quick transactional smile, nothing personal'.[4] The two couples are neighbours and at friendly terms but not close: the older couple have just moved in less than a year ago year and been on two longer trips since.

This is what happens: A woman delivering farm eggs to both households leaves the Weebles's eggs with Peg and Robert because the former seem to be away. Robert remembers the eggs the next morning but decides it too early to pass them on before he drives off to fix the roof of one of his shops in a nearby town. (He takes some pride in doing all the repairs on his stores and their house himself.) He leaves a note about the eggs for Peg and observes on his way that the neighbours' car is in the carport, and the snow in the driveway and yard indicates that they cannot have been out yesterday.

Stopping at the roadside diner to have lunch on his way back, Robert hears of the death of his neighbours, and rushes to the store where Peg works. Later, based on Peg's and the police's report he reconstructs the events. Peg went to deliver the eggs to the neighbours in the morning. The side door was open, and she stepped in, first to the utility room and then the kitchen. The house was warm as if the heating had been on through the night, but oddly quiet. She walked into the very tidy living room, called for them but got no answer. Some sense of disquiet made her walk up the beige carpeted staircase and towards the bedroom. Then she walked out again and drove straight to the police station in the Town Hall. Nevertheless, she arrived at the store before her co-worker, Karen, who only heard about the incident from a customer. The Weebles have been shot, and Peg has found them. 'They were murdered', says Karen. 'It was a murder-suicide', Peg retorts, 'He shot her and then he shot himself. That's what happened.'[5]

Karen, a young woman (described from Robert's perspective as good humoured, alert, efficient) who has known Peg for a long time, is taken aback by Peg's not telling her immediately, of coolly just handling it, going to work, going about her business as if it were an ordinary day. Robert, too, is perturbed. 'Why didn't you get in touch with me?' he asks. 'You were up on the roof', she says, indicating that he could not have been of much help anyway.

Community

Peg's relative silence and composure stands in contrast and potential conflict with the way things are usually handled in the small town: The habitual chatter of acquaintances meeting in the grocery or the local pub, women calling each other to report the present gossip, a weave of exchanges where the individuality of each of them seems to be momentarily given up, their voices merging into the collective, though widely distributed, voice of the town.

The town reacts to the dramatic incident in its characteristic manner: 'It was busy in the store most of the afternoon. People on the street, in the bakery and the café and the bank and the post office, talking. People wanted to talk face to face. They had to go out and do it, in spite of the cold. Talking on the phone was not enough.'[6] Everybody is informed, nobody would 'want not to know'. People are recapitulating the last sightings of the Weebles in town. By the afternoon, speculations concerning motive enter the conversation. The men tend to think it had to do with money: tax debts, bad investments. The women tend to side with the hypothesis that serious illness was involved, or perhaps marriage problems, such as infidelity.

Robert, as a city person and an outsider, has had to negotiate his place in this rather intense communal way of being together. His pleasant reassuring manner helps him blend in, but he is well aware of his differences. His harmonious relation to the local community, like his relation to Peg, seems to be mixed with both idealization and slightly condescending puzzlement. He is highly conscious of the conversational and lexical peculiarities of the locals. Through an earlier incident, where Robert spuriously began to explain a word to Peg, we learn that 'at that time, he had a very faulty comprehension of Gilmore vocabulary – he could still make mistakes about it – and he took too seriously the limits that were usually observed in daily exchanges'.[7] This 'Gilmore vocabulary', as he frames it, is the lingua franca of smooth reassuring social exchange: one where people are not trying to stick out, make a mark, but rather contribute to a seamless social texture. This, as he has had to learn, does not tell you much about people's actual vocabularies, capacities or propensities.

The community-oriented register of talk does not imply or require universal agreement: rather, much of the exchange, especially on this day of social and moral disruption, comes forth as a range of opinions or views voiced to form a well-rounded, comprehensible, plausible account. In the current situation of crisis, the smooth flowing of this talk is interrupted, and yet at the same time it shows itself as all but banal. People crave to talk to each other of what has passed, to share rumours and speculations. There has been a murder and a suicide. The murderer is no longer among the living and thus presents no threat to them in that capacity. He was also from elsewhere: thus, their tragedy might not be thought to reflect back on the safety and moral rectitude of the local community. As a woman says (clumsily) to Robert: 'They weren't Gilmore people, not really.'[8] And yet it is fundamentally disruptive. He was just an ordinary man, nothing he said or did seems to have given note of warning. If Walter Weeble could do this, then anyone could? This kind of thing happens, not just in the generic abstract spaces of the news, rumour or statistics but also in the very concrete space of a house down an ordinary street in their own town.

Knowing and acknowledging

Peg, working all day in the store, wards off curious customers with an emphatic 'can I help you?' Not just the shop clerk Karen but also Peg's younger son Kevin displays amazement at her cool composure and relative silence about the event. Perhaps Robert is particularly alert to their reactions, maybe he even exaggerates them, because he himself is disturbed by her behaviour. He watches her in the store during the day, and at home preparing dinner while chatting with her boys in the evening: as if nothing had happened, although Kevin is trying to wring more gory details out of her. She suggests wine with the dinner however – not a usual thing for them on a weekday – and finally, gives him the whole story after dinner: 'I knew you would want to know.' That is, out of consideration for him, not out of an urgent need to tell.

The first time she shows emotion is later, when her older son Clayton – speculating about whether the Weebles had a quarrel – refers back to when his parents, Peg and her first husband, were still married and used to fight. 'I used to think one of you was going to come and kill me with a knife.'[9] Peg turns 'chalky', looking at Clayton with an expression of 'steady, helpless, unapologetic pain'. Robert tries to intervene with some general soothing explanatory account: 'It's like an earthquake or a volcano. It's that kind of happening. It's a kind of fit. But it only happens once in a long while. It's a freak occurrence.' Clayton takes this analysis to pieces, noting that earthquakes and volcanoes are not freaks and that 'if you want to call that a fit you would have to call it a periodic fit. Such as people have, married people have.'[10]

Robert hasn't been in such a marriage: Peg and he don't fight, as he observes to Clayton. Before Peg, he had consecutive serious affairs with married women, and he knows something about the venom that can overcome you in a relationship. Early on he has confessed to Peg that his previous life was characterized by the avoidance of relationships with real life possibilities. 'Errors of avoidance that I mistook for errors of passion', he says. But perhaps there is more than a bit of the error of avoidance in his relation to Peg too?

Some readers might be beginning to see that the relationship of Robert and Peg is highly amenable to what some will recognize as a Cavellian reading in terms of knowledge and acknowledgement. While told in the third person and initially in an external narrator's voice, it quite soon eases into Robert's perspective and his very quiet, almost subconscious struggle with himself and his relation to Peg. For those who are not familiar with Cavell's work, I will give a brief outline of what this means. In a number of key texts,[11] Cavell discusses misplaced epistemic demands in Shakespeare's drama. Some of Shakespeare's most interesting characters are haunted by the desire to be ascertained of facts about their loved ones: Othello's of his wife's fidelity, King Lear of his daughter's love. For each of them the epistemic demand, the need to know for sure, is an avoidance of acknowledgement of the other person, and for each of them it leads to their doom. They fail to see that what they crave is already right in front of their eyes, nothing hidden, nothing to be added. Cavell thinks of this as the moral core of philosophical scepticism, a feature which in his eyes redeems scepticism as a philosophically interesting topic, though not quite in the way traditional epistemologists would have construed it. This 'moral core' is not just a way of addressing scepticism but also a central ethical theme in its own right – one with deep affinities with Iris Murdoch's work on 'attention'.[12] They share the notion that attending to another, being attentive to them, acknowledging them, even knowing *them*, as real separate persons, should not be conflated with knowing everything about them, or seeing everything there is to be seen about them. Such expectations may well be a form of epistemic evasion of the other and her separate reality, and thus a distinctive kind of moral failure.

Cavell is not suggesting that knowledge is never relevant for proper acknowledgement of the other or the healing of a human relationship. Obviously, there are cases – for example, of suspected infidelity or found out lies – where crucial bits of knowledge can do the trick. He is rather saying that there are cases where knowledge simply will not do, where we are mistaken in demanding knowledge, or where no knowledge – no plain credible facts – can achieve what we need, because the fault is in our mode of relating, in the nature of our demand on the other and in ourselves. Knowledge is not enough for acknowledgement. As Cavell puts it: 'If I say … that the slack of acknowledgment can never be taken up by knowledge, I do not mean to say that the imagination can never be fired by information, rather that you cannot always know when the fire will strike.'[13]

Robert is, like everyone else, unsettled by the event, and in this state of mind suspicion and distrust creep in. He starts noting incongruences in his wife's behaviour after her discovery, and inconsistencies between her account and the police report. The gap between what he gets and what he finds reasonable to expect risks widening into a generalized distrust and sense of alienation. We learn that Peg, early on in their relationship, in exchange for confidences 'offered him facts' about her previous life: how she comes from a large family, how she and her husband lived with his parents on a farm, how they moved into town to a noisy place by a car wash, how he was away for his job as a truck driver and how he eventually 'went up north'. In the current situation, again, she offers him facts, but no confidences, no emotional splurge. Furthermore, the 'facts' she offers concerning the sight on the crime scene are, inexplicably, not quite right. Her coolness, which he has previously considered refreshing, now begins to look like a disconcerting lack of intimacy. Yet it is as if Robert's affability keeps the uncanny distrustful emotions in check. On first reading the story, I interpreted Robert as being profoundly disturbed by these events, but when I went back looking for formulations confirming this, they were not there. They are carefully kept under the surface, in Robert's consciousness as well as in the lexical makeup of the narrative. The organization of the text (the scenes and details delivered) builds up suspense, but only his sense of relief at the end of the story definitely gives him away.

The ending of the story offers a path of reconciliation without epistemic resolution. Robert lets go of the need to know exactly what happened and what Peg saw, realizing that this is something he will never, in some strict sense, know.

> There was one thing he was going to ask her just before Clayton came in. At least, he was turning the question over in his mind, wondering if it would be all right to ask her. A discrepancy, a detail, in the midst of so many abominable details.
>
> And now he knew it wouldn't be all right; it would never be all right. It had nothing to do with him. One discrepancy, one detail – one lie – that would never have anything to do with him.[14]

He has, in the midst of the moral commotion of the events, been overcome by an urge to know for sure and – in absence of access to the contents of Peg's mind – by a kind of moral scepticism that seems to contaminate not just his relationship to Peg but his trust in the whole small-scale, small town form of life he has built with her, far away from his previous urban and potentially more glamorous circles.

With Peg it always seemed like what you see is what you get. She is happy to continue working in the store, to raise her sons and spend her free time taking evening courses at the local high school, diligently handing in her course assignments with 'her earnest statements, her painfully careful small handwriting'.[15] She wants to stay in the modest house where she lived when they met 'in a straggling dead-end street without trees or sidewalks'.[16] Robert once said that she is the most self-contained person he has ever met, and indeed, she doesn't complain, she doesn't dwell on injustices or lacks in her past; there is no drama around her, like there was around his previous more flamboyant big city girlfriends. He appreciates Peg and what she stands for almost as a negation of what he knew before. But it is hard to overlook the condescension in his perspective on her, which has much to do with what looks like a casual assumption that there really isn't much more to her person than what meets the eye. He seems to assume, in spite of himself, that her interiority is as neat and smooth and prim as her exteriority, and that the signs of her lack of formal education are evidence of some sort of charming naivety. As they have a happy domestic life together, he assumes she would confide in him.

In the essay *The Shame of Murder* Susan Warwick also considers Peg's own work of acknowledgement, which in her reading works as a form of healing of the wound opened up by the deed.

> In Peg's 'steady, helpless, unapologetic pain' can be read the experience of ethical shame. In her initial denial of the legitimacy of her son's felt fear about the possibility that the violent exchanges between his parents might result in his murder, Peg endeavors to push aside recognition of that pivotal point between murder and responsibility. But as she finally and fully looks at Clayton, acknowledges his vulnerability, we understand the deaths of the Weebles have led her to confront, without apology, the steady and helpless pain of her own involvement in and responsibility for the suffering of others.[17]

This appears as one psychologically possible reading of what happens with Peg in the scene, but it is perhaps too explanatory regarding the movement of her mind. We see Peg in this scene through the eyes of Robert, who, of course, will see the parental guilt, as probably most readers do. But there might be more for him as well as the reader to take in here. Peg's life shows a trajectory of disorderly environments and a strenuous effort to build – for her sons and herself – an orderly life that better fits her temperament. But she does not strike me as someone who would deny responsibility for the suffering of others. Thus, the belated acknowledgement of her son's suffering seems a weak explanation for her pain, which is, I think, meant to remain opaque to Robert, yet suggesting many possibilities. If we take seriously the marital theme of the story, we might come up with a different and complementary interpretation. Maintaining a good, calm orderly life is not – even in the most favourable conditions – always easy and may come at different kinds of personal cost. Robert, with his friendly air, is a good help to her. But the desired marriage-peace seems to be premised on a form of superficiality: it seems to require that she plays a role she has been given and that she has willingly taken. So perhaps the part of the pain not explicable in terms of plain and acknowledged parental guilt is due to the less acknowledged personal cost of her self-assigned role. It is not always easy to live, ever after, a life where fighting, or even quarrelling, is not an option. Also, it is not easy to live in a relationship (and in a world) where her composure seems to make her invisible.

Thus, there would, in her pain, be a direct message to Robert, which he – given his current trajectory of acknowledgement – may be able to sense, if not quite yet to read.

Community again

The argument thus far has moved from the communal level to that of a specific relation between two people. The former seems to set the stage for the other, and some would read this step as one from superficiality (gossip) to depth (seeing the other person properly). This is, however, not my line of thinking, for reasons that have to do, not just with the story but with a distinctive perspective on moral life (and the task of moral philosophy). The one-on-one and the communal perspectives are equally important for understanding the moral action of the short story, and indeed for understanding moral life overall. I am particularly interested in the kind of broader communal activity generated by the events. The people congregating in the pub – even the curious people driving past the Weeble's and Kuiper's houses – are involved in a most important kind of moral work: that of making communal moral meaning, that is, finding interpretations that make sense to them individually and at the same time contribute to a kind of shareable moral universe. Such a universe consists partly of normative conceptions that could be formulated in some moral code, perhaps complemented by a list of virtues. But it also consists in a shared imaginary of moral lives and situations, and something like a casuistry of meaningful, comprehensible actions, choices, attitudes and judgements. When life in the town goes on 'as usual' people draw on elements of this moral universe quite unreflectively or with little effort, to make moral judgements and decisions that are meaningful to themselves and legible (if not always agreeable) to others around them. Like cases are filed with like cases. Small alterations to (or modernizations of) the 'common knowledge' occur over time, often without much ado. But when something ethically unacceptable, unexpected and shocking occurs, a new rift appears in the moral weave of the community, stimulating fervent activity around the event. The activity may seem banal, but its function is vital for the preservation of moral community, that is, a community where people – in spite of disagreements – can remain morally comprehensible to each other.[18]

It should be clear that different individuals' participation in this kind of negotiation can be of varying kind. In case of a murder, proximity to the event is likely to make a difference: the finder of the body, neighbours, friends and those who have had regular professional contact with the people involved are likely to be differently affected than those unconnected to the event. People of a similar age or situation as the victim or perpetrator may feel more affected than others. Previous experiences and traumas are likely to play in. Temperament, occupation and the nature of one's social relations are likely to make a difference for how and to what extent one takes part in the general talk. Do you have a ready circle of friends you always vet things with? Are you a regular at the diner? Are you a reverend, a doctor, a shop clerk or something else?

But there is no telling in advance how such differences play out at an individual level, and how individual efforts of coming to terms will add to a shared evaluative and descriptive account of 'what happened'.

Also, the work done by different people can be of very different quality. The people driving by the Weeble's house in their cars during the evening are easily imagined as giving way to low impulses of morbid curiosity or perhaps, in some cases, obsessiveness. People gathering in the diner are easily pictured as seeking comfort or clarity, perhaps avoiding the uncanny feelings that creep upon them in solitude. People calling their friends may be pictured (and picture themselves) as imparting vital information, gossiping or assuaging their own anxiety. Some show what we would recognize as moral rectitude by refraining from participation, while others may do so by lending an ear to a friend who is upset, although their impulse would be to have nothing whatsoever to do with the thing. The work done by Robert and Peg respectively should not be conceptualized in contrast to the work done by people in the pub, on the phone, in the cars and so on, but rather as continuous with it, as individual tokens of a movement with collective dimensions.

Furthermore, the communal view achieved through the heated social activity should not be conceptualized as a collective opinion or a verdict of the herd. The debates going on over causes of the murder show differing imaginaries that are likely to give rise to differing conclusions. The result is rather something like a shared space of agreement or disagreement, where different positions gain familiarity and comprehensibility in the eyes of others. Of course, some will feel excluded or isolated because their view does not fit within the range of vented or ventable options. (Imagine the deeply, morbidly depressed person who thinks the Weebles are lucky to be done with the business of living, or the bitter violent misogynous man who thinks she deserved it.) But the range of acceptable and thinkable options changes with time, and in the course of ongoing negotiations, in responding to new realities and experiences. It could be said that moral community consists both of shared registers of ethical judgement and interpretation, and of the places and practices for ethical venting and renegotiation. Deprive people of their places and practices, and the shared ethical framework will soon become a dead letter, unresponsive to moral experience. (Totalitarian regimes seek to destroy the places for all but the most banal moral vetting, creating a deep sense of moral alienation and distrust between citizens.)

I noted earlier that a central part of Robert's work in the story consists in acknowledging Peg as a full person, with aspects of an inner life that he cannot aspire to get access to. I also pointed to what Robert had learned about 'Gilmore vocabulary': that the limited expressions used in the maintenance of social bonds tells little of the actual vocabularies or capacities of its users. Both observations point further to the importance of not underestimating people (their public face is just a slice of who they are and what they can do), but also – perhaps paradoxically – to the significance of the work done in the public persona: the face we show to the world; the face with which we participate in everyday more or less public negotiations; the words we use in them and the words we do not use.

While the ongoing social and moral activity in the story is more intense and urgent than the regular chatty, well-wishing Gilmore talk, the difference should perhaps rather be seen as one of degree than of kind. The current talk is an inflexion or continuation of ordinary everyday talk. It is made possible by the fact that casual talking habits and relations already exist, and that there are assigned places and channels for it. It also, in its turn, makes the continuation of Gilmore talk possible, by assuaging distrust and building community, when the sense of security of its members is shaken. (Again, universal agreement is not needed for a working sense of community.) By talking themselves through the days and weeks following an upsetting event, people regain a sense of shared normality, which is the prerequisite of trust, which again is the prerequisite of community.

Ethical liminality

It may sound like something of an exaggeration to say the moral life of the town is upended by the event. Moral assessments are firm and of the expected type: condemnation of the act, acknowledgement of its element of tragedy. It is not a source of any kind of controversy over moral norms: discussions revolve around 'what happened'. Yet the sense that this kind of thing should not happen, should not be possible, gives rise to a sense of moral insecurity or groundlessness that needs to be dealt with.

Ethical disruption, with ensuing renegotiation, is a very normal part of ethical life. Such disruptions include experiences of serious moral transgression; quotidian unexpected scenes of moral disagreement; experiences (individual or collective) such as unemployment which may change people's sense of moral agency; large-scale ruptures such as war, which upend conceptions of moral duty and permissibility. Some such experiences cause a kind of loss of moral ground or security that pushes the individual to experiences of moral liminality.[19]

Given the relative frequency of morally disruptive moments in people's lives, I would not suggest that the experience of rupture in the texture of habitual moral life would as such qualify as a liminal experience. People confronted with such ruptures may go through a range of experiential, emotional and interpretive states. They may become afraid, assertive, numb, querulous, depressed and so on. Such plurality of experiences forms the palette of any ethical change or rupture at a societal or group level. We could say that many of them are part of 'ordinary' morality. To make good use of the concept of ethical liminality, we need to use it sparingly. Yet, there is a type of experiential possibility in the register of responses to moral rupture that well deserves to be called liminality, and which is portrayed in Robert, not least on his solitary walk through the snowy landscape at the end of the story.

In the evening Robert intends to join the crowd that has gathered in the diner where he first learned about the incident. They will all be talking about it and will ask him about Peg. So, instead, he walks past – further away from the town and its busy community – taking in the snowy landscape, thinking about a discrepancy between Pegs account and that of the constable in the diner, who had seen the crime scene. Peg had told her that Robert's leg was sticking out into the upstairs corridor, but this wasn't at all the position the police officer described. (As far as we can tell, Peg has tidied up the scene in her account, perhaps even in her own mind. Out of discretion, decency or squeamishness? We may not know.) Yet, as he gathered earlier, he will never be able to ask her: there is something fundamentally private, untouchable, about this.

Then something in the landscape captures his attention. He approaches a large snow-covered shape close to a woodlot, not able to figure out what he sees. Only when he gets very close does he realize that he is looking at a pile of abandoned, snow-covered cars. The description of his walk is very matter-of-factly – no fear or fright or alienation mentioned. Yet the combination of discrepancies in testimony and the visual confusion makes the scene dense with underlying disquiet, which seems to dissolve at the resolution of the visual puzzle.

> He thought of himself telling Peg about this – how close he had to get before he saw that what amazed him and bewildered him was nothing but old wrecks, and how he then felt disappointed, but also like laughing. They needed some new thing to talk about. Now he felt more like going home.[20]

The solitary walk and bewildering sight have yanked him out of a previous state of generalized distrust and unreality. He has, in his own way, had a 'fit' of the kind that married people apparently have. Not a freak occurrence, but perhaps a 'periodic fit'. What happens there in the snowy landscape is a kind of emotional and experiential bringing home of the acknowledgement of Peg that began with the insight that he could never ask her about the details of what she saw. It is, however, not an endpoint to that acknowledgement, but rather a kind of beginning. He needs to go back and talk to her, not about this, but about other things.

It seems like he needed to be on his own, with himself, in order to come to terms with what happened. Not going into the diner seems crucial here in terms of the reparation of the crack in his relation to Peg. Yet the diner is not represented as the place of the unthinking mass, but as a place of perhaps too many individual others trying to make sense: a place where his own sense-making might at this moment be devoured by the urgency of other people's needs. Placed as he is, too close to the events, solitude helps him to get back on course. Differently placed, of course, he might have gone in and done his share of the general sense-making, an activity which the story never disparages.

Thus, very concisely put, the story reads as a low-key exploration of moral community, in its individual, one-on-one and collective dimensions. It is about how community is threatened by a transgression, about the efforts made to regain community when relations are endangered, but also about how new moral possibilities (in this case, the possibility of a more substantial relation between spouses) are opened up through the trial. It also gestures towards the ethical disruption of relations as an unsettling of the self: for a moment, Robert does not know himself. Very discreetly, he comes apart: he reacts out of character, while clinging to the external trappings of who he intends to be.

This summary pushes us towards the inevitable question of novelty. What, if anything, is philosophically new in this reading? The register of knowledge and acknowledgement, and of seeing the other 'properly', is well-trodden ground in the moral philosophy inherited form philosophers such as Cavell, Murdoch, Diamond as well as Levinas and Buber. Reading the story in those terms adds, I think, to our understanding of the story, but the story read in those terms does not necessarily add much to insights already in circulation in philosophy. The relation of person to self – the theme of Michel Foucault's later volumes of *The History of Sexuality* – is so sparsely explored here that it only adds up to a substantial contribution in conjunction with the other things on offer.

Attention to the communal meaning-making, which is going on in the background, is less prevalent in the work of philosophers today and goes against a long tradition in philosophy to disregard anything that looks like chatter as philosophically and ethically unimportant. Ethnographers have, however, perhaps always recognized the societal importance of ongoing 'Gilmore talk', and the Cavell-inspired anthropologist Veena Das is one of those who have drawn philosopher's attention to it.[21] Das's thematic eye is relevant for us here also because she has worked on communities torn apart, or torn to pieces, by major political upheaval and violence. In these conditions we see how banal 'ordinary talk' forms a vital part of morally and existentially necessary community making, of reparation, and, indeed, survival.

Munro's story is interesting in this context for how moral liminality and a straying from moral community take place, and is overcome, almost imperceptibly, in conditions that – apart from the murder-suicide – must be described as peaceful. If we take the story as credible and reflective of our moral lives more widely, we must see it as a pointer towards the simultaneous fragility and resilience of moral community: a resilience premised on constant active maintenance, rather than on static permanence. Yet it also points to how this community is built up of individuals and individual relationships, all irreducibly different from each other, and equally objects or subject-objects of (potentially transformative) maintenance. And thus moral life – that is, life – opens up as a very busy place. I share this appreciation of business, I think, with authors such as Iris Murdoch,[22] Cora Diamond[23] and Martha Nussbaum,[24] all of whom have seen this aspect of moral life as a strong argument for attention to literature in moral thought (a caveat for Murdoch who did not want her own novels to be considered 'philosophical' and thought that 'philosophical novels' generally fail, but insisted on literature as deeply intertwined with morality, moral life and moral experience).[25]

But something none of them has perhaps emphasized, although I believe Murdoch partly shares this sense, is that the business, the busy-ness, of moral life does not necessarily take us 'back' to established truths inscribed in our hearts or in the stars, but to new places, places opened up for us by the parallel work of others, and the work we do with them. The triad of I to self, self to other and self to collective, is to be seen more as a heuristic aid to looking at the activity, than an account of the fundamental nature of morality.[26]

What kind of reading is this?

In lieu of a more elaborate conclusion, and given the plurality of scholarly backgrounds among those who might read this chapter, I want to give a brief account of its scholarly genre. It is a type of relatively low-key philosophical reading that aims to illuminate some themes that caught my attention when reading the story, and that resonate with my broader interests in moral philosophy.

It quite candidly addresses figures such as Peg and Robert as people, with inner lives, histories, significant relations, emotional temperaments and intellectual hang-ups: people whose 'lives' we can talk about in order to get clearer about some points of moral life or philosophy. When I first approached authors using literature for moral philosophical purposes about two decades ago, I found this practice quite casually and candidly adopted among philosophers in this field, often inspired by big names such as Stanley Cavell, Cora Diamond or Martha Nussbaum. The critique such authors received from other philosophers usually had less to do with their handling of literature than with the philosophical views they put forward: views that sometimes seemed to question the whole received practice of moral theory.[27] One had to go to literary scholars to hear the ultimate judgement: that, in fact, their whole take on literature was misguided, either because it skewed literary works to answer the questions of philosophers, or because they stupidly enough talked about literary characters as if they were like any one of us.[28]

Surely philosophers are not the only ones to speak of literary works led by their own interests and engaging them as they found them (characters and all). Many keen readers who lack the prejudice of a certain kind of humanist education certainly do. But it seemed like such practice, in those years, lacked the kind of respectable academic justification that would have made this kind of reading acceptable to literary scholars. Rewriting my doctoral dissertation for publication, I added, prompted by one of my examiners, a chapter where I sought to address recent critiques of moral philosophical readings of literature. Eventually, the publisher's referee found this chapter spurious and out of sync with the rest of the manuscript, and I dropped the topic. The worry shared by many critics – that the philosophers' understanding of literature was somehow fundamentally flawed – was perhaps never in the end a key issue in my primary context of moral philosophy.

For people working in a similar vein in the disciplinary context of literary studies the resistance to such readings seems to have been more substantial. The ensuing years have seen a literary critical rehabilitation of some of the very faults that were considered fatal in philosophical readings such as the above. Toril Moi in *The Revolution of the Ordinary: Literary Studies after Wittgenstein, Austin, and Cavell and Uses of Literature*, Rita Felski in *The Limits of Critique* and *The Uses of Literature* and both of them together with Amanda Anderson in *Character – Three Inquiries in Literary Studies* have paved the way for literary critical styles of reading where responding to and living with characters, and engaging their experiences as resonant with our own, are rehabilitated from naive mistakes to the very stuff that draws many of us to literature in the first place. Describing their joint venture, the trio writes:

> We are all interested, for example, in how fiction connects to ordinary life and the responses of lay as well as academic audiences. We are inclined to treat works of fiction as potential sources of insight rather than as examples of unknowingness or complicity

> that need to be corrected by a theoretical metalanguage. We are interested in undoing conventionally formalist approaches to literary form.[29]

They contrast their preferred type of readings against what they see as the prevalence of overly theoretical readings, perhaps above all readings guided by a hermeneutics of suspicion and a 'textual politics' 'that automatically correlates literary form to a troubling of norms or subverting of dominant ideologies'.[30] At the centre of their account is a positive valuation of the individual reader, with their particular concerns and sensibilities, including – as in the philosopher's case – concerns born out of other intellectual projects than the pure study of literature.

The professional repertoire of literary theory and scholarship should, in their view, be at the (more or less) trained readers' disposal, to be discerningly used to express and inquire into whatever one finds important and interesting in literary works, including things that may appear naive from some savvy literary theoretical perspective. Drawing importantly on Cavell among others, the reading practices they highlight are very similar to the moral philosophical readings in anglophone ethics on both sides of the turn of the millennium: especially those inspired by Wittgenstein, Iris Murdoch, virtue ethics and late twentieth-century anti-theoretical currents.

I read 'Fits' as a low-key study of the fragility and simultaneous strength of community both at a group level and in relationships between individuals. To be – that is, to work as – such study the text does not need to be intended for such use, and the reading may (as I indicated in an endnote before) include elements that were unplanned by the author. Literary authors vary in the level of awareness of what they are *doing* in ethical or philosophical respects, in and through their portrayals of characters moving through situations. Sometimes the writing of fiction may be a conscious act of moral philosophy or moral psychology, with moral or philosophical aims. More often, however, I believe, authors feel unease at such labelling, not least because they are easily interpreted in overly moralistic, simplistic terms.

Some authors like to insist on the moral philosophical work done by the literary or fictional work itself. Nussbaum calls upon Henry James's authorial intention when exploring the 'Aristotelianism' of his mature novels.[31] Cavell again likes to stress that film is a form of thought in its own right and that the thinking he derives out of Shakespeare is already there in the play discussed. The former is motivated, I think, by a strategic need to emphasize the parallelism between philosophy and some literary works (in terms of intention). The latter is motivated by an emphasis on the work he is looking at, and to bracket the question of authorial intention. Writers on literature differ in this respect depending on their philosophical or scholarly aims, as much as on the specific works or authorships they engage.

The philosophically most interesting fictional works, as I see them, tend to be those that avoid ostensive standardly philosophical ethical points and invest their energy in complex worlds and portrayals that in some way or another resonate with the readers current ethical, existential or epistemic experiences and troubles, or the tensions characteristic of surroundings in which they live. In this sense, fictional narratives representing very different genres can be 'about reality', and are addressed by readers as being so, just like philosophy, history or biography are, though by other means. This aboutness is what keeps philosophical readings of literature, as well as readings in ordinary language criticism, going.

This aboutness is also what makes 'Fits' work the way it does: its 'people' are concisely but carefully described so that we can easily picture them; bits of their background, temperament and perception of the world are portioned out so that we get to know them. Yet, at the same time, they have a convincingly crafted space around them, they are, using Auerbach's phrase 'fraught with background', although Munro provides them with much that should make this impossible: geographical, temporal and social specificity, exact descriptions of looks and so on. Auerbach's phrase is relevant because it evokes, not just the potential depth of a distinctive minimalist style of narration that he associates with the Old Testament, but also a distinctive form of engaging narratives: one where a large part of the work of reading is interpretive engagement that goes beyond the words on the page. As Auerbach puts it, the difference between biblical and Homeric narratives is that

> the human beings in the Biblical stories have greater depths of time, fate, and consciousness than do the human beings in Homer; although they are nearly always caught up in an event

> engaging all their faculties, they are not so entirely immersed in its present that they do not remain continually conscious of what has happened to them earlier and elsewhere; their thoughts and feelings have more layers, are more entangled.[32]

This is to be read in contrast to 'the Homeric heroes, whose destiny is clearly defined and who wake every morning as if it were the first day of their lives: their emotions, though strong, are simple and find expression instantly'.[33]

The possession of complex background invites rich interpretive engagement from the reader. What we are told about or shown of Munro's characters brings them to life; what we are not told or shown invites imaginative engagement and interpretive effort, which brings them to life even more. I will not go so far as to state that the genre of short story that Munro excels in is more biblical than Homeric (although such an argument might not be unreasonable). I merely mean to highlight the feature that makes these stories amenable to the kind of reading provided earlier, while at the same time pointing to the ordinariness of the practice of interpretations that grant characters morally significant 'background'.[34] What is more 'ordinary' in communities deriving from Christianity than the interpretation of narrated characters and events for purposes of ethical illumination?[35]

As Rita Felski[36] puts it, 'Characters are hybrids patched together out of fiction and life'. Characters that invite imaginative engagement beyond the page have life beyond the page, as far as most readers are concerned. The invitation happens in the individual reading, which is also where its fruits are reaped for the consumption of others. The nature of the invitation will depend on the nature of the reader. A reader interested in the substantial moral interiority of individual people, and the constitution of moral community, may turn to authors such as Munro, who have a keen eye for human exchange, and make their characters come to life beyond the page. Isn't there, then, a risk for tendentious over-interpretation: of filling the gaps in the text with one's own private fantasies, or professional hang-ups, agendas and hobby horses? Surely there is, but hardly more so than in other types of readings: all readings go beyond the text, and what kind of going beyond we or our potential readers come to find meaningful is to be seen case by case.[37]

5

'A match in a dark wilderness': Philosophy, literature and morality

Christopher Hamilton

1. I begin with two quotations. The first is from E. M. Cioran in *A Short History of Decay*:

> I turned away from philosophy when it became impossible to discover in Kant any human weakness, any authentic accent of melancholy; in Kant and in all the philosophers. Compared to music, mysticism, and poetry, philosophical activity proceeds from a diminished impulse and a suspect depth, prestigious only for the timid and the tepid. Moreover, philosophy – impersonal anxiety, refuge among anemic ideas – is the recourse of all who would elude the corrupting exuberance of life ... We cannot elude existence by explanations, we can only endure it, love or hate it, adore or dread it, in that alternation of happiness and horror which expresses the very rhythm of being, its oscillations, its dissonances, its bright or bitter vehemences .... We do not *argue* the universe; we *express* it. And philosophy does not express it.[1]

The second is from the great Spanish novelist Javier Marías who, referring to William Faulkner, said in an interview

> that when you strike a match in a dark wilderness it is not in order to see anything better lighted, but just in order to see how much more darkness there is around. I think that literature does mainly that. It is not really supposed to 'answer' things, not even to make them clearer, but rather to explore – often blindly – the huge areas of darkness, and show them better. So in my opinion it does not really matter if subjects are unanswerable (all of them are, possibly), as literature is not expected to solve riddles or mysteries, but just to show them – perhaps putting them in a slightly new light, perhaps calling attention to overlooked aspects of them.[2]

Between them, these two quotations express something that seems to me right – right about the nature of philosophy and right about the nature of literature. And they open up, I think, a helpful perspective on the fraught relations between philosophy and literature (explicitly mentioned by Cioran, implicit in what Marías says). In what follows, I aim to explore the suggestions made in these two quotations and my focus will be on the relations between philosophy and literature in terms that are largely those to do with morality.

2. Philosophy prizes certain traits of mind and character and encourages these in those who practise it: judiciousness, the capacity for close attention and analysis, steadiness and calmness of approach, balance, emotional equilibrium, critical distance, the ability to make distinctions and see differences and much that is related to these. It scorns excess, the extremes, deep and unbridled passion, rapture, ecstasy, anger and despair. And because philosophy is like this it has the ambition – whether or not it conceives of itself specifically in these terms or not, say, as therapeutic – to enable us to live better. For, in encouraging the powers of mind and personality that it values so much, it seeks to get those who practise it to live in accord with such powers, to cultivate them – intentionally or otherwise – in their life and being.

Philosophy's desire to teach us how to live with less waste, less foolishness, is hardly one that one would be disposed to reject outright. Who could seriously fail to see how destructive such things are in a human life, in human life? There are enough, more than enough, of all of them. But what happens to philosophy, so understood, when it turns its attention to literature? Actually, it may not turn its attention in that way at all, seeing itself above it, like the highly distinguished philosopher who once told me in conversation that, apart from those he was forced to read at school, he had never read a novel in his entire life. His reason was that there are no arguments in novels. When I replied that it all depends on what one thinks counts as an argument, the conversation ground to a halt. That philosopher's view is much less a minority view among practitioners of the discipline than one might suppose, though few express it so brazenly. Many philosophers think, explicitly or implicitly, that thinking about life can get by perfectly well without literature, even if it serves some other purposes – entertainment, pleasure or the like. But if philosophy does turn its attention to literature, what happens? It will be likely – I do not say that this must or always will happen, but the intellectual pressure is clearly in this direction – to recruit literature to its project of our becoming more balanced, more reasonable and judicious, less foolish and so on. In a helpful summary, Elisabeth Schellekens[3] enumerates the kind of thing that philosophers often suppose we can gain from commerce with literature: 'understanding and insight into situations we might not have experienced directly', which understanding we might apply to the extra-textual, real world, and through this deepen or expand our knowledge of the world, enabling us to judge better specific situations we confront in various ways; a refining and development of the emotions and our imagination, including where these allow us a deeper understanding of those around us; and moral education, for example, in being better able to empathize or sympathize with others precisely because we exercise these capacities in our dealings with literature.

Now, taken just in that way, there is no reason why, for example, literature should not develop one's emotions and imagination in ways that are quite contrary to philosophy's ambitions. I might, for example, thrill to Michael Kohlhaas's relentless and (self-)destructive pursuit of justice for himself in Kleist's novella and get a sense of how wonderful it is to live so passionately and without restraint; or become fascinated in Huysmans's *À rebours* by Des Esseintes's frivolous aestheticism and amoral life as a dandy, his madly unhealthy life being part of the fascination; or admire Jean-Baptiste Clamence's relentless and merciless self-laceration and laceration of others in Camus's *La chute*: at least this man has seen through the monstrous hypocrisy of bourgeois culture and can live out a fully justified and delicious misanthropy; or delight in Joana's utter selfishness in Clarice Lispector's *Near to the Wild Heart*, for she carries it off with such panache, such style and such a wonderful sense of the delicious sensuality of the world; or grasp the utter mediocrity of the life of most human beings in the relentless monologue that Thomas Bernhard's narrator offers in *Der Untergeher* – anything but being so second-rate!; and so on. But these are, in fact, never the kinds of examples philosophers tend to give when they tell us that we can expand our sympathies, educate our emotions and the imagination, better grasp others' subjectivity through engagement with literature. Philosophers always present examples that are at the least friendly to morality and often are directly morally educative. For example, Martha Nussbaum has argued that novels encourage compassion and empathy, claiming that 'the novel ... promotes mercy through its invitation to empathetic understanding ... [T]he novel cultivates a moral ability that is opposed to hatred in its very structure.'[4] And she writes: the genre of the novel, 'on account of some general features of its structure, generally constructs empathy and compassion in ways highly relevant to citizenship'.[5] Or again, Frank Palmer and Jenefer Robinson are two of the thinkers who claim that we can, through imaginative identification with characters in a novel, find that our emotions have been educated: Palmer focuses a large part of his discussion, for example, on how we come better to understand through acquaintance with Shakespeare's *Macbeth* 'what is it about murder that makes it so dreadfully appalling';[6] Robinson's focus, using the example of Edith Wharton's novel *The Reef*, is on ways in which one might learn from the work about what it really means to mistreat another;[7] and Noël Carroll has claimed that literature can help us deepen and clarify the moral knowledge we already have – the examples he gives make it clear that he is sure what moral knowledge we have and thus how some literature can nourish such knowledge while other literary texts 'mislead or confuse moral understanding and [hence] deserve criticism':[8] the correct moral outlook is anti-racist, anti-sexist, in favour of equality between men and women, sensitive to claims of justice on behalf of those who are marginalized and so on.

Philosophy tends to neutralize the kinds of responses I have referred to earlier, those that are of doubtful moral value, as Carroll does – or simply to ignore them in favour of others that are more morally congenial.[9] Why is this? I think there are two main reasons. The first is that philosophy readily understands morality as the enemy of excess, disorder, exuberant passion and as friendly to order, judicious judgement, balance, reasonableness and so on. This is, indeed, a powerful image of morality that we have. And it dovetails seamlessly with philosophy's investment in certain traits of character. Further, it is clear that morality is of extreme importance in human affairs, and philosophy always has its eye on those things of most import in human experience. So it is as if philosophy and morality were made for each other. It is in part this that Nietzsche had in mind when he said that philosophers have always come to a halt before morality. It is also in part to register his disdain for the way philosophy has of going about its business, and to oppose that, that he took Dionysus, the god of excess, as a central figure in his thinking.

The second reason is that many philosophers who wish to recruit literature to its project seem to suppose that, in educating the emotions, the imagination and so on, literature could or even is likely to influence the behaviour of those who read it. This is certainly the view defended by Martha Nussbaum, and other philosophers clearly accept it with more less enthusiasm. It thus turns out that they have good reasons for eliding or criticizing works that present exciting, appealing, thrilling images of ways of living that are indifferent or hostile to morality. For, of course, since they think that literature can influence one's behaviour for the good, it can also do so for the morally bad: it would be implausible in the extreme to suppose that its influence could only be to morality's advantage.

Now, everything here will turn on what one means both by 'morality' and by 'behaviour'. There are weak (broad) and strong (narrow) readings of these claims. On a weak or broad conception of morality, which one might think of as ethics, it seems to me clearly true that one's behaviour, again in a broad or weak sense, can be influenced by literature. Some critics such as Samuel Johnson, F. R. Leavis and Lionel Trilling have thought of literature as being morally educative in this sense and I largely agree with this approach. Richard Posner puts this well when he says that

> people steeped in literature tend to compare their day-to-day experiences with the literary counterparts of those experiences and to derive some of their expectations concerning other people's behavior from the behavior of characters in literature. They use literature as a template for life … Imaginative literature contains wisdom and psychological insights.[10]

The sense of *morality* (*ethics*) in play here is thus broad and concerns how it is that one makes sense of things in one's life, how one sees things fitting together or failing to do so and the like. And the sense of *behaviour* in question is just that: what one thinks, how one interprets oneself and others and so on. I shall return to this later. However, the sense of these terms as intended by the theorists I have mentioned is significantly narrower than that. What they mean by *morality* is, roughly speaking, *caring about others*, being *concerned about their interests*, *promoting their welfare* and the like, with the corresponding sense of *behaviour*.

But how plausible is it that literature could have this latter kind of effect on us, getting us to care more about others? I think that there are many reasons for being deeply sceptical about such a possibility. For, to make good its claim about what literature can do for us, philosophy will have to show some such thing as that, through our imaginative engagement with, and our empathetic relation to, characters in a piece of literature – a novel, say – we can become more morally sensitive to those around us and to the situations in which we find ourselves. We will have to suppose that, by identifying with fictional characters and the situations in which they find themselves, we enter into their problems, difficulties and so on and thus exercise our imagination in such a way as to mean that we are better able to be kinder, more just to others in everyday life. However, I take it that it is completely obvious that human beings, in the overwhelming majority, are extremely bad at learning from the mistakes, failures, forms of foolishness and blindness – or, indeed, come to that, from the moral successes and achievements – of the flesh and blood human beings around them. In fact, they are extremely inept at learning from these even in *their own* case. So, the idea that, somehow, they *would*, after all, be rather good at this when it comes to fictional characters seems extraordinarily unlikely, let alone that they could then apply all this to those around them in a way that redounds to others' moral benefit. Added to this is the completely obvious fact that there are plenty of people who have a rich, insightful, sensitive, nuanced relationship with literature and yet are morally utterly mediocre in everyday life – just as there are people who never go near a novel, a theatre, a poem or the like and yet are morally speaking sensitive and generous. And, indeed, if reading literature, seeing plays and so on allows us insights into others' subjectivity, such insight, in a person so disposed, might well help him or her to be all the more exquisitely cruel, spiteful or mean to others. Whence the confidence that insight into others' minds will be recruited to ends friendly to our moral life?

But we do not live in hermetically sealed boxes. There are transactions, exchanges, between a person's inner life and his or her overt behaviour and treatment of others, of course, and, *in a person already disposed to take others' concerns into account and for whom literature is important*, it is *possible* that this disposition be nurtured by trafficking with *some* (probably not very many) novels, some poetry and so on. And such a person is likely to wish to condemn a great deal of literature since novels, plays and so on are full of characters and events that, from a moral point of view, can hardly be said to pass muster – or reinterpret them so that they come out as friendly to morality. The latter is a standard moralizing move, where – to take the case of one of the examples I gave earlier – it will turn out, say, that Bernhard's narrator in *Der Untergeher* teaches us of the perils of obsessive concern with brilliance – 'I must be the best or I *die*; I stake *everything* on this' – its selfishness and its indifference to others, so that the novel comes out to reinforce some already held moral views. Carroll invites us to interpret literature in this way, although he does not consider that specific example. But that would clearly be an unhelpful moralization. Actually, Palmer takes such an approach with *Macbeth* – why, after all, as Nietzsche pointed out, could one not thrill to the play in a quite different way?

> *The morality of the stage*. – Whoever thinks that the effect of Shakespeare's plays is a moral one, and that the sight of Macbeth irresistibly induces us to shun the evil of ambition, is mistaken; and such a person is mistaken once again if he believes that Shakespeare himself thought so. He who is truly obsessed by an ardent ambition takes *delight* in seeing this picture of himself; and if the hero is destroyed by his passion, this is the most pungent spice in the hot drink of this delight. Did the poet see things

> differently? How royally and with how little like a scoundrel does his ambitious hero run his course from the moment of his great crime! It is only from this moment that he becomes 'demoniacally' attractive, and that he encourages similar natures to imitate him. – There is something demoniacal here: something which is in revolt against advantage and life, in favour of a thought and an impulse.[11]

Plato, I am sure, would have agreed with Nietzsche and would have wanted *Macbeth* banished. And it is not to the purpose that Nietzsche imagines a spectator of the play who is already possessed of deep ambition, for Palmer is imagining a spectator who is not so disposed, but one friendly to moral concerns. Neither shows anything about the educative power of the play outside the context of the dispositions of the spectator in question – which is the point I made earlier about the possible morally educative value of literature in one already disposed to take others' concerns into account.

The truth, as it seems to me, is that the idea that literature might help in one's moral education – again, in those who care for literature: there can be no plausibility in the claim made by Martha Nussbaum, for example, that we all need to read (certain) novels for our moral education or that all novels could contribute in this way even in those who love literature[12] – can never be more than a *hope*. To my mind, Christopher Ricks, in a discussion of Keats's 'The Eve of St Agnes' gets it about right:

> As to the question of whether there can be carry over of sympathies from literature into daily life, here one is necessarily proffering a trust and a hope rather than an assurance or a substantiation. When Keats not only lets us see so vividly the undressing of Madeline and Porphyro's watching it, but lets us share his richly intimate equanimity, he gives us an example of how we should – in the largest sense – behave. His art, though not didactic, is concerned to educate our thoughts, feelings, and sympathies, and it does so by being exemplary. Of course such an example can be resisted, ignored, or crushed by all the things in life which can make it gratifying to behave ill and feel ill will rather than to behave well and to feel good will. But to say this is simply to say what is true of anything that might hope to help

> by example ... I grant that when in daily life one subsequently comes up against those usual embarrassments which are an invitation to ungenerosity one might not be in the least assisted by having entered into an imagined meeting – in art – with such an embarrassment. But that one might not be assisted is not to say that one could not be and is not to say anything about the (undiscoverable) odds; the trust in art's power to enlarge our sympathies (and not just when ensconced in art) is not different from the trust in bringing up children with love and respect.[13]

There is an immense delicacy in this, a willingness to be mistaken, an invitation to conversation and a lack of urgency that make this exemplary as a piece of philosophical literary criticism. The tone is one of exploration, suggestion, possibility, and it reveals a deep humanity. I share Ricks's hope, but it is that, a hope, and nothing more. I shall return to this question of hope later. For the moment, I wish to turn to the quotation from Marías with which I started.

3. What does Marías mean by speaking of the darkness that surrounds us? Consider one of the absolutely central questions of philosophy, woven deep into its history, and so woven because it has the same place in human life: freedom of the will. There have been, of course, innumerable discussions of this issue, and some philosophers have been sure that they have found a solution, one that shows that we do possess, alternatively do not possess, freedom of the will, and that they have provided the reasons to justify the position at which they have arrived. But what is completely plain is that no such putative solution has commanded assent among philosophers: over and over again, a purported solution has been subjected to criticism and counterarguments, further defences of the original view have been constructed, further critiques have been developed and so on. Part of these critiques is often that the putative solution is not plausible because, even if the argument works, all it shows is that we possess such and such a capacity or ability or whatever, which the philosopher in question supposes to be freedom of the will – but it is not. In other words, it is not just that philosophers disagree with each other about whether we have freedom of the will, subjecting each other's arguments to what often seems to be devastating criticism, it is also that philosophers cannot even agree on what it is that they are talking about, that

is, what freedom of the will is in the first place. For that itself is a philosophical question, and there is no more agreement on that than there is on whether we possess it. The net result of this is that we are as in the dark about the nature of freedom of the will, and whether we possess it, as we have always been, that is, right from when human beings began thinking about the issue at all. This is not to deny, of course, that much that is of intense importance and interest about our lives has been brought to the surface through the relevant discussions, much that we might not otherwise have seen, but there is nothing here that can sensibly be called progress – not, at any rate, of the kind that might issue in a solution agreed on by all parties that one could reasonably think settles matters.

This kind of pattern is repeated over and again in philosophy with respect to all its major areas of exploration. Why is it that human beings find it so much easier, as they plainly do, to be destructive rather than constructive (history is a slaughter bench, said Hegel)? Are we fallen creatures, as Christianity teaches us? How do the material circumstances of our lives enter into and explain our destructiveness? Do human beings really, after all, enjoy inflicting suffering on each other? If so, why? How could this be so? How can we, individually and collectively, create conditions in which we are less destructive? Is this possible? Does suffering have some real meaning in some kind of teleological scheme of history? Or is it devoid of meaning, something we just have to grin and bear, as it were? What are we to make of suffering of which we can make no sense and of what it leads us to do to ourselves and each other? How are we to make sense of human beings' relentless incapacity to learn from history, their making the same mistakes over and over again? Why are we so morally and epistemologically limited? Is there really such a thing as a moral law or some kind of natural law, and, if there is, how are we to understand it? How is it related to our nature? Do we, indeed, have a nature? If so, what is it and how should we relate ourselves to it? Is death just a final end we must accept, or can we make any sense of a life after death, personal or otherwise? Can our fear of death be reduced and, if so, how? Does morality have a foundation in, say, the concept of moral obligation? And what is a moral obligation anyway, or a foundation to morality? How do our obligations relate to human desire, need and sense of purpose? Is there a distinct category of experience or action we can rightly call *evil*? If so, what is it and how is it related to other moral notions? Indeed, is evil a *moral* notion or something else? Are human beings evil creatures and how are we to deal with this if we are?

I take it as completely obvious that these questions are among those – and there are countless others – that go to the heart of reflection on our condition. And I further take it as completely clear that there is nothing remotely resembling consensus on the answer(s) among those philosophers (and others, though the qualification is otiose, since anyone who reflects on these matters is a philosopher: we are, in that sense, all philosophers) who have reflected at length on them. We may have a different way of thinking of these matters from that of, say, the Greeks, but we are no clearer than they were about them, not even if we import into them, say, considerations from the natural sciences to which they could not have had access.

This, I think, is at least part of what Marías means by the darkness that surrounds us. We simply do not have answers to the questions I have indicated. Despite the claims to certainty on these matters that so many philosophers have made, and continue to make, these claims are, in my view, clearly, in the end, a bluff. I repeat that this does not mean that we cannot learn much from philosophers' explorations of these matters, but what we learn actually usually makes the questions all the more intractable and difficult of solution. We are profoundly mysterious to ourselves, so I am saying, with Marías, and we know this. Philosophy is an attempt to clear away the darkness, but it does not do this. Moreover, in my view, it could not. And the reason for that is again suggested by Marías: it is because there are, in fact, no answers to the questions indicated. It is not a contingency that philosophers have not been able to provide solutions to the questions we human beings ask of ourselves; it is not a matter of no one's having come up with the 'clinching argument', as one prominent philosopher once told me when I was discussing such matters with him (arguments for the existence of God, as it happens). There is no such thing as a clinching argument on such issues, and the comment of the philosopher in question displays a whole conception of the human condition, the nature of reason (of thinking), of the notion of one person's thinking for another that, however hallowed by the philosophical tradition, strikes me as absurd and alien. To my mind, it is simply part of what we are – our ontological condition – that we remain mysterious to ourselves, that we do not have answers to the kinds of questions I have mentioned. In *Culture and Value*, Wittgenstein remarks in the same spirit:

> If anyone should think that he has solved the problem of life and feels like telling himself that everything is quite easy now, he can see that he is wrong just by recalling that there was a time when this 'solution' had not been discovered; but it must have been possible to live then too and the solution which has now been discovered seems fortuitous in relation to how things were then.[14]

Imagine that someone now genuinely thought that he had found the solution to the problem of free will. He must suppose that everyone else who disagrees now with him, and all those billions of human beings who lived before him, were in error, that he, and only he and those few who agree with him, can enlighten all of the present time and all of history with the truth. Apart from any suspicion of hubris (to put it mildly) that this raises (could he really think that all those countless others were and are mistaken and that he now, finally, thank God!, has arrived at the truth?), the view in question supposes that somehow, now, the whole human condition has been, thanks to his discovery, lifted out of a state of benighted ignorance and that we can live henceforth in the light of the knowledge he has provided – even if most people cannot understand the subtlety of his philosophical reasoning. That seems to me, as it seemed to Wittgenstein, obviously absurd, but the desire and aim to arrive at such a condition is implicit in the ways many philosophers go about their business, though very few of them would express it in this way. And I remark again that 'philosopher' here means (potentially) anyone who reflects on such matters since there is in all of us, more or less pronounced, as the case may be, a desire to find a solution to the problems that beset us. The style of thinking I am criticizing is not alien to our condition, it is part of it, but unless and until we see it in this way, we shall give in to it. To put the point another way, it is part of our condition to wish to transcend that condition, and the philosophical imperative as I have described it (there are other ways of doing philosophy, and I shall come to that), is an expression of that and needs to be challenged in its own terms. That challenge needs to be understood, in my view, as a recall to our humanity, which is a response to the fact that so much philosophy is *not* written out of, or written for, the humanity of the philosopher and those for whom he writes, but as if from, and for, a disembodied intellect. Too much philosophy, in my view, carries a hostility to, or an attack on, the human condition, which hostility is itself part of our condition but which needs to be explored and placed in the context of the rest of what we are (which is pretty much most of what we are) – weak, vulnerable creatures of flesh, blood, sweat, shit and tears: which, of course, terrifies us and explains in large part why we want to transcend ourselves. Too many philosophers, seemingly without really acknowledging this – perhaps, even, without noticing it – just get on with things as if we were not the vulnerable creatures we are with a desire to shore ourselves up against that (philosophy, I am saying, of course, is part of that shoring up operation).

If we were to answer the kinds of question I raised as being central to philosophy and to what we are, we would, I am saying, no longer be human beings at all. But this does not mean that we can give up asking those questions and seeking to answer them. Our condition is this: we are burdened by questions that we are driven to seek to answer, knowing that we cannot answer them. It seems to me that Pascal was absolutely right when he said:

> We have an incapacity for proof that can be conquered by no dogmatism.
> We have an idea of the truth that can be conquered by no scepticism.[15]

We live, as William James has it, 'on the shambles', and one aspect of this is our longing for truth that we cannot have but the search for which we cannot abandon.

4. I think, then, that this is roughly what Marías means by 'the huge areas of darkness' that are characteristic of our condition. And the spirit of much philosophy when it deals with literature is that of a hope to recruit literature in a task to dispel this darkness. This is well brought out by Jane Adamson, who, in an interesting discussion of the relations between philosophy and literature, notes that from, say, the 1970s onwards, many philosophers in the English-speaking

world have explored the need philosophy – particularly moral philosophy – has of literature. She writes:

> Philosophy's turning to literary texts in search of what Iris Murdoch calls 'more concepts in terms of which to picture the substance of our being' thus implies a recognition of the value of literature's 'messier' kind of moral inquiry. It implies a recognition that *literature works against tidiness*. Yet the problem is ... that philosophy's drive to definiteness, clarity, and the like makes it so averse to ambiguity, opacity, inconclusiveness. Willy-nilly, *philosophy works against untidiness*.[16]

The consequence of this is that

> although philosophers often acknowledge the differences between philosophy and literature, the differences come just as often to be treated as negligible, or dissoluble, or even entirely compatible. Frequently, they get suppressed, or dropped from view. One upshot is an overtidy picture of the relationship, in which philosophy assimilates literature into its system virtually without trace, and thus without evidently benefiting in the process. An alternative outcome, also unbeneficial, is an overcosy notion of their coming-together, as lean philosophy and rich literature join in a marriage of happy complementarity.[17]

I have, of course, been exploring a line of thought much like Adamson's. But if there are no answers to the questions philosophy poses, then, when it gets hold of literature to help it out, it is hard not to feel that it has missed the point. As Marías says, literature's job is not to solve anything. What, then, is it? Marías says: It is to *show* our problems. What does this mean?

I take it that one aspect of this is to remind philosophy (remind us), indeed, that there are no answers to the deepest questions of our condition. There might, for sure, be plainly absurd, foolish or shallow putative answers that we may (philosophically) freely and with clean conscience dismiss – though literature may be as interested in these as in any that seem more plausible, exploring what is at stake in them in various ways. Literature might, say, find a certain character's foolishness and absurdity of great interest – comic, say, or enlightening about irony and conceptions of superiority. Be that as it may, one magnificent example of a reminder that there are no answers is to be found in Virginia Woolf's *The Waves*. 'Let a man get up and say, "behold, this is the truth", and instantly I perceive a sandy cat filching a piece of fish in the background. Look, you have forgotten the cat, I say.'[18] So says Bernard, a central character in the novel. He is a spinner of stories, in love with words, struggling always to make sense of himself and others through narrative. Yet he comes to distrust words and stories, the way in which they provide an order that is not there in life:

> But it is a mistake, this extreme precision, this orderly and military progress; a convenience, a lie. There is always, deep below it, even when we arrive punctually at the appointed time with our white waistcoats and polite formalities, a rushing stream of broken dreams, nursery rhymes, street cries, half-finished sentences and sights – elm trees, willow trees, gardeners sweeping, women writing – that rise and sink even as we hand a lady down to dinner.[19]

It is only a pretence that

> life is a solid substance, shaped like a globe, which we can turn about in our fingers. Let us pretend that we can make out a plain and logical story, so that when one matter is despatched – love, for instance – we go on, in an orderly manner, to the next.[20]

'Life is not susceptible perhaps to the treatment we give it when we try to tell it.' And he speaks of the 'incomprehensible nature of this our life'.[21] But *The Waves* does not insist on this. It insists on nothing. It asks us, rather, to dwell with such a thought, allow it to seep into our being, turn it around in our mind, permit it to cast some light on our individual life – in other words, it *shows* us the problem. And this is the kind of thing literature will often do. For sure, it may be the case that, usually, literature does not *explicitly* remind us that there are no answers. It is modernist literature that is most likely to do that; novels, say, that are often themselves armed from the inside against our being able to come to a completely clear understanding of what they are saying. But even classic literature – say the classic nineteenth-century novel – works against tidiness, as Adamson says. For it might show how things came to a (more or less) satisfactory conclusion in some given context, for some group of people, but it will make no claim that this can be repeated elsewhere, and it will often trace the immense cost in terms of suffering that will need to be paid to arrive at that conclusion. Literature does not in that sense give any answers. So, apart from the fact that the classic nineteenth-century novel will often end with nothing that could be thought of as answer – think of, say, Thomas Hardy's novels in this context – even when something seems to work out, as say, in George Eliot's *Middlemarch*, where Dorothea marries Will Ladislaw, it is clear that the cost, moral and material, to Dorothea here is immense. That she is willing to pay it does not show that anything has been resolved or a solution found. It is rather that she accepts a compromise she can live with. The lesson here, if there is one, is that all of life is a compromise, there are no solutions or answers, and that we must all somehow seek to be grown up enough to accept the compromises of our life. But the novel gives no real sense of how one is to do that in one's own life, for that is not its aim at all. It does not provide moral lessons, not even when the authorial voice makes comments about our condition; it just *shows* us: 'We are all of us born in moral stupidity, taking the world as an udder to feed our supreme selves.'

Further, it is extremely unclear how we are to understand the effect that, say, a novel's narrative might have on one as the reader. There seems to me to be something deeply mysterious here. I might learn, say, to stay with *Middlemarch*, something valuable about Dorothea's idealism and how it leads her into a disastrous marriage with Casaubon, but it is very hard to see how this might help me make much sense – except, perhaps, at a very general level: Am I being too idealistic or naive here and, if so, about what? – of my own romantic and erotic involvements. Or is the idea that, in exercising my imagination in following Dorothea's travails – and those of Casaubon too, for that matter – I am better able to note and understand others' behaviour in such involvements? But how, exactly? I might, of course, think of someone that she is behaving naively and idealistically in getting involved with some stuffed shirt of an older man, and this might call Dorothea and Casaubon to mind, perhaps even in some detail, but what does that show? Will it evoke my compassion? Perhaps. But it might evoke my contempt or frustration too. And would I not have noticed the naivety without having read *Middlemarch*? That seems unlikely: Dorothea's case may have taught me something about naivety, but the case of the young and idealistic woman getting involved with the stuffed shirt would have taught me that without my ever having even heard of George Eliot. My point here is not to deny that reading a masterpiece like *Middlemarch* has had an effect on me, for it certainly has. I am, rather, saying that it is very unclear what that effect is supposed to be and how we are to understand it. It seems to me that it is infinitely more subtle, elusive and resistant to articulation than philosophers often like to suppose. Lichtenberg says in one of his aphorisms: '*Ich vergesse das meiste was ich gelesen habe, so wie das, was ich gegessen habe, ich weiß aber so viel, beides trägt nichts desto weniger zu Erhaltung meines Geistes und meines Leibes bei.*' ['I forget most of what I have read, just as I do most of what I have eaten, but I know that both contribute no less on that account to the conservation of my mind and my body.'] That seems to me right: all the things I have read, including an enormous amount of literature, have helped shape my sensibility and temperament, my outlook on life. But I really do not know how: I have forgotten most of it, most of it I do not think about much in explicit terms, and yet it is all *there*. It has helped make me what I am with my specific patterns of response to others and to myself, my sense of the world and so on, but how exactly this is so seems to me elusive.

Or again, to take another example, Tolstoy is immensely enlightening about jealousy in his exploration of Anna and Vronsky, as is Proust in his of Swann and Odette, as is Shakespeare in his reflections on Othello, and all this can deepen my sense of what jealousy is (I hope it has). Yet it is far from clear how one puts in discursive terms what it is that they show, beyond some obvious banalities, for it is a matter here of living with, being in the presence of, the texts in question, much as I can have a deep sense of what it is to be with a certain friend, say, without feeling that putting that sense in discursive terms would be adequate at all to the experience – though, of course, there can be better or worse ways of making the attempt. And it is also far from clear that my knowledge of, my feeling for, these texts has helped me cope better with moments when I experience jealousy in my own case, made me more reasonable or judicious or less hasty and so on. For what it is worth, I record here my sense that it avails little. Perhaps more exactly it is that I am better able to understand my jealousy – or that of others, for that matter – but I am far from sure that I have become more sensible, level-headed or the like in dealing with it. My better understanding might, after all, make it all the more intractable: whence the confidence that clarity of insight into emotional states makes them more amenable to my managing of them? It might make me realize more deeply just how resistant they are to me in that way.

In any case, as Charles Altieri has argued, what we can grasp from Proust's exploration of Swann is not something about how terrible and destructive jealousy is and how it can be educated to more morally benign purposes. Rather:

> For Swann, jealousy is emphatically not a disturbance or form of unpleasure leading him to pursue actions that might eliminate its cause or gain revenge on its objects. Instead, Swann seems to pursue jealousy, intensifying it and actively attempting to appreciate the intricate shifts in sensibility it creates for a love affair .... In his hands then, jealousy becomes an art form attuning him to every nuance in Odette's behavior.[22]

What Proust does is to subvert the usual platitudes about jealousy and its destructiveness, its excess, and allow us to enter into a sense of its distinctive value.[23]

Jealousy is, of course, an inner state, a condition of the soul. And, just as I may feel that my sense of what jealousy is has been deepened or changed by what Shakespeare, Tolstoy and Proust show me, so I may feel this for many inner states: grief, longing, despair, anger, frustration, joy and so on. And I am sure that my understanding of these, in myself and others, has been enriched by all the literature I have read, by all that it is has shown me of these. But putting in discursive terms what that is would, I feel sure, betray my sense of what this literature has given me. And it is certainly far from clear that it has made me more judicious, level-headed, reasonable, still less that it has made me kinder or more generous to others. Altieri has spoken of the possibility of 'simply coming alive by participating in the mix of passions and projections that powerful imaginative writing elicits',[24] and that seems closer to my experience and is central to what I mean by the idea that literature has enriched my life. But that is no solution to anything, no answer. It has enabled me, perhaps, to muddle through, but it is a muddling through and nothing grander.

5. Perhaps I am a peculiarly hopeless, recalcitrant case. Perhaps others, through reading literature, are more able than I have been to get through life without making a mess of many things, including important things: reading Nussbaum, Palmer, Robinson, Carroll and others certainly gives the impression that they take themselves to have become wiser, more sensitive, more reasonable through all the literature they have read, as well as more open to others and their needs. Perhaps they do not mean to give this impression, and I am sure that they are much less sure of themselves from the present point of view than they seem from what they write, but that is, in part, because they are writing as philosophers, which, as I have suggested, encourages an authorial voice that has got clear on things, has understood, has answers and solutions. I shall return to this later.

I suspect, in any case, that the philosophical voice misleads us into misdescribing what is going on in us in our responses to literature. For, as I have said in quoting Altieri, literature can make one come alive in all kinds of ways. I feel more alive in relating my gloomy moods to Philip Larkin's or when my own life is revealed to me by, say, his sense, looking at others, that 'Something is pushing them / To the side of their own lives'; I cannot think of some lines or images in Shakespeare or Auden or Eliot or Hopkins without being moved and excited or consoled; ever since I read Conrad's *Lord Jim* when I was a young man, I have carried it around with me as a marvel of writing, psychological insight, pity and horror; I return again and again to Kafka and Büchner as authors who astonish and appal me at the same time; I carry inside me fragments of Italo Svevo's *La coscienza di Zeno*, and they make me chuckle and smile – at myself and others; Virginia Woolf gives me a sense of a kind of mystical unity behind all things; and so on and so forth. I am quite certain that many of those theorists whose lives, like mine, are steeped in literature, have such experiences with the books they love. But then, when one tries to think about all this in a philosophical voice, one gets misled. For philosophy, as I have been exploring, likes to think in terms of solutions and answers. But what literature has to teach, in my view, is one's own weakness and vulnerability. If you think your knowledge and love of literature has made you in some way a better person, morally wiser, stronger and so on, then, to my mind, that is *already* a betrayal of anything literature can teach you. For what it will teach you is that *there*, in the moment of your foolishness or indifference or pain, what will help you make less of a mess of things for yourself and others, or bear them better, is very largely a matter of *luck*. If you think literature has made you stronger or better, you have tried to turn it into a *force*, a *power*, quite contrary to what it has to offer. That is why I earlier agreed with Christopher Ricks's view that we are dealing here with *hope*. But hope is no force, has no power. That is why it is hope. To hope is to know that how one copes with, makes sense of, some ill in one's life, moral or otherwise, is a matter of forces outside one, of contingencies and chances. Or we could put the point this way: great literature shows us, among other things, as Murdoch and others say, the difficulty of living. But in showing us that difficulty, in making it imaginatively alive for us, it does nothing to remove that difficulty. At best, it says: keep going; you will start your life from a point of mess and confusion, from a point where you understand little and are confused, and you will go on in this way, but that is what living is; it is not a matter of removing confusion so much as making it productive. It is as if thinkers such as Murdoch think that productive confusion is not really confusion after all. But it is. The difference is that one can see the confusion a little more clearly, but that is not the same as making it go away.

I think it would be fair to say, therefore, that the points I have been making are partly conceptual-cum-psychological concerning the relations between philosophy and literature and also partly ethical. I think, that is, that *one ought not to think* that involvement with literature helps to make one morally better since that idea is itself a form of moral complacency and self-congratulation, one through which, as I said previously, one seeks to turn literature's showing of our weakness into a power, allowing one to suppose oneself better armed against making a moral mess of things – which, apart from anything else, is more likely (because it is a form of complacency) to lead one to make an even bigger mess of things, probably all the while imagining that one is coping better. Among the most seductive thoughts to which human beings are prone is the terrible error of supposing oneself to be good. As some of the theorists I have mentioned see literature, it can, I think, only encourage that thought and should be resisted.

6. In an autobiographical essay, Gabriel Josipovici writes: 'Only fiction, in the right hands, can awaken in us the sense of how little we know of ourselves and the world, and how intense is our desire to change that condition. By so doing it brings us back in touch with both ourselves and the world.'[25] It will be clear from what I have said so far that I share with Josipovici – as I share with Marías – his sense of literature (fiction). And when Josipovici adds that we have an intense desire to change our condition by knowing it, knowing ourselves and the world, more intimately, more completely, fully, he expresses, I take it, the same basic thought that I articulated earlier, namely, that it is part of our condition to wish to transcend that condition. Josipovici suggests that only fiction can give us a sense of how deep this is in us, and there seems to be me something right in that, but also something wrong. For philosophy, I have suggested, is deeply characterized by the desire to lead us out of our condition, so it is unclear to me that it is right to say that only literature (fiction) can give us a sense of how deep this aspiration is in us. However, I think it is right to say, nonetheless, that philosophy, generally speaking, covers its tracks in this regard. That is, it is characteristic of the philosopher's way of going about things that he or she does not dwell on and take time over the ways in which we are possessed of so intense a desire to change our condition because we know so little about ourselves and the world. Rather, the philosopher, so to speak, sets out from the beginning seeking to remedy that situation, seeking to provide solutions to the questions that torment us. It is this, I think, that can give many – I am one of them – that peculiar sense that one can so often have of philosophy as a way of thinking that somehow averts its eyes from what is deeply troubling in the human condition, as if it had started too high up, and despite its assumption that it is the most fundamental way of thinking about the human situation. Of course, the point is subtle and must be understood aright, for it is certainly true that philosophers regularly set out the problem with which they wish to deal, and they sometimes do so in painstaking detail. And even when the background concern is left less explicit, it shimmers through as the philosopher sets to work. But the sense that philosophy is often in flight from the really troubling aspects of the human condition comes through nonetheless, and it does so in the fact that the philosopher so often claims, after all, having thought about the issue for so long, and having marshalled all the relevant arguments for and against, to *know*. That sense, which is, as it were, the controlling spirit of philosophy, its ideal that haunts it, therefore often lends to philosophy a sense of unreality, as if it took itself to be dealing with the deepest problems of our condition but somehow failed to see them clearly. In that sense, I think Josipovici is right: literature reminds us how little we know and has a better measure of the intensity of our desire to change that because *it does not claim that it can do so*; it does not claim to *know*.

For me, therefore, this raises the question of what a philosophy would look like that refuses the claim to knowledge. Now, in one way, I would say that that is what the best literature already is. It *is* philosophy. I said previously, in referring to the philosopher who did not read novels, that his reason for doing so was that there are no arguments in novels. And philosophy surely must deal in arguments. Yet the question remains: What counts as an argument? If you think that an argument – ideally at any rate – appeals to nothing more than the intellect and has no dealings with the peculiar vicissitudes of a person's life – his or her particular experiences, emotional sensitivity, temperamental dispositions and so on – then, of course, you will think that there are no arguments in novels, for no novel worth reading could conceivably appeal only to the intellect in that way. And it is because so much philosophy depends on the notion of argument that appeals in just that way that it becomes a largely technical exercise where, providing the intellect is functioning well, there is no difference in principle for philosophical work between a fifteen-year-old adolescent with no experience of life and a grown man or woman with a wealth of such experience. And this is another reason why philosophy so often feels as if it were fleeing the deepest problems of human life, because that view of argument – of what it is to reason (properly or responsibly) – immediately seals philosophy off from notions of the kind of depth and insight that can come from living, that is, from wisdom. For 'philosophy' means 'love of wisdom', but if anyone really took that seriously then he would not think of argument and reason as philosophy does. And if you think that an argument should aim to engage the whole of a person – his or her temperament, sensibility, experiences or lack of them, emotional subtlety and sensitivity and so on – then you will be likely to think, as I do, that literature is philosophy. For that is what literature appeals to: it aims to appeal to the whole human being, not some specific aspect such as the disembodied intellect. This is in part why the effect literature has on one is a lot less clear than many theorists seem to suppose: it seeps into one and its effect is very largely mysterious.[26]

But what if one were to set out to write philosophy aiming to prescind from the claim to know? What would such a philosophy look like? It would involve, I think, a striving for a certain style, a style which conveys precisely that weakness, that vulnerability. There can be no clear way before the fact of what that style might be. Indeed, each attempt at writing in the way in question will no doubt demand a different approach, a new attempt at finding the appropriate style. And the best example of that I know is Montaigne – and it is significant, I think, that he is utterly ignored in virtually all mainstream philosophy. It is not unimportant, of course, that Montaigne wrote essays – *attempts*. And the best analysis of the essay I know is Theodor Adorno's 'The Essay as Form'. Adorno's reflections are far too rich to summarize here, but essentially he argues that the condition of *unknowing* is central to the essay. Contrasting it with philosophy with its 'ideals of purity and tidiness ... an airtight and thoroughly organized science', Adorno says that the essay 'unapologetically lays itself open to the objection that one does not know for sure how to understand its concepts'; 'it has to pay for its affinity with open intellectual experience with a lack of security that the norm of established thought fears like death'. 'It thinks in fragments, just as reality is fragmentary ... Discontinuity is essential to the essay' and it welcomes 'the same spontaneity of subjective fantasy that is castigated in the name of objective discipline'. It challenges the fact that 'the academic guild accepts as philosophy only what it clothed in the dignity of the universal and the enduring ... [I]t arouses resistance because it evokes intellectual freedom.'[27]

It is striking that, although Adorno is talking about the essay, he could be talking about literature. Indeed, Adorno's essay on the essay is in a collection of his pieces entitled *Notes to Literature*. It is clear that he thinks of the essay as a form of literature – even as he clearly thinks of it as a form of philosophy. And in all this it is not that literature and the essay do not offer arguments for various views, opinions, ideas and the like. The crucial thing is *the spirit in which this is done*. That is why I said that style is central here, because it is the style of writing more than anything, I think, that makes clear the spirit in which things are being approached. One can certainly advance a view and argue for it but do so in a spirit that is porous, open-textured, undogmatic, ever aware of one's limitations as a thinker and human being. The alternative to 'an airtight and thoroughly organized science' is not the anarchy of mere personal opinion – and the fantasy, or fear, that it is is part of philosophy's neurotic need of 'purity and tidiness', which in this way blinds itself to the fact that virtually all of human life and thought takes place between its obsessive fixation on a certain idealized conception of objectivity and mere personal opinion, an area into which the personal does indeed enter but as what Stanley Cavell calls 'mastered subjectivity' or others would call wisdom – or the hope, the striving, for such.

7. Jospovici says something else that I wish to quote here to end. In a book review of a work on Kafka, he quotes the author who claims that Kafka 'decisively shaped our conception of the twentieth century, [and so] might suggest fruitful strategies for coping with the twenty-first'. Jospiovici comments: 'But who ever imagined that writers should give us "fruitful strategies for coping", even if we knew what that meant? They have quite enough on their plate trying to say what they feel they have it in them to say.'[28] Now, the trouble is that plenty of people have imagined what Josipovici implies no one but the foolish would imagine. That has been my complaint about a certain way of speaking of literature. Philosophers find it almost impossible, so to speak, to leave literature alone without trying to make it do something other than that which it is doing. T. S. Eliot once famously remarked:

> The chief use of the 'meaning' of a poem, in the ordinary sense, may be (for here again I am speaking of some kinds of poetry and not all) to satisfy one habit of the reader, to keep his mind diverted and quiet, while the poem does its work upon him: much as the imaginary burglar is always provided with a nice piece of meat for the house-dog.[29]

Put in those terms, one might say that philosophy gets distracted by the piece of meat and supposes that this is all that is on offer. It finds it incredibly hard simply to let literature work on us and has little to say about what that is. Philosophy throws us the piece of meat – and then says that that is all there is to eat. This leaves us hungry, with a feeling that much of what is truly important has been left out. And so all I have wanted to do here is to do something to begin to clear a space in philosophy to allow literature to be what it is and not another thing.

6

Ways of flourishing: Literature and moral philosophy

Anthony J. Cascardi

Over the last few decades, if not longer, academic criticism has struggled to make the case that literature can play a role in making us better human beings. The reasons for this struggle are of no minor importance and have as much to do with the question of 'literature' as with questions of morality. The reassessment of the literary canon instigated in the aftermath of structuralism by the proponents of Marxism, feminism, critical race theory and postcolonial studies pointed to a set of deep-seated biases about what counted as valuable in the way of literature and about claims that literature could play a role in the moral improvement of human beings. More directly stated, the idea that literature ought to be prized (read, taught, preserved) because it would make us better people came under great pressure in light of the rising consciousness (a) that what counted as 'literature' was limited largely to the writings of dead, white males from a relatively small number of First World countries, and (b) that any claims to moral improvement were undercut by the theological premises and social costs associated with that limitation, namely the unjust suppression or simple ignorance of other voices and the ways of being they represented.

These reassessments brought the academic engagement with literature far closer to the world of praxis than had previously been the case. For, regardless of whether earlier approaches to literature were grounded in structural analysis, in aesthetics (which largely meant stylistics and 'close reading'), myth criticism or in literary history, the resulting attention to the text was by and large disconnected from the many questions of social justice towards which criticism has more recently turned. Setting aside the conceptual limitations involved in isolating literature from the social and political worlds, it strains credulity to recognize that academic literary criticism did its best to steer clear of politics, even in the face of writers like D. H. Lawrence, George Orwell and E. M. Forster. It was, of course, hard to ignore Conrad's critique of Belgian colonialism in the Congo in *Heart of Darkness* or Dickens's assessment of the effects of the industrial revolution on British society, but in the innumerable instances where the social and political engagements of literature are not self-evident, criticism was for decades content to bypass such issues, failing not only to identify them in the texts themselves but failing also to consider the prejudices at work in identifying what counted as valuable in literature in the first place. Whether in search of high-minded justifications rather than for merely skills-based validations, it seemed always possible to appeal to the general notion that reading literature somehow contributed to making us better human beings. Especially in the pedagogical context, one ought to take 'making' in the sense of 'creating' or 'fashioning': literature, it was long thought, ought to play a crucial role in the formation of moral human beings.

There is no doubt that proponents of the various forms of praxis-oriented criticism could argue equally well that we do far better in shaping good human beings by taking the opportunities literature affords to address questions of social justice, of economic (in) equality, of gender bias, of the suppression of subaltern voices and the like than any alternative appeal to the moral value of literature could provide. And yet, while recognizing the force of these arguments, something (more than one thing, in fact) is missing. In asking about how and why what came to count as valuable in the way of literature came about, and what it left out and in asserting the political value of literary criticism, the specificity of literature is apt to be lost. I do not mean to suggest that a reshaping of the canon needs to come at the cost of a clear sense of what literature is, for the notion of literature has, since its invention, always been subject to revision. Rather, I mean that in bringing forth the political work done by literature and those who study it, the questions of why any of this is *literature's* work to do, and of why it matters that this work is done in and by literature (as opposed, say, through policy documents or political manifestos), remain unanswered.

There is yet more to say before sketching what I believe a convincing set of alternatives might be. Much, though not all, praxis-oriented criticism can trace its roots to modes of thought related to what can broadly be described as 'critical theory'. To be more specific, it is closely aligned with the tendency within critical theory to appeal to the strategy of 'immanent critique'.[1] While clearly anchored to the work of the Frankfurt School, critical theory is in fact a far more capacious notion that encompasses a wide spectrum of self-reflective postures designed to guard against the authoritarian intellectual impulses to which so much thinking seems to be prone. And yet, much praxis-oriented criticism seems liable to lose sight of its connections to self-reflective thought. The results may appear rote, in spite of efforts to enter into a dialogue of contestation with opposing views.

If any of this is true, then we need some other way of articulating the moral value of literature, one that neither falls back on the problematic and outmoded tenets of past decades nor leaps over questions of morality altogether in the course of earnest efforts to engage in the practice of politically oriented critique. Such an alternative situates literature in between the spheres that Hannah Arendt[2] called the *vita activa* and the *vita contemplativa* and is what I propose to outline in the pages that follow. In doing so, I take the following principles as a guideline. First, that in whatever we say about morality, it must be recognized that we, as human beings, are faced with a dissociation between our biological and our moral ends, such that we cannot calibrate what is good in a moral sense on the basis of what is natural. Such a statement may well not have been regarded as true in the pre-modern world, or in any context where the order of nature is regarded as ordained by God (as, e.g. in arguments about a host of issues made by the religious right). But it has been taken as overwhelmingly valid throughout much of the history of the modern West, and I take it as fundamental for what I wish to argue here. We are creatures who cannot rely on the idea of a species-specific *telos*, but who must continuously invent our own goals. And if we think as broadly and generally as possible about how such goals might be characterized, then it makes sense to say that one of our fundamental goals (if not indeed our single goal) puts us in the challenging position of finding ways in which we might flourish while leaving open all the specifics about what shape that 'flourishing' might take. (One might also characterize this as a liberal view about human nature, recognizing that 'liberal' here is meant to invoke the liberty we enjoy to shape our own ends.) My suggestion is that literature can afford us with a crucial means to achieve this goal, and, moreover, that literature can help us broaden the scope of this endeavour by ensuring that in pursuing our own flourishing we do not diminish the opportunity of others to do the same.[3] While this may not align precisely with Kant's idea that a moral maxim should be something we can apply not just to ourselves but to everyone, such that it could be held universally, it nonetheless does align with the form of the golden rule that says we should not preclude others from achieving the same happiness we would seek for ourselves.

I take Aristotle's *Nicomachean Ethics* as offering what remains one of the best articulations of human flourishing available to us today. Flourishing is about being able fully to achieve the excellence of human being. The term that Aristotle uses for flourishing is *eudaimonia*. Though the translation is imperfect, it helps convey the idea that a good human life is a life in which we fully express our human capacities, that is, the things for which we are best suited. It is, Aristotle says, the condition of 'living well and doing well'.[4] Human flourishing involves something more than *life* and, likewise, more than mere sentience, both of which we share with other animals. For Aristotle, it involves 'a life, concerned in some way with action, of the element that possesses reason'.[5] And, he adds, 'the characteristic activity of the good person is to carry this out well and nobly'.

The relationship between the idea of human excellence that Aristotle holds and his ideas about literature is nonetheless not without its difficulties. While Aristotle does offer some memorable literary examples in *Nicomachean Ethics* (e.g. the misfortune that befalls King Priam as told in Homer's *Iliad*), any teacher or student of literature will recognize that there is a world of difference between adducing literary examples, as Aristotle occasionally does, and the experience of reading a literary work. And in spite of the fact that Aristotle invokes some literary examples to illustrate his ideas about ethics, the question of how we learn and transmit human 'excellence' remains tangled in a conundrum, since Aristotle also believes that only those who are on the path towards goodness will be able to pursue *eudaimonia*.[6] It is for this reason not surprising that contemporary thinkers who are broadly sympathetic to Aristotle have pointed to the importance that literary texts be *available* within the culture; if they are not in fact available, it is the task of those who teach them to try to make them so.

Perhaps more important is the fact that literary texts work by imaginative invitation rather than by what is conventionally understood as rational argument. Moreover, they do so not for the purpose of leading us to draw a conclusion about a particular issue (e.g. 'Was Antigone unjustly punished?', 'Should Hamlet have acted more rapidly?', 'Was it wrong for Emma Bovary to betray her husband Charles?'). Their invitation is, rather, to develop the powers that themselves make us human. These are the powers of imagination, of intelligent feeling and of (self-)reflection. My argument is, first, that we act in the development of our potential as human beings, hence act morally, when we develop these powers and, second, that literature can play a key role in this process. Furthermore, the capacity for self-reflection that literature develops can help ensure that the pursuit of our own happiness (*eudaimonia*) will also allow others to do the same. Indeed, there is nothing in the development of *my* capacity for intelligent feeling that, on the face of it, would preclude *yours*; on the contrary, the work of intellectual feeling called for by literature is bound to encourage an openness towards ways of thinking, feeling and imagining that may well be inconsistent with one's own. And so, while literature may not necessarily persuade one to change one's mind about a particular issue under consideration (e.g. justice, revenge, adultery), it will certainly draw one to open oneself to unfamiliar ways of understanding (of thinking, feeling, imagining) that in turn will encourage us to reflect on our understanding.

In proceeding, it bears explaining that the idea of human 'excellence' ought to be regarded as a regulative ideal, not a goal with fixed parameters. Similarly, 'virtue' and 'goodness' are rather like muscles to be exercised than goal-posts to be reached. They form part a conceptual web that includes the notion of 'perfection*ism*'. Perfectionism is typically associated with ethical and moral theories that characterize the good in terms of the development of human nature in the pursuit of excellence (and not necessarily with the aim of achieving it). The political philosopher John Rawls, for instance, characterized perfectionism as aiming at 'human excellence in art, science and culture'.[7] We might call this 'human nature perfectionism', in contrast to 'objective goods perfectionism', which Derek Parfit by contrast characterized as the achievement 'the best *things* in life'.[8] There is nothing about 'human nature perfectionism' to suggest that the good for human beings is itself perfection and still less that perfection is attainable. This point has been made emphatically clear in Stanley Cavell's writings on perfectionism in association with Emerson. Indeed, the grain of Cavell's thinking about (and with) Emerson goes against attaching any fixed, metaphysical interpretation to the notion of a self to which 'excellence' might be attributed;[9] in *In Quest of the Ordinary*, he characterizes the Emersonian self as a work always in progress, directed ultimately by itself. This is one implication of the fact that the 'external' criteria that religion once may have provided to us are no longer available, at least not in Emerson's secular world:

> The idea of relying in Emerson's word *self-reliance* knows its relation to the idea of binding or bonding in the word *religion*, so that the self's (perpetual, step-wise, circle-wise) construction of the self, say in 'Self-Reliance', has to pass through an idea of the self's alliance with and rallying of itself, its self-authorizations, as on a path, or succession, in the aftermath of religion's dominance.[10]

'Self-reliance' means that any transformation of the self must happen in accordance with an ideal that is internal to the self rather than one that comes from without. And, as Stanley Bates aptly said on this subject, 'we need to remember that what is "internal" and what comes "from without" are themselves not fixed and permanent categories. If the transfiguration of any particular state of the self is to be possible, then these categories will be capable of transformation.'[11] If this would seem to place us on slippery ground, then the answer is that any other ground would be false, in just the way that Nietzsche characterized metaphysics as offering a kind of comfort that is false.[12] It is the risk of this lack of comfort but also this reward that literature (and the humanities writ more broadly) afford us. To cite a recent thinker on this point, we are thereby made free for a 'poetic reinterpretation of authenticity as well as opened up to the possibility of giving up the concept altogether and living according to other concepts ... The point of the humanities, then, is not some goal external to it. The point of the humanities is that it itself is a mode of flourishing.'[13]

Reaching back across time, the long arc of history supports the idea that there is no single moral purpose that human beings are designed to serve nor a particular moral goal towards which human beings ought to strive. Literary history similarly highlights the contingent nature of our striving towards excellence (where 'contingent' simply means that all particular aims are made up by us and so might well be transformed). And if literature is indeed to be our guide to human excellence, then any assertion about what specifically is good for us – beyond being more human – has to be stated provisionally or with enough self-conscious irony to make overturning and improving upon it a very real and welcome possibility. Acceptance of the contingency of human aims is essential to the complexion of the 'ironist' personality that Richard Rorty characterized in *Contingency, Irony, and Solidarity*, that is, someone who 'faces up to the contingency of his or her own most central beliefs and desires – someone sufficiently historicist to have abandoned the idea that those central beliefs and desires refer back to something beyond the reach of time and chance'.[14]

This account of what 'excellence' means for human beings is as value-neutral as the account of truth offered by modern pragmatist thinkers, including Rorty, for whom truth is just 'what works' – that is, works best – in the way of ideas.[15] This implies a recognition of the fact that there are no higher, metaphysical principles authorizing a conception of what is good for human beings – none beyond the ones we ourselves establish,[16] and is consistent with the belief that we do well to inject any claim to moral authority we might assert with a healthy dose of irony. Without irony, any virtue – whether courage, temperance or justice – is likely to be hubristic.

The further development called for by these initial ideas can be organized around three topics, each of which draws on a well-established set of philosophical discussions. The first concerns the premise that literature helps cultivate our capacity for intelligent feeling both in intensity and in nuance. Here, Nietzsche is a crucial ally. The second concerns the premise that literature helps cultivate our capacity to think and feel in unfamiliar ways. Here, Bakhtin's work is of particular value. The third concerns the premise that literature helps cultivate our ability to think and feel with others. Here, arguments from sympathy advanced by a suite of Enlightenment figures (including Hume and Smith) are particularly useful, though they can fruitfully be supplemented by reference to the philosophical problem of 'other minds', which has been a nagging issue for thinkers ranging from Descartes to Wittgenstein. I should aver that in mentioning these particular figures I have no illusion that the entirety of their thinking would be consistent with the views about literature that I am constructing, much less that they could all be reconciled. Nonetheless, I do believe that the positions I take from them can, together, give us a plausible picture of how literature furthers the cause of human flourishing. Moreover, when taken together, they offer us a richer picture of human flourishing than any one of them on their own can provide.

As to the first of these arguments, imagine a case for *eudaimonia* where our goal as human beings is simply to increase the capacities that make us human – including our perceptual and psychological awareness, our self-consciousness, our emotional responsiveness and our historical understanding. We become better human beings, striving towards excellence, to the extent that we perceive more acutely (in both sensory and psychological terms), understand more deeply, feel more intensely and think more carefully. Nietzsche's secular critique of morality can provide a background for this claim. In response to the question 'What is good?', Nietzsche replies: 'Whatever augments the feeling of power, the will to power, power itself, in man.'[17] And conversely, in response to the question 'What is evil?', he answers, 'Whatever springs from weakness'. And, perhaps most relevant to the issues raised here, he asks, 'What is happiness?' and answers, 'The feeling that power increases, that resistance is overcome'.[18] I would propose that we can substitute 'intensity' for 'power', notwithstanding the fact that Nietzsche himself did not regard it as among the greatest of goods; indeed, he wrote that 'not the intensity but the duration of high feelings makes high men'.[19]

Expanding on Nietzsche, Luc Ferry has written that 'it is intensity that has primacy; the will to power carries the day against all other considerations [in Nietzschean morality]: "There is nothing to life that has value except the degree of power!"'[20] Ferry goes on to explain that this does not mean that there is no such thing as value. Quite the contrary. 'We also need to comprehend, as is clear in

Nietzsche's critique of the Socratic cure and of romanticism, that genuine intensity has nothing in common with unleashed passions or the emancipation of bodies; it resides in the harmonious and classical integration of the vital forces; in the serenity, the calm, but also the lightness that oppose Mozart and Schubert to Schumann and Wagner.'[21] Intensities are linked to qualities, not to facts. The *how* is what matters, and not the *what*. Ferry goes on in this vein: 'Like one skilled in the martial arts, the man of the grand style moves in elegance, at a thousand leagues from anything that seems laborious. He does not perspire, and if he moves mountains, it is serenely, without apparent effort.'[22]

An example may help to make the point. Consider Wallace Stevens's 'An Ordinary Evening in New Haven', a poem that I have discussed in a related context elsewhere.[23] Stevens often draws attention to the difference between the world as it *is* and the way the imagination gives the world to us, that is, constructs the world, and may construct *possible* worlds. Stevens's ostensive aim – to express things 'as they are' – thus yields a remarkable potential for the transformation of consciousness through intelligent feeling, and does so in ways that go considerably beyond the expressiveness of the romantic poetry that preceded him. Romantic poetry certainly has its own intensities but, As Charles Altieri put it, Stevens shows how romantic self-consciousness establishes sites of feeling that, at the same time, demand a very different kind of aesthetic intelligence, one that affords us the capacity to participate knowingly in the poet's act of the imagination.[24]

As for the poem in question, Stevens's aim in 'An Ordinary Evening' might appear to lie in expressing a vision of 'pure reality', unadorned, and seen with the utmost certainty. But the work of 'simple seeing' is not at all so simple in the end, and certainly not just descriptive. First, it registers not just perception itself but the effort that seeing demands, making his work 'the fresh inscription of an endless duty', as one critic put it.[25] One might say that there is an obligation reflected in these lines, and that the work of 'simple seeing' requires of us a form of attention that stands to make us better human beings.

In all this, the work of poetry is revealed as a profoundly expressive and creative act. It requires and cultivates something beyond sight, which in the passage cited earlier Stevens calls 'insight'. This is why, no doubt, he also writes in 'An Ordinary

Evening' that 'reality is the beginning not the end'.[26] Poetry draws us to something more, something that engages a set of capacities that mere 'seeing' does not encompass. My argument, extrapolating broadly from what I intend to serve as a salient example, is that in providing opportunities like this, literature asks us to develop dimensions of human excellence that might otherwise be stifled, and that, in doing so, it serves a moral purpose.

What, then, of the claim that literature helps us think and feel in unfamiliar ways, and that there is moral value in this? One could well say that a poem like Stevens's 'An Ordinary Evening' also does this, recognizing that it is not our powers of perception that the poem summons, nor *just* our imaginative powers, but something with which we may be oddly unfamiliar, that is, our own reflective sense of how we imagine things, which generates an appreciation of the powers of insight that the poem calls for. But there is much more to be said on this subject, and for this the work of Mikhail Bakhtin – and in particular his account of 'heteroglossia' – proves especially useful.

Succinctly put, heteroglossia (or 'multivoicedness') describes the assemblage of many different styles of speech. It is, for Bakhtin, a hallmark of the novel, though not exactly an invention of the novel. Indeed, every language (according to Bakhtin) has elements of heteroglossia because every language depends on a past (indeed, on many pasts). Every speaker 'constructs his own utterance on alien territory',[27] meaning that *my words* are never entirely mine alone. Every utterance is part of a dialogue – with the past, and with the language of others and with the objects of the world: 'The word is shaped in dialogic interaction with an alien word that is already in the object.'[28] This dialogue is endless; there is no such thing as the 'final word'.

The novel is, for Bakhtin, the genre that epitomizes dialogic discourse. It is, in his estimation, the genre that depends on the presence of multiple discourses within a single voice. Moreover, it is a genre in which the differences among these many discourses are never resolved, never subordinated to a dominant way of speaking. And since every way of speaking carries with it a point of view, the dialogic novel is also deeply perspectivist. A particular language in a novel is always a particular way of viewing the world, Bakhtin writes, 'one that strives for a social significance'.[29] But in the novel there is no controlling centre of social significance. As a consequence, the novel is open-ended; characters begin as less than fully-formed creatures and have the possibility of evolving as they move towards the future. The contrast between epic and novel could not be any more stark: Bakhtin describes the epic hero as solidified, complete: There is 'something hopelessly ready-made; he is all there, from beginning to end he coincides with himself'.[30] To be sure, this is not true of *all* epic heroes, but the contrast, however schematic, helps sharpen the nature of the (heteroglossic) novel. The protagonist of a novel cannot be reduced to who he or she may be at any single moment. 'He cannot become once and for all a clerk, a landowner, a merchant, a fiancé, a jealous lover, a father and so forth.'[31] The typical novelistic protagonist is a Robinson Crusoe, refusing the fixed role his father (society) has in mind for him, determined to live a life of adventure, bound towards the future, not knowing what fortune or misfortune may be his.

Indeed, Defoe's novel (sometimes considered the first of the genre) is equally unsettled in discursive terms – which is to say that, as a paradigm for the genre, the novel is not defined by any single form of discourse. *Robinson Crusoe*, for example, mixes the discourse of adventure travel, voyages of discovery, spiritual autobiography and economics (just to name a few). To choose another example, Cervantes' *Don Quixote* is a stylistic assemblage that includes the discourses of chivalric romance, popular ballads, pastoral poetry, proverbs and adages, political advice and the so-called Moorish novel. Just as the protagonist (Alonso Quijano) steps out of his role as idle landowner to become Don Quixote and seek whatever adventures might come his way, discourse in Cervantes' novel is subject to the perspective of whoever is speaking – which is to say that on both linguistic and social fronts, the novel resists the normativizing and homogenizing tendencies to which languages and societies seem otherwise to be drawn. 'Perspectivism' has long been identified as a defining feature of *Don Quixote*, and there is perhaps no better example of it than in the discussion about the object that appears to Don Quixote as a battle helmet belonging to the fabled Mambrino (*yelmo*) and appears to Sancho Panza and others as a mere barber's shaving basin, *bacía* ('what seems to thee a barber's basin seems to me Mambrino's helmet, and to another it will seem something else').[32] The matter is brilliantly 'resolved' when Sancho Panza later[33] dubs the object a *baciyelmo*. This example is particularly illuminating insofar as it helps us see that thinking in unfamiliar ways does not lead to social breakdown. On the contrary, what is unfamiliar to each of the characters in this episode is bridged by a new linguistic creation (the *baciyelmo)* – which is also to say that if thinking in unfamiliar ways, and especially in ways that contradict accepted norms, creates challenges for us, we also have the resources to meet those challenges. We are hardly diminished but rather enriched by the creation of the *baciyelmo*.

This last issue leads to a final set of considerations – specifically to consideration of what literature contributes to the project of knowing 'other minds'. The philosophical problem referred to by that name encompasses a number of issues, foremost among them the question of whether we can know, for certain, that other (human) beings are sentient (thinking and feeling) in the way we are and, if we can, then whether we can ever truly know their feelings and thoughts. One version of the problem was articulated by Descartes in the *Meditations*, 'If I look out of the window and see men crossing the square, as I just happen to have done, I normally say that I see the men themselves, just as I say that I see the wax. Yet do I see any more than hats and coats which could conceal automatons.'[34] And *if* we determine that these shadowy figures are human beings and not mere mannequins, then how can we know what they are truly thinking and feeling? Adam Smith elaborated on the problem in these graphic terms: 'Though our brother is upon the rack, as long as we ourselves are at our ease, our senses will never inform us of what he suffers. They never did, and never can, carry us beyond our own person, and it is by the imagination only that we can form any conception of what are his sensations.'[35]

One answer to the problem lies in the argument from the analogy advanced in the work of David Hume, as for example when he writes in *The Treatise on Human Nature* that 'no quality of human nature is more remarkable, both in itself and in its consequences, than that propensity we have to sympathize with others'.[36] It is by means of sympathy that we are affected by the passions and mental states of others, which otherwise 'remain concealed in the minds of others'.[37] This response aligns with Smith's conclusion that 'it is by changing places in fancy with the sufferer that we come either to conceive or to be affected by what he feels, may be demonstrated by many obvious observations, if it should not be thought sufficiently evident of itself'.[38]

If the prospect of our own flourishing must not preclude the suffering of others, then we must be practised in the art of imagining ourselves in the place of others.[39] If poetry affords us the opportunity to develop our capacity for intelligent and reflective imaginative sensation, then prose fiction and drama serve the same purpose when it comes to our capacity to know and feel as others do. One cannot, for example, be fully engaged with the work of Dostoevsky if one does not enter the thoughts and feelings of Raskolnikov, or with the work of Dickens if one cannot do the same with David Copperfield, or with the work of García Lorca if one cannot do likewise with the character Bernarda Alba. These examples could be multiplied many, many times over, and along with them one could offer any number of examples where our ability fully to know a character is impeded by some of the very same opacities that cloud our knowledge of the human others in our midst. The point is not they we ever fully *do* know and feel what another does, but that we are able to imagine what it might mean to be in their place.

The further consequences of that conclusion are among the insights that Stanley Cavell drew from the work of Wittgenstein, aided in large measure by his engagement with the works of Shakespeare. Wittgenstein's articulation of the problem is in the following passage from *Philosophical Investigations*:

> If one has to imagine someone else's pain on the model of one's own, this is none too easy a thing to do: for I have to imagine pain which I *do not feel* on the model of pain which I *do feel*. That is, what I have to do is not simply to make a transition in imagination from one place of pain to another. As, from the pain in the hand to pain in the arm. For I am not to imagine that I feel pain in some region of his body.[40]

Much of Cavell's work in *The Claim of Reason* and in subsequent essays on Shakespeare, as prompted by Wittgenstein, was devoted to demonstrating that the problem of 'other minds', as classically conceived, was aiming for the wrong kind of answer. Whereas the general expectation was that the question could be answered with certainty, following criteria, as a matter of knowledge (as, e.g. in Descartes's *Meditations*), it could in fact only be answered by acknowledgement. This is also to say that conventional responses to the problem of other minds tended to lead us to avoid the responsibility that attaches to the knowledge of others. Knowing others is not enough. What is required is that one take responsibility for acknowledging the humanity in others, which in turn is evident in the way one behaves towards them. Acknowledgement is something we do in relation to others, not a cognitive achievement.

This also goes to say that the distinctive purpose of literature is not to give us knowledge of anything, much less knowledge of others. It can, however, afford us with opportunities to learn what it means to acknowledge others. And in that it increases the opportunities for our own flourishing in the most generous possible way. In pursuit of our own flourishing, not only do we not diminish the opportunity of others to do the same, we engage in a practice where we can imagine what it might mean for others to feel pleasure and pain and, of course, to flourish as well. This is the work of the moral imagination, and it is work that literature does especially well. It is further enhanced by all the other ways in which literature supports human flourishing, including, not least among which are the opportunities it provides for us to think and feel with greater care and intensity, regardless of what the intention of those activities might be.

7

The ethics of narrative art: Philosophy in schools, compassion and learning from stories

Laura D'Olimpio and Andrew Peterson

Introduction

There are good *prima facie* reasons for accepting that children engage in narrative artworks in various aspects of their education and schooling. Whether through subject-based curricula (such as literature, history, geography, social studies, art and drama), through pastoral support programmes or through other educational activities (such as excursions to museums), narrative artworks are a common feature of children's lived experience. Our interest here is the extent to which, and ways in which, children's educational engagements with narrative artworks hold the potential to connect to philosophical notions of the good life and human flourishing.[1]

The question of how one might live a good life has been – and continues to be – a central, shared concern of philosophers and educators. We start by making two suggestions: (1) that humans are storytelling animals; and, (2) that narrative artworks provide a valuable resource for engaging with the stories of diverse others, including regarding the nature of the good life and human flourishing. On the basis of these two suggestions we seek to make two related and further claims of import for education: (1) that educators have a responsibility to engage children in *specifically philosophical* questions about the stories they hear, read, share and explore – that is, questions which engage children with ideas of human nature and what it means to live a good life, and, (2) that engaging in such specifically philosophical questions places certain important curricular and pedagogical demands upon schools and teachers. In order to illustrate the sorts of arguments we wish to make in this chapter, we focus specifically on the virtue of compassion as a morally educative virtue.

To advance these arguments, and following this introduction, the chapter comprises three main sections. In the first, we make some rudimentary comments about humans as storytelling animals. In the second, we offer a deeper analysis of the educational value of narrative artworks. In this second section, we draw on the virtue of compassion to illustrate the arguments we seek to make. In the third section, we explore some core educational implications of our analysis, including the need to give explicit attention to philosophy and philosophical questions in order to maximize the educational value of narrative artworks.

The significance of the analysis we offer lies in the extent to which narrative artworks can, and should, be considered as moral resources for educators; moral resources, that is, which require explicit engagement with philosophical ideas, concepts and questions if they are to provide a formative function. In this way we are making a stronger claim than simply defending stories as sources of entertainment, which is, of course, another valid function of stories. On our reading, we concur with Nussbaum's suggestions that 'certain novels are, irreplaceably, works of moral philosophy' and that 'the novel can be a paradigm of moral activity'.[2] In concurring, however, we are both mindful of, and interested in, the pedagogical implications of such a claim.

We should also note that for the purposes of this chapter, and for reasons of space, we do not provide a precise overall account of the moral basis of stories. While there are interesting and important philosophical and educational debates concerning the relationship between the aesthetic and moral worth of works of art,[3] it will suffice for our purposes here to assume the position defended by Carroll[4] that works of art – such as novels and stories – contain at least some moral content, and such moral content may be evaluated in light of the overall or aesthetic evaluation of artworks. This seems particularly reasonable when it comes to narrative artworks, as Nussbaum notes, which necessarily raise ethical questions pertaining to *life*.[5] Thus, we maintain that narrative artworks contain moral content which may be critiqued and responded to by readers of such texts.

Humans as storytelling animals

Humans are storytelling animals. We tell the narratives of our lives and the world in which we live, and the versions of the stories we tell affect ourselves as well as others with whom we share these tales. The ancient Greek philosophers were aware of this, with Plato worrying about the effects of stories on children and citizens. In Book III of the *Republic*, he refers to censorship and the supervision of storytellers (including the artists and the poets). Aristotle was similarly aware of the power of stories, yet held a more favourable view of their role in society, as evidenced in the *Poetics* in which he speaks of stories as a form of imitation of life, which is natural to children. We learn through imitation, he claims, and then represent the truth we discover in various ways to others. It is through dialogue that we shape a shared understanding of the world we inhabit.

Medieval thinkers St Augustine and St Thomas Aquinas similarly expressed an understanding of the way in which stories can help us to find meaning in life. The example of the role of parables and stories of scripture illustrate how narratives can connect diverse people, uniting them in a shared vision of values and belief. Influenced by these Christian philosophers, and following Aristotle, contemporary virtue ethicist Alasdair MacIntyre defends an account of humans as storytelling animals in *After Virtue*.[6] MacIntyre argues:

> A central thesis then begins to emerge: man is in his actions and practice, as well as in his fictions, essentially a story-telling animal. He is not essentially, but becomes through his history, a teller of stories that aspire to truth. But the key question for

> men is not about their own authorship; I can only answer the question 'What am I to do?' if I can answer the prior question 'Of what story or stories do I find myself a part?'[7]

Indeed, the philosophical tradition of Philosophy for Children (P4C) that was started by Matthew Lipman and the Institute for the Advancement of Philosophy for Children (IAPC) at Montclair State University in New Jersey, United States, sought to return to the idea that (particular) stories were the perfect vehicle for doing philosophy with children for two reasons; they were engaging and age-appropriate. At the time Lipman was writing, the university departments teaching philosophy tended towards content-driven lectures without any emphasis on the pragmatic *doing* of philosophy. The *doing* of philosophy, he argued, was important to teach children philosophical thinking skills, rather than solely learning philosophical content or the history of ideas. The idea that literature could be a vehicle for philosophical knowledge was not new, even if nearly forgotten by the Western analytic tradition of the academy at the time in which Lipman was writing. It is noted:

> For the greater part of their history in Western civilisation, literature and philosophy have been estranged from one another. But this was hardly the case during those early centuries in Greece which saw the emergence of philosophical thinking. Prior to Aristotle, in fact, philosophy was virtually always embodied in some literary vehicle. There were the aphorisms of Heraclitus and the poetry of Parmenides, just as there were later to be the dramatic dialogues of Plato.[8]

Like Lipman, we argue that narratives can be philosophical; they can tell truths and be morally educative. Storytelling, in which authors make use of language and the mode of writing to communicate their ideas, is a powerful medium by which one may express morality and influence others. According to Iris Murdoch, judgements about value(s) are unavoidable in narrative works as 'one cannot avoid value judgements. Values show, and show clearly, in literature.'[9] Value judgements are embedded in our language and the words we use often imply or presume certain kinds of moral evaluations. Murdoch notes:

> It is important to remember that language itself is a moral medium, almost all uses of language convey value. This is one reason why we are almost always morally active. Life is soaked in the moral, literature is soaked in the moral ... So the novelist is revealing his values by any sort of writing which he may do. He is particularly bound to make moral judgements in so far as his subject-matter is the behaviour of human beings.[10]

In the sections which follow we examine in further detail the ways in which particular narratives might be philosophical, conveying truth and values, in a way that may be deemed to be morally educative when engaged with in a certain way.

The educative value of narrative artworks

Drawing upon Aristotle, as well as Iris Murdoch, Martha Nussbaum argues that we can, through imaginative and compassionate engagement with the stories of diverse others, learn to adopt a moral attitude. We can practise this caring disposition when hearing about the experiences of others, even – and perhaps even more so – if these others are fictional characters.

One way we can learn, morally, from narrative artworks, is by practising a 'loving attitude' or caring disposition that eventually becomes a rational habit engrained in our character. By practising this moral attitude in relation to characters in stories, we are protected in a safe fictional space and therefore may find it easier to take the perspective of others. Nussbaum writes:

> The aesthetic activity, which takes place in a safe and protected 'potential space' where our own safety is not immediately threatened, harnesses the pleasure of exploring to the neediness and insufficiency that is its object, thus making our limitations pleasing, and at least somewhat less threatening, to ourselves.[11]

Nussbaum[12] focuses on compassion, which she terms an 'intelligent emotion', as providing an important disposition to be developed through engagement with narrative artworks. Crucial in this regard are the ways in which narrative artworks allow us both to engage with the thoughts, feelings and goals of key protagonists and to use our imaginative capacities to develop the sympathy and empathy for others – including others who are different from ourselves – which compassion requires. Literary artworks are not only lifelike enough, but also best capture the subtleties of real moral dilemmas and thus provide us with a useful proxy in order to practise moral discernment.

To understand this last point, we must appreciate certain features of compassion. The first concerns the extent to which compassion requires some form of harmony between sympathy (the care-based sorrow we feel at the suffering of others) and empathy (the 'imaginative reconstruction', to use Blum's term,[13] of the others' suffering, which blends self-focused and other-focused role-taking.[14] Once these two characteristics of compassion are identified, the realization that one's imaginative reconstruction of an other (in compassion's case an other who is suffering) may be fallible becomes crucial, and moves the compassionate subject to engage further in order to understand the other. Such understanding forms a crucial part in the discernment and deliberation central to *phronesis* (or practical wisdom).

To possess moral virtues means, on Aristotle's account,[15] 'to feel them at the right time, with reference to the right objects, towards the right people, with the right motive, and in the right way'. Given this, understanding the other – and in turn understanding ourselves – in ways which seek to reduce the empathic gap seem crucial, and to this end particular forms of narrative artwork are particularly apt. As Nussbaum suggests, 'only in fiction is the mind of the other transparent. The empathetic person attempts to reconstruct the mental experience of another.'[16] Through engaging with those of others, the compassionate agent adopts a more reflexive understanding of their own thoughts and feelings. Certainly, narratives must be somewhat like our own world and experiences in order for us to identify with, understand and interpret them correctly; if novels weren't at all based in reality they wouldn't make any sense. This is evident as novels often make use of linear time and the characters are humans with thoughts and emotions and act upon a world in a similar way to us. Even science fiction stories have enough similarities to make them relevant and meaningful to their readers. Nussbaum argues that, if we meaningfully engage with and practise an ethical mode of attention to scenarios and characters depicted, this can enable us to engage with and learn, two particular philosophical or moral concerns: (1) moral truth and (2) human flourishing.

Moral truth on this account is wider than that of a solely propositional account. Here Nussbaum draws upon the pragmatist and author Henry James, claiming that moral knowledge restricted to propositions would be incomplete and what is needed is a broader understanding of moral knowledge. Nussbaum argues, 'Moral knowledge, James suggests, is not simply intellectual grasp of propositions; it is not even simply intellectual grasp of particular facts; it is perception. It is seeing a complex, concrete reality in a highly lucid and richly responsive way; it is taking in what is there, with imagination and feeling.'[17]

In illustrating her point, Nussbaum goes into great detail in her analysis of classical works of literature such as Henry James's *The Golden Bowl*.[18] James's work is considered as an example of (perhaps rare) narrative art that is both aesthetically and ethically good. The intricate detail with which James describes the characters, their inner worlds as well as their moral dilemmas is what particularly resonates with the attentive reader, allowing a caring attitude to be adopted to fallible, human characters that we recognize are 'like us' in important respects. As we engage imaginatively with the plight of these fictional others, we care about the decisions they make and the consequences of their actions in the fictional story-world. In this way, the empathetic reader is practising a moral attitude of compassion and sympathetic engagement with other(s) who differ to themselves.

A central idea defended here is that the nuances of moral judgement sometimes escape the black and white depiction of analytic moral philosophy and are better expressed in narrative form. In this way, Nussbaum believes that moral philosophers would do well to consider *A Golden Bowl* a work of moral philosophy! It is the detail and nuance of good narrative artworks that allows for sympathetic engagement with the characters' thoughts, intentions, feelings, behaviour and circumstances.

A key aspect of this sympathetic engagement is the potential of good narrative artworks to engage us in dialogue and reflection about human flourishing and what it means to live a good life.[19] In her work on compassion, Nussbaum identifies *eudaimonistic judgement* as central to compassion.[20] When we exercise this judgement we become closer to the other who is suffering; that is, we come to see them and their humanity as inherently important to our own lives. As Nussbaum explains 'she must take that person's ill as affecting her own flourishing. In effect, she must make herself vulnerable in the person of another.'[21] In this way, when compassion is in action we not only recognize the cause of the other, we bring that cause into our own goals. A crucial part of this process is understanding what human flourishing and conceptions of the good life are so far as those suffering are concerned. As these may be rather different to our own, a fundamental requirement of the compassionate agent is to extend their compassion to those different to themselves and, indeed, to engage with such difference.

In focusing on the value of narrative artworks in relation to moral truth and human flourishing, Nussbaum offers a positive causal link between morality and literature as she believes that *good* literature can assist us in understanding morality, as well as enable the practice of virtuous conduct and ethical decision-making in our everyday lives. By practising a loving attitude towards characters in works of fiction, we care about their plight. If we practise this moral attitude firstly in the safe fictional space, we can then apply it to real-life others we encounter.

This causal argument will only work if we agree with Nussbaum's starting point, that humans are rational and emotional, embodied and contextual. The good life, on such an account, requires others *as well as myself* to flourish, and communities to support and promote healthy policies and institutions conducive to this flourishing (*eudaimonia*). This contextual, empirical approach to moral value entails that the search for exceptionless moral rules is misguided, even if general capabilities, for instance, are useful and worth legislating at a societal or global level. At the level of personal decision-making, the virtue ethicist allows for contextual deliberation of moral acts and will further point out that *how* I act upon the virtue of, for instance, compassion, depends on the situation at hand and the people involved in the moral context under consideration. All of these factors, discerned through practical wisdom, will impact upon the moral appropriateness of the agent's response.

Thus we can see how Nussbaum's 'loving attitude', her version of ethical attention, encourages a certain perspective to be adopted with reference to ethical situations and decision-making.

This loving attitude calls on the love or compassion (a feeling component with a cognitive element as well as a volitional aspect) working alongside the intellect and the imagination. These three elements work together in order to understand the facts of a particular situation, whereby the ethical agent may empathize by imaginatively engaging with the plight of the people in the scenario and then 'seeing' how to appropriately respond. The imagination, emotions and narratives, then, are important to a holistic approach to being human. Nussbaum explains:

> I defend the literary imagination precisely because it seems to me an essential ingredient of an ethical stance that asks us to concern ourselves with the good of other people whose lives are distant from our own ... an ethics of impartial respect for human dignity will fail to engage real human beings unless they are capable of entering imaginatively into the lives of distant others and to have emotions related to that participation.[22]

Engaging students in narrative artworks: The need for philosophy

In this section, we build on the arguments advanced so far to explore some pedagogical possibilities central to engaging students in narrative artworks. Before exploring the pedagogical possibilities, we wish briefly to spend time first setting out some justifications for the place of philosophy within the curriculum of schools, in particular those curricula experienced by children before the age of sixteen. Such justifications are multiple, interconnected and recognize both empirical and normative concerns. The first is the idea alluded to previously that young people *already* engage in various ways with the sorts of questions central to philosophy and philosophical investigation. Whether through familial, community, religious, media or peer-based interactions, questions concerning who we are, how we live our lives, how and why we relate to others and what our rights and responsibilities are (to give just a few examples), are ones which are prominent in the daily lives of young people. In other words, young people are already likely to be philosophically active, but not necessarily with the support and structure to make sense of such activity in a structured and philosophically rigorous manner.

A second reason for including philosophy in the school curriculum relates to the sorts of questions young people are likely to be considering as part of their daily lives, which are also questions which feature within the aims and curricula of Westernized educational jurisdictions, but which may remain under-explored without specific attention and careful cultivation. Our focus on compassion illustrates this point rather well. The goal of educating young people to be compassionate (sometimes also expressed through associated terms such as empathy and care) is not uncommon within official curricula, educational practice and educational literature.[23] It is a goal which transcends narrow educational outcomes relating to economic utility and academic achievement, and which speaks of our relationship to others as human beings.

As Peterson has argued elsewhere,[24] cultivating compassion is not a process which is either simple or straightforward, but rather one which requires careful, targeted and consistent nurturing. Such nurturing involves some level of engagement with concepts, ideas and processes which are precisely philosophical. Let us take an example to illustrate. If a goal of education and schooling is to educate compassionate young people – a goal which we have argued here involves engaging with narratives – then engaging with notions of human flourishing and what it means to lead a good life are crucial. As we have suggested previously, educating about and for compassion involves us in coming to understand – through deliberation with others and within ourselves – *eudaimonistic* judgements. Such deliberation 'requires a capacity for critical reflection, consideration of alternative possibilities, and a genuine concern for truth and clarity';[25] in other words, the development of a particular form of practical wisdom through which young people seek to discern appropriate moral responses within given contexts.

Third, there is a growing body of empirical research which suggests important outcomes for students' cognitive and socio-emotional development through engagement with philosophical ideas and processes.[26] While this is not to claim that trained philosophers are *better*, ethically, than anyone else, the idea here is that practising critical thinking skills is helpful for practical decision-making (*phronesis* – practical wisdom). For example, thinking through ethically relevant features of moral decisions by using fictional case studies or thought experiments encourages us to become more attuned to the contexts in which we must act, including being aware of the ethically salient features when making decisions that affect ourselves and others. When taught and practised in a certain way, namely, dialogically, philosophy is an ideal subject through which to facilitate such contextual analysis and applied decision-making.

In offering these justifications for philosophy in the school curriculum, we are not suggesting that philosophy *necessarily* needs to exist as a separate and distinct curriculum subject. Our weaker claim is that, taught well, philosophy may be engaged with within existing subjects, but this requires explicit cultivation, and preferably by teachers who have themselves been educated in the field of philosophy. Our stronger claim is that teaching philosophy and ethics as a distinct curriculum subject using a pedagogy that prioritizes the students' own questions and includes narratives would allow students to explicitly reflect upon the ethical values, norms and concerns central to *their* good life in a way that is not usually invited or encouraged in other subjects. In both claims, we are suggesting that without explicit focus and cultivation the contribution of philosophy is left to chance, and as a result may be underplayed or neglected altogether.

Philosophical pedagogy using narratives

In the preceding sections, we have argued that humans are storytelling beings and that narrative artworks are of ethical and educative value for the extent to which they provide possibilities for engaging with core moral ideas. So far as the education of children in schools is concerned, however, it seems appropriate to suggest that while narrative artworks provide the *potential* for moral and philosophical learning, such educative outcomes require explicit cultivation in order to be realized in practice. One can readily imagine, for example, a child in school reading Dickens's *A Tale of Two Cities*[27] who does not necessarily engage with the text's central and deep moral content without the requisite support and pedagogical intervention of the teacher. In this section, we suggest some key pedagogical considerations for engaging children with narrative artworks, suggesting as we do so that each of these considerations requires teachers to engage *explicitly* in essentially philosophical questions, in both the construction of materials (the selection and adaptation of resources and associated activities, for example) and their use with children. Indeed, Nussbaum herself is aware of the objection that critics such as Richard Posner aim at her claim that narrative artworks can be morally educative. Posner cites instances of literature-loving Nazis and English professors who are no more moral than anyone else[28] while also reminding us of the importance of a good upbringing when it comes to moral formation. However, Nussbaum needn't deny these examples in order to still defend her position. In fact, she happily grants Posner's point that empathy in and of itself will not sufficiently motivate good action, and such an emotion must be grounded in a good early education in childhood for it to motivate any moral concern for others.[29] Nussbaum simply claims that some literature *can* have a morally beneficial effect, not that it always will. However, for those instances where a good narrative artwork does have such an effect, the reading of that work itself can be deemed a moral act.

A claim defended here with respect to the morally educative power of certain narratives is that fictional stories can articulate moral truth. Again, we ought to respond to the sceptic who enquires that, while adopting a caring disposition towards fictional stories may seem like a nice thing to do, how does that result in moral truth? Furthermore, how does it entail learning about moral truths rather than simply confirming moral truths the reader already knows? This criticism suggests that a reader must already be aware of the atrocities of, for instance, slavery, in order to appropriately empathize with Huck and Jim in *Huckleberry Finn*.[30] Propositional moral truths, or *knowing that* may not be the kind of truths we are learning through our engagement with literature. About this, Posner or the sceptic may be correct. However, drawing upon Gilbert Ryle's distinction between *knowing that* and *knowing how*, we may be learning about the contextual application of morality or 'what it is like' via imaginatively adopting other perspectives and thinking through various scenarios in our minds. This *knowing how* or *knowing what it is like* is a pragmatic aspect of moral knowledge.[31] It is worth noting, though, for the aesthetically and ethically good artwork to have such an effect, the reader themselves must be appropriately sensitive and adopt a loving attitude in order to engage compassionately with the characters and scenario depicted. This is precisely why our focus on how to engage with appropriate narrative texts in the classroom via encouraging students to practise a loving attitude or the virtue of compassion is so important. And on this point of how this may be done, pedagogically, Nussbaum is silent.

If we accept, as we would wish to do, that narrative artworks offer crucial educational possibilities, a further question becomes precisely *which* artworks. At a general level, there is some agreement that not all works of art offer the same educational potential in this regard. That is, while some (good) narrative artworks may have a morally educative role to play, the role of other (less good) narrative artworks is less certain. As Nussbaum notes:

> One can think of works of art which can be contemplated reasonably well without asking any urgent questions about how one should live. Abstract formalist paintings are sometimes of this character, and some intricate but non-programmatic works of music (though by no means all). But it seems highly unlikely that a responsive reading of any complex literary work is utterly detached from concerns about time and death, about pain and the transcendence of pain, and so on – all the material of 'how one should live' questions as I have conceived it.[32]

According to Nussbaum, 'the fact that Sophoclean tragedy inspires compassion for human suffering and the fact that it is great and powerful poetry are not independent facts: it is the poetic excellence that conveys compassion to the spectator, cutting through the habits of the everyday';[33] while Bohlin identifies the challenges educators face from 'the range of negative narrative images and stimuli that feed the imaginations and aspirations of young people', including 'widely popularized books that idealize the fast track to fame and fortune'.[34]

Crucial here is the role of narratives in permitting students to engage with the thoughts, feelings and goals of others, including tracing how these develop and respond to formative experiences. In her work on teaching character through literature,[35] Bohlin refers to such experiences as 'morally pivotal points' – events through which characters 'reassess or refine their life goal(s) or path(s)'. When a philosophical approach is taken, literature and testimony enables students to consider and explore the characters and their actions involved in relation to their own responses in ways which allow and shape reflection on the good life and human flourishing. In this way, narrative artworks engaged with philosophically can allow young people to contemplate how their character and actions – including virtuous actions – represent expressions of themselves. As Bohlin contends, it can provide a tool for reflection on character which 'happens somewhere between the heart and the will, every time characters make a choice, particularly choices that somehow define who they are and mark an important change of focus'.[36]

To frame such explorations, Bohlin helpfully sets out four common features – each of them apt for exploring compassion – upon which teachers can focus in teaching character through literature: (i) 'relationships'; (ii) 'learning from pain and acquiring new pleasures'; (iii) 'thoughtful reflection'; and, (iv) 'courage to face the truth (about reality, oneself, and others)'.[37] To reinforce the point being made here: narrative artworks clearly have the potential to move children to feel and express sympathy, empathy and compassion whether or not these are intended by teachers. This is particularly the case if we start with the narrative artworks that students are already watching and enjoying. However, without an explicit and philosophically aware discussion of those feelings – including their cognitive dimensions – the ethical and educative potential of such artworks are neglected, and are so in ways which restrict children's moral development.

The philosophical community of inquiry

The philosophical community of inquiry (CoI) provides a particularly apt pedagogical tool to foster the explicit and philosophical discussion required to draw out the moral learning of narrative artworks. In a CoI, participants are seated in an inward-facing circle and the teacher facilitates a discussion based on the students' own questions. In order to generate the students' questions, teachers may first use an age-appropriate text. Traditionally, Lipman used novels he wrote, such as *Harry Stottlemeier's Discovery*,[38] which were imbued with philosophical ideas and involved characters discussing ideas and reflecting on experiences that would be similar to those encountered by school-aged children. The relevant chapter would be read aloud, paragraph by paragraph, by those seated in the CoI and then, after a brainstorming session or activity, a central question would be democratically decided upon by the group as the focus for the ensuing CoI. This central question should be philosophical: open, 'deep' and not a question that yields an immediately obvious answer. As facilitator of the discussion rather than the authoritarian source of all knowledge, a teacher's role in the CoI is radically altered. In a CoI, the focus is not on learning philosophical content by rote but, rather, on *doing* philosophy in order to develop critical thinking, caring responses, creativity and the ability to work together collaboratively with respect for diverse ideas in the search for truth and wisdom.

By commencing a CoI with a narrative, the students are encouraged to identify with the main character, such as Harry, and place themselves in the shoes of this character as he seeks to understand concepts and refine arguments. The CoI dialogue that follows is student-led and, ideally, sees participants willing to critically engage with their own and others' ideas, while compassionately responding to the views of others as they are encountered. Far from there being 'no correct answers', the philosophical CoI should see participants move away from the worst answers or arguments and move towards more reasonable, justified ideas while also recognizing a common humanity, even with those with whose ideas one disagrees. As Lipman, Sharp and Oscanyan remark: 'To the extent that philosophy presents a range of alternative views about values, meaning and knowledge itself, it liberates children from the dogmatism of ignorance, outlines relative considerations that have been developed, and encourages that "thinking for oneself" which is so much the mark of a truly educated person.'[39]

Teacher training is central to the aim of a CoI generating a *philosophical* dialogue and thus training the philosophical thinking skills of its participants. Lipman, Sharp and Oscanyan distinguish between a conversation, a good conversation and a philosophical conversation. A conversation may be disjointed and superficial whereas a good conversation may have flow and direction and arrive at a conclusion or resolution. A philosophical conversation is a good conversation that pertains to deep ideas, and seeks to clarify concepts that may be debated or arguments that may not be entirely settled (such as 'what makes a good person?' or 'does God exist?'). The teacher must have training in both the P4C and

CoI pedagogy as well as in the study of philosophy, otherwise they may not develop a philosophical ear to recognize the philosophical nature or potential in children's contributions or questions. To this effect,

> further, in regard to the training of teachers to encourage philosophical thinking, it is the exposure to and the involvement with the history of philosophical ideas that enables a prospective teacher to develop an appreciation for philosophical questioning himself. This sensitivity is essential if one is even to hear the philosophical significance of what children say. If one cannot hear the philosophical dimension, then it is inconceivable to expect the teacher to aid children in coming to a deeper awareness of it themselves.[40]

The role of the teacher, even in a student-led CoI, is thus pivotal in guiding students to critically reflect and compassionately consider the ideas, examples and associated feelings of others as well as their own. Participating in a CoI provides the individual with an opportunity to recognize that they are not an isolated cogito but, rather, 'one among others'.[41] As it is recognized that others are more or less similar to oneself, even when we have different thoughts, feelings and experiences, we feel compassion towards them as we are united by a sense of common humanity.

Splitter identifies three key components of this process that are cognitive as well as affective. These include, first, appreciating my own self-worth, arising from a recognition of my role in the community; second, appreciating that others are also striving for this kind of self-appreciation; and third, 'understanding that self-appreciation and appreciation for others are interdependent and mutually reinforcing'.[42] In seeking shared values that arise from a context, in a time and a place, the group must care about one another if it is to function well.[43] This is further reinforced by Splitter's remark that 'the CoI is an interactive environment whose entire rationale is the wellbeing of its members (in intellectual, moral and affective terms)'.[44] Similarly, the virtue ethicist recognizes individual *eudaimonia* is intrinsically linked to the well-being of the polis[45] or, in this instance, the community, including the school community and the wider community of which the school is a part. By engaging philosophically with narratives within an educational setting, using a CoI pedagogy, children are given the opportunity to practise, in a safe space, the moral attitude of compassion, while developing their techniques of critical reflection; skills that prepare them for the role of living a good life.

Conclusion

We have suggested that we are storytelling animals who learn from the stories of diverse others. Moral agents use rational emotions such as compassion to imagine 'what it is like' for another prior to deciding how they should act. Narrative artworks, such as aesthetically and ethically good novels and films, allow us – and young people – the opportunity to engage imaginatively and compassionately with diverse characters and scenarios in a safe, protected space that is created by the fictional world. By practising what Nussbaum calls a 'loving attitude', her version of ethical attention, we can form virtuous habits that lead to *phronesis* (practical wisdom) and enable us to lead a flourishing life.

On this basis, we have advanced two main educational arguments. The first is the idea that educators have a responsibility to engage children in *specifically philosophical* questions about the stories they hear, read, share and explore. In this way narrative artworks provide insights and stimulus for engaging with ideas of human nature, human relationships and what it means to live a good life. Whether such philosophical questions – which require some level of philosophical understanding on behalf of educators – are best taught through a specific discrete school subject called philosophy or through other curriculum subjects has not been our main focus, given that what seems most pressing is whether philosophy should be taught in schools at all. It seems likely to us that either (or perhaps both) models of curricular inclusion hold particular possibilities. The second main educational argument we have advanced is that engaging children in such specifically philosophical questions places certain important curricular and pedagogical demands upon schools and teachers, demands which can be met by using philosophy as a praxis in the classroom. We have sought to illustrate this claim by exploring how teachers can draw upon narrative art in classrooms in support of a pedagogy designed to promote caring thinking alongside critical, creative and collaborative thinking skills. This may be done by facilitating a community of inquiry, a way of practising philosophy in the classroom, which often utilizes narrative as a provocation in order to generate philosophical questions and dialogue from the students who are participants in the inquiry. Teachers may create a safe space for students to co-construct meaning via active engagement with narratives as a stimulus for students' own ideas. This leads to students participating in meaningful experiences, from which they can learn, reflect and develop virtuous habits. By taking seriously the idea of children as embodied, we can value experiential and affective knowledge alongside a rational, cognitive epistemology. Aesthetic education can work well within this educative approach known as philosophy for children (or P4C) in its search for rational and pragmatic wisdom. For these reasons, philosophy should be included in the classroom and make use of, alongside other texts and stimulus materials, good narrative artworks in order to encourage children to be compassionate as well as critical citizens.

PART THREE

The Genres of Philosophy

8

The literary evolution of the philosophical metaphor of *theatrum mundi**

Sophie Bastien

The *theatrum mundi* metaphor is a conceptual depiction of existence which emerges from reflection on the impermanence and powerlessness of humankind. This understanding provokes a feeling of theatricality, makes us see the world in theatrical terms, as though humans are actors and spectators watching each other. In contrast to physical metaphors, which compare two tangible objects, *theatrum mundi* falls within the category of moral metaphor, based on Pierre Fontanier's early, but still relevant, classification[1]: something from the moral order (i.e. existence) is compared with something from the physical order which appeals to the senses (i.e. the dramatic arts). Having evolved for over two thousand years, this metaphor has been used extensively in Western culture's canonical texts, to the point of becoming ubiquitous. It provides a wealth of hermeneutic considerations, including aspects of metaphysics, politics, pedagogy and aesthetics.

The first part of this essay will trace the philosophical origins of *theatrum mundi*, highlighting its cognitive utility. Using a diachronic approach, it will begin in Antiquity and conclude in the Middle Ages. The second part of the essay will focus on the Renaissance and the seventeenth century using a synchronic and interdisciplinary method, as the theatre metaphor is found throughout the many disciplines of the period. To boot, for the first time in history, the metaphor is extremely prevalent within the theatre itself, more so than in any other discipline: it appears in theatre both as a literary genre (in dramatic works) and as a performing art (on stage). In other words, life's theatricality is increasingly expressed in written plays and made visible through staging. The third and final part of the essay will resume the metaphor's chronological trajectory, laying emphasis on the twentieth century and culminating in the twenty-first century. This passage will demonstrate just how versatile this metaphor really is, its meaning being adapted by writers to suit their respective ethics and place in time. Thus, the evolution of this metaphor reflects the evolution of our perception of the human condition, while, at the same time, mirroring the development of the literary transposition of this perception.

Ancient origins of *theatrum mundi*

A confluence of fruitful concepts

Before delving into Hellenism, the period that gave rise to the theatre metaphor, it is worthwhile to look even further back – to the Old Testament. While it does not contain a conception of a theatrical world, it does demonstrate some preliminary ideas. For instance, life's inconsistency is signified by the metaphor of shadows, while human transience is symbolized by the metaphor of 'passing through', that is, en route to our true destination. Psalm 39 combines both of these metaphors: 'Surely all mankind stands as a mere breath! / Surely a man goes about as a shadow' (5–6). Chapters from the *Book of Job* also feature them: 'Our days on earth are a shadow' (8: 9); 'He [man] comes out like a flower and withers; / he flees like a shadow and continues not' (14: 2). These phrases make the concept of human vanity tangible and concrete, whereas it remains abstract when expressed literally – as in the well-known verse from the *Book of Ecclesiastes* (1: 2): 'Vanity of vanities! All is vanity.'[2] Furthermore, these phrases from *Psalms* and the *Book of Job* fulfil a dichotomous function in service of religious ideology: their manner of describing human life highlights humankind's misery, with the aim of contrasting it with God's glory. Be that as it may, the metaphorical imagery of shadows and passing through are intimately linked to the concept of *theatrum mundi* – practically indivisible from it. This imagery is associated to *theatrum mundi* throughout every era, such that it serves as a mainstay in the development of the trope.

The shadow metaphor is also prominent among the Greeks. In Homer's *The Odyssey*, men are 'shadows that drift ineffectually'.[3] Plato then furthers this image using a dichotomy similar to that seen in the Old Testament: he contrasts the shadow with being, reflection with reality and the cave of men with the light of God. In the 'Myth of the Cave', Louis Van Delft perceives the idea of theatricality;[4] however, the theatre metaphor begins to take shape shortly before Plato. Although its precise origin is yet uncertain, it was likely first introduced by the Presocratics in the fifth century BC. Lynda Christian traces its emergence to the very invention of theatre.[5] As soon as theatre took its first steps as an art form, the analogy was obvious: the world was compared to a stage, and its people to actors. The dramatic arts are the source of these comparisons, and they bring about a revelation, sparking philosophical awareness, thereby becoming cognitively useful.

To better understand how the theatre serves a revelatory function, awakens consciousness and works as a cognitive tool, we must turn to the concept of mimesis. This concept was already being used to reflect on various arts, and Plato was the first to apply it to the theatre, at least to the dramatic text. In his view, imitative discourse is akin to the dialogue of tragedy and comedy.[6] Aristotle then applies the concept of mimesis to the stage. He states that mimesis is the imitation of human actions, and it refers to actors who represent characters in action.[7] Above all, Aristotle sheds light on its cognitive function: first, mimetic activity is rooted in human instinct, and, second, it provides pleasure – that of recognizing resemblance. This pleasure is directly linked to knowledge, given that we learn from what we observe.[8]

In Aristotelian theory, the performing arts are an irrepressible part of our condition. Since they are mimesis of human life, the spectator recognizes the imitated object and consequently reflects on it with new consciousness. If the spectator's new consciousness pertains to the ontological nature of existence – as was the case for the very first theatre-going philosophers – the spectator will express it in theatrical terms and liken life to the theatre. So the relationship is tautological: theatre refers to life, and life refers to theatre. Philology has shown that this interplay is in its embryonic stage in Plato and Aristotle, where it manifests itself grammatically: imitative verbs refer to both the imitated object and to the outcome of mimetic activity, that is, to both model and copy.[9] At first glance, this ambiguity in the founding concept of mimesis is merely linguistic, but it does have philosophical implications. This is reflected in the sometimes ambivalent use of the theatre metaphor, a circular movement in which the compared element and the comparing element become interchangeable (examples to follow). Fontanier takes into account this dual directionality in his definition of the moral metaphor: the mind moves from the concrete towards the abstract or, conversely, from the abstract towards the concrete.[10]

Growth and diversification of the theatre metaphor

In *Laws*, Plato builds on this early conception of world as theatre. On the one hand, he claims that 'we ourselves are poets, who have to the best of our ability created a tragedy that is the most beautiful and the best'.[11] On the other, he asserts that 'each of us living beings [is] a divine puppet'; we are strung along between virtue and vice, and we must decide whether to obey or resist the forces that pull us.[12] As discussed earlier, the dramatic arts in the literal sense gave rise to the metaphor of *theatrum mundi*. But when this metaphor refers back to the dramatic arts (as is the case in Plato's examples), it is in a figurative sense. From this point, the pattern is reproduced, perpetuated and modulated *ad infinitum*.

Once the theatre metaphor is assimilated and established as a thought pattern, it assumes a didactic function. First, it teaches that the theatre of human life is governed by a supernatural power. As does the image of the shadow (in the Old Testament and Plato), it suggests a dichotomy, thereby inducing in humankind a feeling of spiritual humility before the supernatural power in question. In Antiquity, it reflects the pagan world view. For instance, according to Diogenes and his followers the Cynics, and subsequently the Latin Satirists (Horace, Petronius, Juvenal, Lucian), Fortune, who is unfathomable and capricious, assigns roles and costumes to the actors. The Stoics extend the theatre metaphor through their belief that existence is, on the one hand, ordained by the Logos, and on the other, fleeting: with this metaphor, they marry two assumptions. The second assumption – the fleetingness of existence – gives rise to powerful images: we remain on the stage until the final curtain falls; death is the last act in an ephemeral drama. Such images recur in Cicero and other authors of his era, but they are particularly vivid in *Cato on Old Age*.[13] The exit from stage and curtain fall obviously signal the end of the performance, though connotatively they evoke the end of life to illustrate the inevitability of death. Epictetus adds to this that we do not decide the duration of our stay: 'Remember that you're an actor in a play, which will be as the author chooses, short if he wants it to be short, and long if he wants it to be long.'[14]

The randomness of life, underscored here by Epictetus, is the inspiration for many lessons in moral conduct, with numerous philosophers combining metaphorical form and the theatrical content. Such philosophers confer upon *theatrum mundi* an edifying purpose, and based on it, they draw up rules for living. Life is viewed as a theatrical game, yet one must nevertheless play the game seriously. And while Lucretius describes man as a passive spectator,[15] Epictetus advises us to play our part to the best of our ability, whatever that part may be.[16] Similarly, Marcus Aurelius makes this recommendation: 'Make sure your part is not that of the cheap and vulgar line in the comedy.' Through the theatre metaphor, he does no less than summarize the essence of Stoic wisdom: 'What matter if that life is five or fifty years? … It is like the officer who engaged a comic actor dismissing him from the stage.'[17] If man has been called to the stage of life by a power beyond himself, he must be ready to leave it with equanimity,[18] concludes Marcus Aurelius, embroidering the sustained theatrical metaphor that runs throughout his *Meditations*.

This stylistic phenomenon of sustained metaphor is common among the Latin philosophers. In addition to Marcus Aurelius, it occurs with Seneca and Lucian, among others. It sweeps through sizeable texts, and contributes to the evolution of an entire mode of thought, inseparable from its means of expression. According to Éric Bordas, this phenomenon demonstrates the considerable expressive capacity of the mother-metaphor.[19] Building on the same thematic core, the scope of *theatrum mundi* expands, gradually producing offshoots and connections that are coherently articulated. The outcome is a micro-narrative of human life in imagery.

If the theatre represents the world in a nutshell, it successfully encompasses countless aspects of it. One of these aspects is undoubtedly the political. Most of the aforementioned writers were engaged in political life. Cicero and, notably, Marcus Aurelius, were politicians, while several others (Aristotle, Horace, Seneca, Petronius, Lucian) were close observers of politics, and this experience colours their outlook. They clearly grasp that the sovereign's public role places him in a theatrical situation, setting him on stage before subjects who are transformed into spectators. Even the emperor's death is theatrical, as many historiographers have revealed. Suetonius describes how Augustus prepared for his own death:

> On the last day ... calling for a mirror, he had his hair combed and his falling jaws set straight. After that, calling in his friends and asking whether it seemed to them that he had played the comedy of life fitly, he added the tag: 'Since well I've played my part, all clap your hands and from the stage dismiss me with applause.'[20]

At the end of his reign, Augustus understood the intrinsic theatrical nature of his political office. And beyond this office, as death approached, he embraced the intrinsic theatricality of life – as though the sovereign's condition should carry emblematic value and dramatize the common condition. Seneca adapts this idea when he explicitly transposes the theatre metaphor to politics:

> Human life is a play, assigning us roles we can scarcely fill. ... all those fashionable people carried in litters above the heads of the crowd: their happiness is just playing a part. If you strip them of their fine apparel, you will hold them in contempt. ... Do you see that king of Scythia or of Sarmatia, with a splendid crown on his head? ... take away his headdress: much that is bad lies hidden underneath.[21]

The 'litters' and 'crown' represent that which Seneca perceives as the princely figure's stage set and costume, respectively. These mask the fundamental precariousness that is common to all mankind, and from which the prince cannot escape.

After its development throughout Greco-Roman Antiquity, the *theatrum mundi* metaphor is adopted in Christianity, accompanied by the interrelated notion – as seen in the Old Testament – that man is only passing through. In addition, Saint Paul, Saint Augustine and the Church Fathers, align *theatrum mundi* with providentialism, embedding within that belief the dogma of grace. From this perspective, the finite earthly theatre leads to the eternal heavenly Kingdom. In the Middle Ages, this metaphor becomes richer as Christian doctrine matures. In the twelfth century, John of Salisbury ascribes to God the dual role of spectator and supreme judge. Henceforth, the role that men play on earth has value merely as a prologue, and God judges them when death removes their mask.

Variations in the theatre metaphor from the Renaissance to Classicism

Among the humanists

The humanism of the Renaissance places man at the forefront, lending an anthropocentric dimension to the theatre metaphor. Accordingly, the binary dynamic between man and a divine power is less ubiquitous. According to Erasmus, to be human is to be deluded, and existence is reduced to a comedy: 'All human life is nothing but a stage-play.'[22] Montaigne adds a nuance with the flippant remark that man is, 'after all, the fool of the farce'.[23] With these words, he concludes one of his major essays, eloquently titled 'Of Vanity'. In the tradition of Antiquity, the theatre metaphor in the sixteenth century aims to make the concept of vanity tangible.

The metaphor also reflects the head of state's status. In this respect, Erasmus follows in Seneca's footsteps. The 'gold chain' around the neck, the 'crown set with precious gems', the 'scepter', the 'scarlet robe': 'all this lofty costume', this 'splendid apparel', are merely theatrical 'accouterments'.[24] And the palace, which is the focal point of the Empire, the central attraction to which all eyes turn, is the stage set – that is to say, the spatial counterpart to the costume and accessories that are the royal insignia. Notwithstanding, Erasmus takes the metaphor further than his predecessors, noting that the theatricality includes the clergy. 'The life-style of princes has long been diligently imitated, and almost surpassed, by popes, cardinals, and bishops.' 'They play' and 'perform' with all the traditional symbols that accompany their 'garment': 'the linen rochet', 'the gloves', 'the miter', 'the cross', and 'the crosier'.[25] When Erasmus compares the monk or cleric to a 'comedian or pitchman', however, the theatricality stems more from their behaviour than material possessions, which are altogether more modest in clerics than in princely figures. For their 'oratorical artistry', the monk and cleric craft 'their tone of voice', 'their facial expressions', their gestures and gait.[26] Machiavelli, meanwhile, ignores these physical manifestations and focuses instead on the ability to conceal: 'He who has best known how to play the fox has ever been the most successful. But it is necessary that the prince should know how to colour this nature well, and how to be a great hypocrite and dissembler.'[27] The Greek word *hupokrisis* means the acting of a stage player: hypocrisy and theatre are one and the same. Similarly, the Latin root *persona* means stage mask. Thus, etymologically, the *theatrum mundi* metaphor raises the ontological problem of (in) authenticity.

The Renaissance is marked by the emergence of distinct scientific disciplines, and this in turn shapes the theatre metaphor. This metaphor grows in prominence and permeates several fields of knowledge. It serves to aestheticize, so to speak, breakthroughs in those disciplines. In geography, Ortelius publishes the first world atlas, which finally provides mankind with a stage plan for the landscape it inhabits. The title speaks for itself: *Theatrum Orbis Terrarum* (for which the most common translation is 'Theatre of the World', although the literal translation is 'Theatre of the Lands of the World'). The word *theatrum* not only has a geographical function but also an iconographic representation – and in this case, cartographic. Moreover, it does not simply refer to the physical place that is Earth. For a lengthy period, it will also be used as a generic name for map collections. There are two reasons for this use of the word *theatrum*. First, map collections make the Earth a theatrical object to be viewed and contemplated (it should be recalled that *theatrum* comes from the Greek *theaomai*, 'to look upon'). Second, these collections *represent* the continents and oceans on a *stage set* of illuminations and mythological creatures.

With increasing versatility, theatre terminology also influences the very beginnings of psychology in Europe, as evidenced by Zwinger's work, which also has a metaphorical title: *Theatrum Vitae Humanae*

(Theatre of Human Life). The noun *theatrum* appears frequently in medicine, in medical scholarly works. Casseri's treatise on human anatomy is metaphorically entitled *Theatrum Anatomicum* (Theatre of Anatomy). A large part of the treatise is dedicated to engravings that make a spectacle of dissected and dismembered bodies. This theatrical idea would serve as a springboard, as anthologies would be published in the seventeenth and eighteenth centuries under the same title, with illustrations showcasing parts of the body. During the same period, theatres built in European metropolises were also known as *Theatrum Anatomicum*: on a centrally placed dissection table surrounded by stands, the insides of a cadaver are displayed for viewing by students and the general public. The theatricality even extends to animal biology, with, for instance, a treatise entitled *Theatrum Insectorum* (Theatre of Insects).

In the theatre, at last!

After a 2000-year trajectory, at the turn of the sixteenth and seventeenth centuries, the *theatrum mundi* metaphor is finally articulated in the theatre – and abundantly so in Shakespeare. To begin, Shakespeare gives his venue a name that is apparently very simple and nevertheless laden with meaning: 'The Globe' pithily sums up the *theatrum mundi* metaphor, but inverts it. More precisely, this name is reminiscent of the topographers' vision of Earth as theatre, only now the theatre is likened to Earth. This inversion underscores the two-directional nature of this metaphor, which, as previously seen, was already at play in Plato and Aristotle. This dual directionality is expressed in *The Tempest* by Prospero, who uses the word 'globe' between two comparisons:

> These our actors
> … were all spirits, and
> Are melted into air …;
> And like the baseless fabric of this vision,
> … the great globe itself,
> Yea, all which it inherent, shall dissolve;
> And, like this insubstantial pageant faded,
> Leave not a rack behind.[28]

In addition to giving his theatre a highly significant name, Shakespeare affixed to the venue's entrance the following maxim, which was penned by John of Salisbury to summarize verses by Petronius: *Totus mundus agit histrionem*. The maxim is famously translated in the much-quoted line, 'All the world's a stage', which effectively encapsulates *theatrum mundi*. And yet, the whole excerpt from which this line is drawn is germane. In *As You Like It*, Duke Senior states the following:

> This wide and universal theatre
> Presents more woeful pageants than the scene
> Wherein we play in.

Jaques's answer is perhaps made more memorable by the sweeping effect of its anaphoric determiner 'All':

> All the world's a stage,
> And all the men and women merely players.
> They have their exits and their entrances,
> And one man in his time plays many parts.[29]

Antonio's musings in *The Merchant of Venice* are similarly lucid:

> I hold the world but as the world, ...
> A stage where every man must play a part.[30]

While I have quoted three of the Shakespeare's comedies (*The Tempest*, *As you like it*, *The Merchant of Venice*), this vision of the world also resurfaces in the tragic mode. Following the death of his wife, Macbeth comes to this momentous revelation:

> Life's but a walking shadow, a poor player
> That struts and frets his hour upon the stage,
> And then is heard no more. It is a tale
> Told by an idiot, full of sound and fury,
> Signifying nothing.[31]

King Lear is no less sombre when he mentions 'this great stage of fools'.[32] This short but powerful line echoes the conclusion of Montaigne's essay 'Of Vanity', but in a more serious tone.

Shakespeare's repeated use of the vision of the world as theatre is surely related to his drawing inspiration from history, as evidenced in his ten 'Histories', but also in a few of his 'Tragedies'. As Seneca and Erasmus observed, history demonstrates how the royal apparatus – with its stage sets, costumes and accoutrements – is in itself a pompous spectacle that only makes sense with an audience. And Machiavelli examines the prince's hypocrisy, a masquerade that is not physical but behavioural. Like thinkers before him, Shakespeare (especially in *Richard II*, *Richard III*, *Macbeth* and *Coriolanus*) depicts various facets of political theatricality as hyperbole for the theatricality that permeates life on the whole. To this conviction, he adds the alleged presence of a transcendent Spectator. This inconspicuous but key component sets Shakespeare apart from the Humanists discussed here, although it links him to the tradition of Antiquity and the Middle Ages. The divine is often invoked by Shakespeare through various forms of discourse, such as prayer, prophecy and curse. However, *theatrum mundi* confers upon the divine the position of spectator. In a vertical scheme, the divine presence becomes the spectator perched atop the *theatrum mundi*, perpetually overlooking the human spectacle. On the one side, the king is looked upon by his subjects, over whom he has dominion; on the other side, he is overseen by a transcendent power that looms over him. This higher additional plane, which surpasses the earthly realm, suggests that the king is a human being and therefore has an inherent weakness. As such, *theatrum mundi* underscores the dichotomy between the king's political power and his smallness, his underlying misery.

Further, in Shakespeare's dramatic works, the transcendent Spectator is not merely passive: he intervenes as Providence. In other words, the One who is above all else an observer becomes an actor. Thus, as John of Gaunt states, God sanctioned the coronation of Richard II; and Richard II prays to God several times. After his fall, in the extreme solitude of his prison cell, the deposed king reaffirms the existence of the celestial Spectator:

> the searching eye of heaven is hid
> Behind the globe.[33]

In *Richard III*, the celestial Spectator is vested with the ability to discern the truth behind masks, which seems to reassure Queen

Elizabeth, who seeks to transcend the world's deception by appealing to an 'all-seeing heaven'.[34] The celestial Spectator's ability to discern truth gains traction in *Macbeth*. This ability is confirmed when the porter discusses the truth-like lie: 'An equivocator ... yet could not equivocate to heaven.'[35] More noteworthy, Lady Macbeth believes the sky is spying on her: 'Heaven peep through the blanket of the dark.'[36] This watchful gaze certainly does not reassure Macbeth. Just a slight extrapolation is enough to attribute to the watchful gaze the status of judge, or even of vigilante, when it comes to this usurping couple. By contrast, in *Coriolanus*, the dynamic between the celestial Spectator and the earthly subject is lightened. It is played down by the protagonist's assertion that there is no threat posed by the divine gaze and nothing serious in the human spectacle. The divine gaze is even entertained by the human spectacle:

> The gods look down, and this unnatural scene
> They laugh at.[37]

The tone and content are radically different here. The gods maintain their presence as spectators, but they recede into insignificance. This is perhaps because, even before *Coriolanus*, Shakespeare's *King Lear* questioned Providence and the merits of its interventions, and this is especially evident through the words of Gloucester:

> As flies to wanton boys are we to th' gods;
> They kill us for their sport.[38]

After Shakespeare, the expression '*theatrum mundi*' became associated with a specific trend in European dramaturgy at the end of the sixteenth century and the first half of the seventeenth century, at the height of the Baroque period. This new dramaturgical trend extended the theatrical vision of the world beyond Shakespeare's usage, both thematically and structurally. As for the latter, Shakespeare had already developed the structure of the play-within-a-play. But, as Georges Forestier notes,[39] this device now becomes a transposition to the stage of the theatrical conception of the world. The innovation consists in presenting *theatrum mundi* on stage by making it visible to the public through the device of the play-within-a-play. Ethics is thus complemented by a corresponding aesthetics, achieving an equality of content and form.[40]

Moreover, the dramaturgical trend of *theatrum mundi* deepens the religious theme from a Christian perspective. The Baroque ethos holds that reality is a deceptive façade; there is an acute sense that it merely consists of appearances, and that nothing is substantial where mortals are concerned – as it is the case in the metaphorical titles of Calderón's plays, *La vida es sueño* (*Life is a Dream*) and *El gran teatro del mundo* (*The Great Theatre of the World*). According to this ethos, the stage of life may be deceptive, but another exists of greater importance and veracity. The Baroque version of the theatre metaphor thus serves Christian doctrine, and reciprocally benefits from it. It bestows on God several functions: (1) He is the Author of the play – that is, of Creation. (2) He is also the stage director, assigning roles to actors and lending them costumes. He nevertheless grants them free will, so they perform nothing less than their destiny. (3) He is a spectator who observes the actors as they play their roles. (4) He is a judge who awaits the actors at the end. They arrive naked before him, as the costume was loaned to them only for the duration of their role. In short, this theocentric parable is didactic, designed to edify the faithful and bolster their religious fervour. It is used emphatically by Lope de Vega and Calderón, as well as in martyrdom dramas, whether in Spanish, German or French.

In the seventeenth century's prose of ideas

Alongside an emergence in the theatre which happened over the course of a few decades, the theatre metaphor underwent a multi-millennial evolution in the prose of ideas. While philosophical prose is typically a less artistic format than drama, it is often nonetheless replete with stylistic work and imagery to capture the reader's imagination. Even a philosopher as thoroughly rational as Descartes resorts to such linguistic devices. The 'Preliminaries' in his early writings introduce the beginning of his career with the following words: 'Actors, taught not to let any embarrassment show on their faces, put on a mask. I will do the same. So far, I have been a spectator in this theatre which is the world, but I am now about to mount the stage, and I come forward masked.'[41] His philosophical enterprise thus proceeds with caution, and the language he uses here is performatively cautious, by way of its metaphorical detour of donning a mask. It is more artful than admitting his fear of suspicions of heterodoxy or the deterrent effect of Galileo's struggles.[42] The opening of the 'Preliminaries' can be interpreted that way: 'The fear of the Lord is the beginning of wisdom.'[43] Drawn from *Psalms* (111: 10), it evokes the transcendent principle that traditionally underlies *theatrum mundi*. Later, the *Discourse on Method* again conveys the reserved attitude indirectly through the use of metaphor: 'I did nothing but roam from one place to another, desirous of being a spectator rather than an actor in the plays exhibited on the theater of the world.'[44] Interestingly, Descartes does not use the *theatrum mundi* metaphor as philosopher: it is not to discuss man in general, but about himself in particular. Expressing himself with the pronoun 'I', he individualizes this metaphor and centres it on his own case – an original formulation up until this point.

The Age of Classicism explores the human condition through theatricality. It values metaphor as a device because it enables the intellect to grasp the enigma of existence. But the theatre metaphor is no less complex for the moralists. First, it sheds light on the game that holds sway at the heart of social relations. It is concerned with lies and pretence: man performs on a vast proscenium and masquerades before others. Second, the theatre metaphor becomes internalized, gaining psychological resonance. 'We become so accustomed to disguise ourselves to others that at last we are disguised to ourselves', writes La Rochefoucauld.[45] The mask is no longer an instrument of deception on the worldly plane; it has now become the self. *Theatrum mundi* penetrates the human heart and gives rise to the theatre of conscience. Third, the theological backdrop gets starker: predestination is a fact, the stage is set and man is guilty. He is an actor because he is a sinner, condemned to the theatre as he is condemned to evil. The theatricality signals the Fall. The austerity of this moral ideology was inspired by Jansenist axiology, with its Augustinian prodromes.

As for La Bruyère, he revisits the lineage of Antiquity and the Middle Ages by focusing on the transitory nature of existence, which is implied in *theatrum mundi*. He emphatically reminds us that as actors we are merely finite beings:

> The world will be the same a hundred years hence ... there will be the same stage and the same decorations, though not the same

> actors. ... Others have already made their entrances who will act the same parts in the same plays, and in their turn make their exits, whilst those who have not yet appeared one day will also be gone, and fresh actors will take their places.[46]

In that vein, the preacher Bossuet draws directly from the Old Testament by coupling the interrelated metaphors of passing through and shadows to support the idea of vanity: 'Does not man himself pass for a shade ...? And as he himself is nothing solid, so also does he pursue vain things.' Against this background, the theatre metaphor assumes a sombre tone: 'Just as we have seen others go before us, so others will see us pass, and they will present the same spectacle to their successors. ... the play would have been no less well played had I remained behind the curtain.'[47] In contrast, with La Fontaine and the playful approach adopted in his *Fables*, *theatrum mundi* becomes lighter, secular and humorous – all the while retaining its moral underpinnings. It is then recovered in a very different context. Indeed, in a popular science work on astronomy, successful at the end of the seventeenth century and which prefigured the Age of Enlightenment, Fontenelle asserts: 'Nature always appears to me in the same point of view as theatrical representations.'[48]

Contemporary transformations in the theatre metaphor

As previously noted, among writers from Antiquity and the Renaissance, there are many examples of the language of theatre being applied to politics. This rhetorical practice becomes even more pronounced in the eighteenth century, in the wake of the period's historiographical advances and profound reflections on history. Montesquieu's style, and later Gibbon's, tend to portray Rome as a theatrical stage upon which various scenes from a performance follow in succession. Consider this short excerpt from Montesquieu: 'This is the place to set before ourselves the spectacle of things human ... in the history of Rome.'[49] And Gibbon concurs: 'The public scenes displayed before the Roman people.'[50] In these excerpts, the theatre vocabulary refers to the setting, the site of events. But this figurative sense overlaps with the literal one, to the extent that there is almost an equivalence between the two meanings. This merging of the political and theatrical realms continues to occur in the language used up to the present day. More recently, Ariane Chebel d'Appollonia's book on the political history of the mid-twentieth century opens with a chapter aptly titled 'On the Theatre of the World'.[51] It examines 'the spectacle of a science dedicated to organized killing'.[52] Reflecting on the following decades, Roger-Gérard Schwatzenberg's essay bears a title that could not be more crystal clear: *The Spectacle State*. Schwatzenberg analyses the behaviour of rulers, identifying a trait that is similar to, yet distinct from, that which is underscored by Machiavelli: the ruler builds an image, creates a persona.[53]

In fiction, Balzac, in the nineteenth century, consciously selects *The Human Comedy* as title for his gigantic multivolume collection. This expression is antithetical to Dante's title for his poetic masterpiece, *The Divine Comedy*. These two succinct titles nonetheless share some common ground: their manner of conceptualizing the universe is theatrical, and they encapsulate it using the term *Comedy*. In Dante's Middle Ages, however, the universe cannot be fathomed without 'divine' intervention, whereas five centuries later, the Balzacian title is reduced to the earthly, 'human' world. But regardless of the ideological lens under which *theatrum mundi* is placed, there is an underlying belief that spans centuries: the Creator's eye is always watchful. Lynda Christian uses this belief in particular to explain the *raison d'être* of *theatrum mundi*: 'This basic assumption means a desire to grant order to the experiences of life by making them part of a larger, if unknowable, plan conceived by a great power. If life is a play, it must have an author, a producer, a director, and a caster of roles.'[54] Even when the theatre metaphor stems from secular or sceptical thought, melancholy or dysphoric emotion, this belief has the power to soothe. Ultimately, the metaphor of *theatrum mundi* reveals a need for the absolute. It employs physical images that appeal to sense perceptions as means to clear a path towards this absolute.

Until the twentieth century, the theatre metaphor continues to be used in various literary genres because it continues to inhabit thought: it helps the mind to grasp the human journey more clearly and visualize a cosmic order. Over the course of the twentieth century, however, a radical shift takes *theatrum mundi* in an unprecedented direction. The ancient metaphor comes back, but in a manner that challenges the spiritual foundations provided by thousands of years of literature. It departs from schemata that linked it to a deity, in whom the actors found their protector and hope of salvation. Up to that point, Georges Forestier explains,[55] if man felt powerless on the stage of the universe, he was nonetheless conscious of a supreme deity. But twentieth-century man does not have this consciousness and is thus prey to a new metaphysical anguish. With the disappearance of a supreme deity, a great void is created, if not an abyss. Anne Larue notes that the contemporary variant of *theatrum mundi* highlights man's position on his planet: the dead end position of a human being abandoned by grace.[56] This version of the metaphor not only expresses the fragility of existence (like the previous versions) but, above all, the senselessness presiding over existence. It lays bare a spiritual despair: there is no longer a transcendent gaze that bestows meaning upon the world's theatre, and actors are now left to fend for themselves. The Creation becomes nothing more than pure illusion, trapped within its own theatricality, without remedy or consolation, other than human recourse. Thrown onto the stage with no exit, man finds himself condemned to the role of an actor. He is seeking an essence and finds nothingness. Behind the mask, lies a hollow, a gulf. Inauthenticity proves to be fundamental.

This is the premise of the theory of the Absurd, which Albert Camus outlines in his essay *The Myth of Sisyphus*, acknowledged as 'one of the great, seminal heart-searchings of our time'.[57] Camus aptly explains his theory with the theatre metaphor: 'This divorce between man and his life, the actor and his setting, is properly the feeling of absurdity.'[58] 'The stage sets collapse', he writes.[59] For Marie-Louise Audin, the paradigm of the theatre in *The Myth of Sisyphus* exposes an incomplete mystical quest.[60] Some of the excerpts from Camus's essay prove her right: 'All existence for a man turned away from the eternal is but a vast mime under the mask of the absurd';[61] in this world without a judge, 'we can achieve nothing that will transcend the fatal game of appearances'.[62] The metaphor draws a parallel between the mortal state and the essence of theatre. A causal connection can be made: in retrospect, death, the final act, makes us see the road we have travelled as theatre – a theatre from which we feel God's complete absence. This intrinsic theatricality, in its new form, is a major manifestation of the absurdity of life. More than ever, the theatre metaphor achieves an effect that appeals to the sensitivity of the receiver, through the potential pathos of its message. Because ultimately, what is at stake in this absurd theatrical game that is life? 'The possibility of nothingness is always there ... the imminence of universal darkness', writes Howard Pearce. 'The specter of unreality, of darkness, meaninglessness, and despair lurks on the horizon.'[63]

Moreover, Camus inverts the comparison, which aligns him with Shakespeare, who named his venue 'The Globe'. In addition to comparing life to the theatre, Camus compares the dramatic arts to life, because the dramatic arts provide an image of life's precariousness. Camus also compares the actor to man, because the actor is the prototype of man, demonstrating that 'there is no frontier between being and appearing'.[64] One year after the publication of the *Myth of Sisyphus* (1942), Jean-Paul Sartre publishes *Being and Nothingness* (1943). He follows in Camus's footsteps, asserting that man is perpetually performing and that playing a theatrical game is his natural state. From this ontological fact which governs man, Sartre discerns an insufficiency: a lack of being.[65] Without essence, man has no more tangible substance than the fiction of theatre. Ever more versatile, the *theatrum mundi* metaphor becomes a vehicle for existentialist thought. And it subsequently feeds the Theatre of the Absurd – which takes its cue from Absurdist philosophy with even deeper pessimism. The authors of this theatrical movement share a conviction regarding life's evanescence and emptiness. In Samuel Beckett's view, any attempt to communicate is a horrible comedy,[66] and according to Arthur Adamov, we are mere puppets subject to incomprehensible cosmic laws.[67]

Many post-Sartre philosophers have defined existence as a theatrical game. Among them, Kostas Axelos remains a major reference, as evidenced by the recent republication of his book *The World Game*,[68] as well as Gilles Deleuze in his essay 'The dramatization method' and his book *Difference and Rehearsals*.[69] The idea of existence as a theatrical game is also widespread in the anthropological community, uncovering a myth which has endured since Antiquity – as is the case with another recently republished reference work, Jacques Henriot's *Under Color of Play*, whose title quotes Claude Lévi-Strauss.[70] Sociologists, for their part, study theatrical forms of play within social relationships, with efforts including Jean Duvignaud's *The Game of the Game*, Erving Goffman's *The Presentation of Self in Everyday Life*[71] and even a devoted sociology journal special issue entitled *Theatricality and*

Society.[72] And according to psychoanalysts such as Jean Gillibert, with his study of the 'theater of Being',[73] the self, like a stage product, does not exist in itself, but through an audience that observes it. Moreover, many literary critics and, *a fortiori*, theatre scholars, are influenced by Pirandello and consider man a 'character in search of an author' – to quote the title of the famous play.[74] Ruby Cohn explains this idea: 'The post-Pirandellian world of ambiguous relationship between person and role twists Descartes' "I think, therefore I am" to "I play, but am I?"'[75] In short, in the modern world, dramatic rhetoric is always constant in its recurrence; however, in the twentieth century, it assumes aesthetic and intellectual functions that are as diverse as they are novel.

That being said, our era has transformed *theatrum mundi* into metaphysical aporia by dispensing with its transcendent Spectator. By definition, the spectator is an essential part of the act of theatre. Consider Eric Bentley's minimal definition of theatre, which cuts straight to the point: 'A impersonates B while C looks on.'[76] Without C – the requisite gaze – the *theatrum mundi* is deprived of a vital organ. In other words, without transcendence, the spectator role is by necessity limited to other humans. Actors and spectators are therefore on the same plane – that of humanity – and they converge in reciprocity. In the twenty-first century, with mass media and technological tools at everyone's fingertips, changes are afoot. The spectator role is blurred with the self, which further reduces it. The inflated ego is revealed and, with it, the projection of the self through a narcissistic mirror. These tendencies are reinforced through the blurring of distinctions between self and the means of exhibiting self, as suggested by the conspicuous names iPhone, iPad, YouTube and the like. The stress on the personal pronoun within these labels implies an equivalence between the private individual (artificial or deficient) and the stage persona (without which the private individual cannot exist). The personal pronoun also implies that the persona possesses its audience. Today's *theatrum mundi* is therefore egocentric, even if paradoxically, through technological tools, spectators can be located around the world at the very same time. But perhaps there is a causal connection between this egocentricity and the fact that the spectators are innumerable and dispersed.

***

Generally speaking, metaphor is one of many figures of speech, but it is also much more, because its value extends beyond that of a figure of speech. As Jean Molino observes, cognitivism contends that metaphor is not ornamental but necessary: it is an irreplaceable tool for consciousness, creating meaning that could not be conveyed by other means.[77] Given that a purely intellectual approach does not suffice, metaphor appeals to another faculty. The case of *theatrum mundi* is conclusive in that respect. Its meaning is profound, but would be inaccessible without the metaphor's mediation. This specific metaphor *stages* its subject in order to articulate it. As Louis Van Delft points out, it evokes imagery that the receiver can instantly visualize on his mental screen.[78] Anne Larue notes that it fulfils a didactic function in which the concrete comparator traces a short and effective route to an abstract idea.[79] It is assuredly a convenient way of making the world more intelligible.

Its literary, linguistic and aesthetic evolution do not follow a linear route, as my account demonstrates. Rather, its evolution follows extremely varied, shifting and dispersed paths, because this metaphor has the flexibility and adaptability of Proteus, like the very theatre to which it refers. Hellenism, Stoicism, Roman decadence, Patristicism, Humanism, Elizabethan Baroque, the Spanish Golden Age, Christianity, Classicism, Pirandellism, Absurdism, contemporary atheism – to name but a few – are all conduits for it. And publications of every kind – philosophical treatises, literary essays, geographic atlases, medical manuals, plays, sermons, popular science works, political writings, historiography and so on – provide it with as many platforms. Its variations emerge from so many points of view and mobilize so much seemingly disparate knowledge. It acts as the common denominator shared by various bodies of knowledge and points of view. As a result, they can stand out as equals that are part of a cultural whole and a collective imagination. Van Delft asserts that the term *theatrum*, more than any other, is a treasure trove that not only contains a wealth of texts but also an entire culture.[80]

This all-encompassing term alone converges related metaphors – shadow, reflection, illusion, appearance, passing through, and so forth – and thematically fuses them, as a conceptual crossroads where they all coexist. All these related metaphors belong to the term's semantic field insofar as they connote vanity and transience. The dialectics of being versus appearing and reality versus fiction also contribute to expanding its semantic field. Naturally, the term *theatrum* includes all the elements of the practice of the theatre profession: stage, set, spotlight, prop, costume, mask, make-up, character, role, acting, play, act and scene, curtain up and down, enter and exit stage, and so on. Secondary metaphors (which are subordinate to the mother-metaphor) derive from these elements of theatrical art. In short, *theatrum mundi* stands as a dominant macro-metaphor and branches out into implicit micro-metaphors, for which it serves as a reference point that enables synthesis.

However, a question arises: in being rehashed *ad infinitum*, has this *topos*, with all its corollaries, become a trivialized cliché? And is its survival under threat? More than a learned notion, the metaphor has been assimilated into our intellectual instincts and is anchored in our psychic responses. And yet, it is by no means reduced to a mechanical formulation that has lost all impact: it has a vibrancy and has retained its dynamic properties and evocative potential. Positioning theatre as analogy for the human condition results in subjective and even affective impact that makes it effective. Its semantic weight awakens our consciousness to the futility to which it refers. Howard Pearce understands the metaphoric process of *theatrum mundi* as follows:

> Reality is called into doubt by being related to the problematical dimensions of theater. ... The privileged reality that we accept as certain, substantial, and enduring is converted by the protracted metaphorical relations. ... the metaphor reduces the distinction between the real and the fictional and raises the ontological question. It opposes positivist certainty and closure ... opens rather than resolves the question of reality.[81]

The *theatrum mundi* metaphor was born of a metaphysical desire to remind of man's smallness and lack of control over everything other than appearances, images, shadows. It is an accurate and ingenious way to communicate the ontological insecurity to which human being is constrained According to Van Delft, it has endured because it is compelling and has an impact on the imagination and memory.[82] Ubiquitous in Western culture, not to say worldwide, the metaphor maps a near-continuous trajectory in the history of literature and thought – one that never ceases to renew itself.

9

The dream of reason: Giannina Braschi's ethics of in-betweenness

Grace Whistler

Introduction

Puerto Rican poet, essayist, novelist and academic, writing in Spanish, English and Spanglish, Giannina Braschi is a unique voice in the literary world. Not only are her writings full of fiery political critique and visceral realism, she also writes with a magnification and distance comparable to Joyce. What is of most interest to this chapter, however, is how she crosses borders with her writing – between genres, between languages, between consciousnesses. Drawing on the work of Goya, and critique by Nehamas, this chapter demonstrates Braschi's quest for that fruitful and dreamlike state between imagination and reason, where artistic creation takes place, and the human can reach her full capacity as an ethical animal.

Yo-Yo Boing![1] is a free form, unrelenting dialogue – it is more of a disembodied play than a novel in any conventional sense. It is nevertheless peppered with magic-realist allegories, foul-mouthed parables and drifting lines of poetry (of Braschi's as well as others). In the midst of this enveloping (and at times disorientating) trans-genre experience, Braschi's voice speaks her intentions clearly: 'I'm here to present thoughts, not to explain them.'[2] And while Braschi tells us openly her purpose as a writer (as though she wants us to think in real time about what and why and how we are receiving her text), she does not condescend to prosaically explain her philosophical positions, and perhaps this is why she 'do[es] n't think it's harder to be a philosopher than an artist'.[3] Besides, Braschi is never exclusively one or the other – her poetry and prose are philosophy in motion – and it is for this reason that we can situate her so fittingly among the likes of Tahar Wattar, Mary Shelley, Albert Camus, Iris Murdoch, Alice Munro or any of the other authors considered in this volume for their ability to span the chasm between the abstract and the tangible.

El sueño de la razon

Braschi's inspiration comes from innumerable sources, including philosophy, Golden Age theatre and pop culture, but of these abundant threads she weaves so adeptly, it is a briefly cited aquatint copper plate that this essay shall use as a springboard. *Los Caprichos*, by Francisco José de Goya y Lucientes, is a collection of eighty aquatint copper plates. No. 43 of this collection is titled 'El sueño de la razón produce monstruos', which is usually translated as 'The sleep of reason produces monsters'. This title would appear, on first reading, to champion Enlightenment values, but Goya also included a seemingly contradictory caption: 'La fantasía abandonada de la razón, produce monstruos imposibles: unida con ella, es madre de las artes y origen de sus marabillas'[4] – roughly, 'imagination abandoned by reason creates impossible monsters, united with it, it is the mother of the arts and the origin of their marvels'.

The critic who has addressed this ambiguity most fully is Alexander Nehamas, who emphasizes the idea that reason and the imagination should be indivisible in human creative endeavour. He writes, 'the sleep of reason does not represent the imagination's taking over. On the contrary, reason is asleep when the imagination deserts it. ... their relation is symmetrical. It is only when both work together that each is fully awake.'[5] Indeed, *Los Caprichos* are themselves a work of the imagination – 'It is only on the basis of the imagination that we realize that reason is "asleep"'.[6] For Nehamas, it is 'that combination of reason and imagination that makes us

FIGURE 9.1 *Francisco de Goya y Lucientes,* El sueño de la razón produce monstruos, *1797–9, Etching, Aquatint on paper, 153 mm x 215 mm, Museo Nacional del Prado, Madrid (catalogue no. G000744). ©Photographic Archive Museo Nacional del Prado.*

truly rational and therefore human'.[7] While this standpoint (that it is human nature to draw on both reason and imagination) hardly needs any further justification, if we look closer at No. 43 – both the image and its caption – Goya seems to explore this relationship with a richness that even Nehamas doesn't account for.

From a purely translational perspective, there seems to be an issue with the equivalency between 'sueño' and 'sleep'. In Spanish, 'sueño' is more commonly used to refer to a dream, whether literally asleep or not. In that light, any 'dream of reason' seems like an inherently imaginative activity, perhaps suggesting a certain naivety or vanity in the Enlightenment aspiration towards rationality. In aiming to be purely rational, we may lose the benefit of those softer faculties of imagination and feeling – but is Goya suggesting this dream even more dangerous than that? Is the consequence of this divorce from the imagination the production of 'impossible monsters', as the title seems to suggest? The figure in the image is presumed to be reason, asleep and surrounded by monsters. But the shape these monsters take tells yet another story of ambiguity. Our sleeper is flocked by unsettling creatures in the gloom – but on closer inspection, these beings are eerily reminiscent of the owl of Minerva. Perhaps these inhabitants of the twilight between reason and imagination symbolize inspiration and indeed wisdom – burdens which have the potential to be both profoundly enriching and unsettling in equal parts.

Interestingly, Braschi quotes this very caption in *YYB*, and in the English translation which bilingual (translingual?) Braschi closely oversaw, we read 'as Goya said, the dream of reason creates monsters'.[8] But how then, does Braschi navigate this space of obscurity, and draw on these *gemelos*, these twinned human faculties of reason and imagination? And to what end? These are precisely the issues to be explored in the remainder of this chapter – the philosophical aims behind her creations and the form they take are examples of the marvels of which Goya speaks.

As was mentioned towards the beginning of this chapter, Braschi is not shy about her aims as a writer. Braschi has spoken frankly about this in interviews and reviews, telling us, 'Poetry has been cloistered in a convent for far too long ... set her free to ... date and mate with other genres ... All great writers have worked outside of the limits of their genre, be they philosophers or poets.'[9] And elsewhere,

> When I started writing, this was my main concern: get out of poetry. Let poetry walk the streets of New York. Make her cosmopolitan. See the world. Not in these estrofas, not in these stanzas, which are camisas de fuerza [straightjackets]. I have to get out of poetry. ... I have to be taken out of context to be understood. I belong where I don't belong.[10]

She also praises this exploration of genre in other writers, and makes claims about what an experience of such texts can do for the reader. She says of Nietzsche that he 'crosses the line between poetry and philosophy ... the poet-philosopher fills you with ideas, without allowing the craftsmanship of his language to override the intuition of inspiration. ... [He] says what he has to say and then disappears at the end of the text, leaving you inspired to develop your own thoughts.'[11] Alongside this affirmation of tenacious experimentation with genre in herself and others, she also tells us her stance on the relationship between feelings and ideas when it comes to writing, 'I have ideas, feelings – above all, feelings, because my ideas come from my feelings'.[12]

This commentary on genre is almost ubiquitous in her prose and poetry, too, in which she is often (either explicitly or implicitly) a character. *YYB* is replete with such instances, but here we get more of a sense why this practice is so important. Human life is messy, and Braschi is searching for a mode of communication that does it justice, 'I can't fit life into rhyme scheme. Rhythm is free. ... what is immortal in the novel is not the form, which is long dead, but the context. ... No verse.'[13] As such, she claims we understand things better when they aren't clear cut, and don't follow predictable patterns. She talks of a 'melody that had no melody, because it was amorphous, and gave it a form of expression that the masses could understand'.[14] The reason we may understand writing like this better is that we too come from this twilight between imagination and reason, and poetic writing speaks to this fundamental part of us – 'poetry ... sees in the dark. And it creates twilight. Beyond twilight, it loses sight. To shine a light is to bare her stitches. No one wants to see the history of its wounds – the myth is what matters – obscurity and transcendence.'[15] This metaphor of dwelling in twilight is present in secondary sources on Braschi too. One critic writes, 'the poet chases down intuitions, glimmers of half-formed thought that do not necessarily conform to fully formed ideas. ...

[and puts] that disorder into words'.[16] The result is a literary marvel that speaks to the messiness of the whole human and her faculties, both imagination and reason.

Braschi, as we are beginning to see, defies convention – not merely in her refusal to conform to the expectations of traditional philosophy, but also in the form of her prose and poetry. She is, as one critic puts it, 'the poet trying to woo her way into Plato's Republic'.[17] In *YYB*, there are instances in which commentary becomes prose becomes poetry, performative, free and indirect:

> With so many categorically presumptive adverbs that leave the mind on a precipice precipitating precipitately, you don't need so many ly's to precipitate if you go straight to the point without beating around the bush and spread your wings and fly, you fly straight like and arrow and hit the thought, bull's-eye, and you're brilliant, sparkling like a flawless diamond (sorry, but I love little flaws), you don't know what I'm talking about but that doesn't stop you from contradicting me ... The truth has no subclauses or subterfuge, crutches or canes ... No, I won't say no to subjunctive clauses or to double brackets that close when they're supposed to, or to single brackets that say open, searching in vain for the cat's four paws of the subjunctive clause in the wolf's jaws where they'll never see the light of day, and I won't say no to either side that thinks it speaks the infinite truth because neither one crosses the dividing line or because two parallel lines never meet their grief.[18]

Throughout her works, Braschi 'affirms the unique status of the artist whose function is to reconnect with truth and authenticity through the aesthetic'.[19] She wants cross dividing lines, between genres, between perspectives, between people, and, as we will see in the following paragraphs, this is motivated by a desire to forge connection, and an ethics of in-betweenness.

Plurality, connection, ethics

This entire volume revolves around a suggestion by some thinkers that literary and narrative works may be able to fulfil some of the functions of more conventional moral philosophy. The idea here is that, in engaging imaginatively with a given text, its characters, their inner lives and the situations they find themselves in, readers may be able to develop their capacity to understand others which could help them to grow in a way that is empathetically and morally fruitful. Among the most famous proponents of such a standpoint is Martha Nussbaum, who goes as far as to say that the act of reading is in itself a moral activity. She writes,

> The activities of imagination and emotion that the involved reader performs during the time of reading are not just instrumental to moral conduct, they are also examples of moral conduct, in the sense that they are examples of the type of emotional and imaginative activity that good ethical conduct involves.[20]

This way of being with a text is something like what Krista Ratcliffe calls 'rhetorical listening' – 'a stance of openness that a person may choose to assume in relation to any person, text or culture'.[21] As Braschi writes in *Empire of Dreams*,[22] 'You'll open the door to poetry because poetry doesn't know what it's looking for'.[23]

But by no means are all critics in agreement with this view – 'Reading deeply in the Canon will not make one a better or a worse person, a more useful or more harmful citizen', as one such commentator suggests.[24] Alexander Nehamas even weighed in on the debate, making the point that not all the phenomenological experience we may gain from engaging with a text is transferable to our personal lives, and not every imaginative engagement will be ethically productive. Having read great literature, 'You will have become more complex, subtle, nuanced, unusual, individual, and more open to different ways of thinking and feeling – but certainly not, for those reasons, a better [person]. Perhaps you will even be, just for those reasons, worse on that front.'[25] Looking to imaginative works for moral education, he suggests, is merely a symptom of our misguided emphasis on pure reason: 'Neglecting the values specific to the imagination forces us to look to the arts either for information or for the kind of moral edification that an incomplete conception of rationality – reason bereft of imagination – has imposed upon us.'[26]

Other chapters in this volume will examine the arguments for and against looking to literature for moral reasons in much more detail, and no doubt its readers will formulate their own opinions.

Meanwhile, this chapter merely seeks to expose the substantial contributions of an author who endeavours to blur the boundaries between the literary and the philosophical, and suggest an ethical aim behind these efforts. It is clear by now that Braschi is working at the boundary between genres. What I am suggesting in this essay, is that she does so not only for aesthetic purposes. Concurring with Aldama, I suggest that 'Braschi ... creates new aesthetic objects that trigger new perceptual, emotional, and cognitive relations between the narrative and the reader', and that this 'cross-genre aesthetic persuades readers to step close to the discomforting and ontologically different'.[27]

We have already seen some examples of Braschi's conceptual and trans-stylistic work, but up until this point, we haven't seen so much of how she attempts to bring about this ethical engagement from her readers. One important consideration (which we have already touched upon more generally) is the idea that literature may bring us closer to understanding the other. As she said in an interview, 'I'm interested in the multiplicity of voices. I want to hear all the voices of the people.'[28] In *YYB*, she echoes the voice of some of her critics:

> – *She thinks dialogue is everything. She should work on description. Take someone's face for example and describe it. Because she loses track of her themes.*
>
> – And you lose track of your characters.[29]

And it's true – as readers we are often completely adrift in a sea of dialogue, reaching out instinctively for something to hold onto, a firm point of reference. But that's exactly Braschi's intention. Dialogue in which utterances aren't concretely anchored to specific persons allows the reader to float freely in-between perspectives. The result is a lively, perplexing experience of inter-consciousness. And it's no accident:

> I'm not frivolous. I'm doing a portrait of reality. If I am observing the funeral of a famous man, I must talk from the point of view of the widow, with no distance from the sorrow, the journalist, with distance enough to appeal to the masses with melodrama or soap opera, and the artist with the most distance so I can objectify it, but I should also become the dead man.[30]

There is no order, no hierarchy of experience, resulting in a curious levelling effect, and as Braschi writes, 'Greatness isn't better. Sometimes it's worse.'[31] This constant back and forth in *YYB* is ever present – even in the novel's title. With 'yo' meaning 'I' in Spanish, the bounce of a yo-yo is a metaphor for an 'ontological ricocheting' of the self.[32]

But meanwhile, in solitude, the self is a blank slate of possibility:

> *Looking at the blank verse in the mirror every morning ... right through the blank verse because it's blank without verse or phrase or paraphrase – sound or mute – blank or empty – the eyes of the verse fill the blank verse and open each window of my verse, my veracity, my versatility.*[33]

It is only through dialogue with other perspectives that we take shape. As Braschi said in another interview, 'Do you know what inspires dialogue, the confrontation with another human being? It spawns so many ideas, it airs out what you have inside.'[34] This dialogue bridges a phenomenological gap, forging new ideas and perhaps even revealing deeply held beliefs and feelings which we may not have previously been aware of.

Along with *YYB*, *United States of Banana* is another example of her writing which 'suggests the utopian potential of the aesthetic as an ethical alternative'.[35] This 'novel' is an intertextual pastiche, incorporating philosophical dialogue, commentary on Puerto Rico's political status and epic adventure – all against the backdrop of post 9/11 New York City. Its *dramatis personae* include the likes of Zarathustra, Segismundo, Hamlet and 'Giannina' herself. But as much as the work is performative (and indeed a performance) of Braschi's philosophical mission, it is nevertheless a cerebral manifesto. She asks, 'Can't there be a work of art that is a great event and that at the same time creates a new value?'[36] In another aesthetically pleasingly self-referential loop of logic, *USB* is an attempt to do just this. Braschi writes, 'Yes, we will break the divisions between genres and genders and races. Fuckers. You will not divide us anymore.'[37] With this ragtag band of philosophical, literary, and real-life characters, Braschi creates a unity out of difference:

> Originality is to go back to the origins – and that's why I go back to the exceptional – what is extra – what gives gifts – generosity

> and light. The writing that goes overboard and over borders – and that is on the edge of breaking – and finds a light – and beams.[38]

Here Braschi is suggesting that this is a light that only art can shine on the tenebrous ambiguity of human reality – we are 'obliged to seek out a compromise with mimesis and rationality in order to reaffirm real emotion via the expression of an ethical universal', one which 'can only be mediated through the romantic imagination of the artist', as one critic writes.[39]

Braschi's purpose as a writer, throughout her works, is to bring together different experiences, different perspectives, different consciousnesses. Her intent is that, by exploring the inner life of the other, through the artistic imagination, we are able to understand and therefore better empathize with the lived experience of the other. As a Latinx writer of queer fiction, and perhaps even more particularly a Nuyorican, she resides very much at the borders and in-between spaces of American identity. But this is what gives her such a valuable vantage point to create art that bridges divides and sparks dialogue, because, by their very definition, borders delineate and define why things are the way they are. *USB* is an especially poignant example of this, it is,

> a book about camaraderie, compañerismo, even the generosity of love ... a book about the multiple networks of horizontal rhyzomatic relations that the incitement to be singular and different, not to fit, can create. Thus its revolutionary consigna, its avant-garde, manifesto-like call to action is to 'understand' – but not by placing oneself at a distance, by towering above the other to comprehend, to apprehend, to appropriate, to grasp ... to re-create ourselves by expanding and reconnecting with others in unexpectedly new, appositional, singular, and horizontally asymmetrical ways ... it attempts to imagine and foster ... new forms of interaction, communication, and cooperation.[40]

But is not just through her stylistic innovation and philosophical endeavours that Braschi is a bridge-builder. It is of course evident that Braschi is interested in language as a means of crossing the divide between consciousnesses, but this doesn't just mean 'literary' language – it is something more fundamental than that, also evident in her code-switching and translanguaging between English, Spanish and indeed Spanglish. The following paragraphs will show how Braschi attempts to create an ethics of in-betweenness through the use of these languages, with relevance to the visceral realities of cultural identity.

As Braschi writes in *YYB*, 'I was sick 'n tired of being misunderstood ... I wanted to make sense. I wanted to feel like the common denominator.'[41] This is why she attempts to formulate a 'new American language. Wave farewell to all the separatist rhetoric and atavisms.'[42] To Braschi, keeping these languages and their cultural inheritances separate stands in the way of ethical progress, in the way of us moving towards a sense of community with our fellow humans, regardless of their background: 'It doesn't really matter which side because the right is to the left of the right where the left is writing what the right was just saying because both sides are falling on their asses at the same time because they're both writing in the same tongue, left or right.'[43] To Braschi, this is not just her duty as an artist (someone who is able to draw on both reason and imagination to aid her communication), it is also her obligation as a polyglot: 'We have to start tearing down the walls dividing our two Americas. And we – you and I – have be the spokesmen because we're bilingual. ... We have an obligation as poets to speak words of truth.'[44]

Braschi's linguistic exploits are the antithesis of ubiquitous Puerto Rican stereotypes such as those popularized by *West Side Story*'s 'America', in which nostalgia for island life is counterpoised by aspirational consumerism.[45] Instead, she 'resists uniform monolingual expressions and also reminds readers that Latinx identities and experiences ... are shaped across a linguistically nonbinary hemispheric Américas'.[46] Nevertheless, not all scholars (even those praising her invention) seem to wholly affirm or appreciate the deliberate linguistic and authorial choices she makes. One critic writes of her 'random' and 'contaminated and contaminating use of Spanglish', and her 'unauthorized appropriation of the Western canon'. Her supposedly 'irreducible alien perspective' is characterized by the 'irregular sentences uttered by her immigrant community', and 'her pastiche digresses ... until her alien compost gets caught in a grinding recycling process in which literary echoes and icons can float freely, never to be assimilated nor fully appropriated'.[47] Meanwhile, another commentator backhandedly comments that her 'semi-fluency becomes a surprisingly expressive resource'.[48] By now we have seen a great deal of evidence that Braschi is not semi-fluent – she is at least doubly fluent, and willing to subvert linguistic expectations in order to communicate and encourage ethical engagement.

But to merely comment on Braschi's subversiveness would miss out on some of the joys and subtleties of her writing. Yes, she is radical – her boundary blurring with gender, sex, ethnicity and politics defy expectation – but the freedom and pleasure of her writing comes from a place of irreverence and a performance of identity that plays jump-rope with conventional boundaries. As we have seen, Braschi is not nostalgic for a romanticized vision of island life, or losing her Puerto Rican identity in the midst of New York – she is Nuyorican, her identity forged in the mess of colonial postmodernity, but nevertheless positive and definite, colonizing the city of colonizers. In the following section, we will see how her affirmative playfulness manifests itself within her texts.

Word games

As we have seen, Braschi takes the task of poetry and art more generally to be a serious one: she believes in art's ability to bridge divides, linguistic, political, experiential. She writes, on the suggestion that poetry 'is a luxury', 'Ask Plato who threw the poets out of the Republic. ... What is a luxury? Is an air conditioner a luxury? I would love to be as luxurious in my poetry as an air conditioner in August.'[49] But, just because this task is an important one, it doesn't mean that it is without joy, just as a breath of fresh air on a hot summer's day. According to Braschi, confining poetry to the aesthetic domain is what has made it a useless luxury, but,

> poetry has been a useless art for too long. ... Poetry should jump out of the system ... out of good and bad, beauty and ugliness, right and wrong. Poetry is fun. Poetry hasn't been fun for ages. It should give pleasure. We've grown accustomed to unhappy poetry. My poetry is happy not to be sad. I steal pleasure from toys, movies, television, videos, machines, games – and put the fun back in function so that the work runs like and engine that clinks and clanks, tingles and tangles, whirs and buzzes, grinds

> and creaks, whistles and pops itself into a catabolic dämmerung of junk and scrap.[50]

Braschi succeeds in this, and of course the work that this quotation is derived from is itself 'a rhetorically supercharged romp through genres, registers, canons, popular cultures, and dramatis personae'.[51]

Of course, Braschi is able to achieve this feat because she is fluent in many registers – an artist and an academic, high-brow and pop, cerebral and scatological. But Braschi also wants us to get comfortable with the experience of dwelling in twilight – she wants us to accept 'the impossibility and unnecessariness of complete understanding'.[52] At times, her writings can be a place where artistic irreverence meets playful synaesthesia. She writes, 'I don't have themes. I have flavors ... My favorite is the pink one',[53] and 'hot and cold conversations create words in color from all angles of my body'.[54] And almost childishly, elsewhere,

> – Art is history. If you don't remember, you don't have a past.
> – Who wants a past? I want the future. ...
> – Future is an illusion. A bubble.
> – Bubbles are nice.[55]

The point here is not to send us some highbrow hermeneutical mission to discern once and for all what she is 'on about', rather, we are encouraged to let the text to wash over us, leaving an impression, but one which only makes sense if we allow our gaze to become a little less focussed. It is, as Ashbaugh writes, 'a charming and humorously delightful pleasure' to not have to 'burrow into the work in search for some profound meaning', instead we become free to experience the movement of the text 'according to Braschi's circuitous grace'.[56]

Braschi also achieves this effect with her use of translingual portmanteau, neologism and nonsense which undeniably carries its own form of sense. To unpack some of Braschi's innovation, here we will turn to Gilles Deleuze's work on nonsense and portmanteau in *The Logic of Sense*. Deleuze defines portmanteau as neologism which is derived from 'contracting several words and encompassing several senses'.[57] The imaginative effect of encountering portmanteau words, for Deleuze, rests on the idea of 'disjunctive synthesis' – disparate meanings, senses, experiences are unified to create something which transcends its individual elements.[58] Layer upon layer of half-registered phonetic echoes create an effect which is greater than the sum of its morphological parts. In Deleuze's own words, '*disjunctive* or portmanteau words ... perform an infinite ramification of coexisting series and bear at once upon words and senses, or syllabic and semiological elements'.[59]

As a sort of case study for this suggested function of portmanteau, Deleuze introduces the example of the word, 'frumious' from Lewis Carroll's nonsense poem, 'Jabberwocky', from *Through the Looking Glass* (2010). He writes,

> The necessary disjunction is not between fuming and furious, for one may indeed be both at once; rather, it is between fuming-and-furious on one hand and furious and fuming on the other. In this sense, the function of the portmanteau word always consists in the ramification of the series into which it is inserted. This is the reason why it never exists alone. It beckons to other portmanteau words which precede or follow it, and which show that very series is already ramified in principle and still further ramifiable.[60]

The original Spanglish edition of *YYB* is especially replete with instances of such layering of meaning, but as Jones points out,[61] some of this deliberate linguistic muddling is edited out in the English translation. For example, in the following layering of alliterative portmanteaus, 'in mutinity – in mutility – immotivated by the immobility of immutability',[62] bringing to mind the sounds of 'mutiny', 'mutilate' and 'emotive', they are translated into 'in mutiny – in futility – unmotivated'.[63] Also, when 'you obliviated the Indians',[64] is levied at a British interlocutor, using a past participle of 'obliviate' (which strictly means 'to forget' in English, but used here to echo 'oblivion' and 'obliterate'), it is simplified to 'obliterated' in the translated edition.[65] Some such instances do, however, make it into the English edition, such as, 'immortability ... morbality ... mortability',[66] in which 'immortality', 'morbidity' and 'morality' resonate, with other possible meanings ever lurking behind the continual wash of sound.

This cumulative wordplay is also ever present in Braschi's most recent book, *Putinoika*,[67] a timely exploration of plague and politics through the lens of Greek tragedy. Riffing off the homophony between 'Pan', the merry faun-god of Greek mythology, and the prefix 'pan', meaning 'all' (also Greek in origin), Braschi writes: 'Pan will come out and sing – no matter what – even if it has to go negative with the demic of the Pandemic added to the bread of life.'[68] Here Braschi affirms a resilience and joyfulness of being that is embodied in the human will to live even in the darkest of times. This is again an example of a kind of false portmanteau, deliberate etymological *faux amis* of which Braschi is particularly fond. Elsewhere in *Putinoika*, she toys with phonetic echoes in the name of Antigone, the idealistic Theban princess who is caught (in Sophocles' rendering) between the dictates of the gods and familial ties. Braschi writes, 'Why the agony of the anti and the gone? I'll make a drama of myself in two parts … Let bygones be bygones.'[69] Perhaps this passage, on first reading, doesn't make much sense – but what we do get is a palpable sense of inner conflict and contradiction. As Deleuze would put it, 'the gift of meaning occurs, in this region which precedes all good sense and common sense. For here, with the passion of the paradox, language attains its highest power.'[70]

Deleuze is conscious of conventional philosophy's difficulty in formulating compelling examples of the illogical – 'the mistake made by logicians, when they speak of nonsense', he writes, 'is that they offer laboriously constructed, emaciated examples, fitting the needs of their demonstration, as if they had never heard a little girl sing, a great poet recite, or a schizophrenic speak'.[71] The experience of reading Braschi can be like any one of these – and at times, all three at once. But while all these adventures in language are interesting and pleasing in their own right, we know that her aim, in each case, is to bring people together through her writing. In *Putinoika*, Antigone declares, 'We are obliterating hatred. We are uniting sets of tragedies and creating a comedy. But I am not laughing. I am open to multiple possibilities',[72] and soon after, Athena proclaims that 'plurality will head the state'.[73]

Conclusion

The reception of Giannina Braschi's writings thus far has been somewhat divided. It is true that her work is at times challenging and complex, but this is absolutely to her credit. Her writing is joyful, in her compositions she is 'pouring out everything with abundance and gratitude',[74] and she is doing so with an ethical vision in mind. Braschi wants to uproot her readers from their biases, experiences and times, bringing them together through immersion in her texts. There are some things about the human experience that are difficult to communicate in any logical, sensible way, and this is undoubtedly the stuff great literature is often founded upon – a 'complex *theme* which does not allow itself to be reduced to any propositional *thesis*'.[75] Braschi's goal as a writer is not to simplify the complexities and ambiguities of human life, but instead to find a mode of communication which does them justice, endeavouring to, as Deleuze puts it, 'reach a secret point in which the anecdote of life and the aphorism of thought amount to one and the same thing'.[76]

By means of word games, trans-linguistic and trans-generic invention, her readers are invited to transcend boundaries between self and other, across time and space – between reason and imagination. As Stavans put it, 'Braschi crea una lexicography that is and isn't atrapada en el presente', because 'She destruye la lengua only to reconstruirla en un juego de echoes y re-echoes'. We may not always know exactly what her words mean, but it doesn't matter, because in this twilight between imagination and reason, 'Nada is what it sounds'.[77]

10

The sorrow of the lone one: Existential despair in Mary Shelley's *The Last Man*

Katalin Nun Stewart

Introduction: Human existence and suffering in literature

Philosophers have not always been so good at recognizing the value of literature for their field. Especially in connection with questions of ethics, value and meaning, literature provides a wealth of illustrative examples of characters and situations that could serve as a great resource for philosophy to draw from. In this sense literature can be seen as an outstanding medium for posing and critically discussing philosophical questions.[1] In what follows I wish to demonstrate this with the example of a novel with a rich philosophical content, namely, Mary Shelley's *The Last Man* (1826). Despite the profound philosophical reflections that this work contains, philosophers have made no use of it. In this chapter I will try to rectify this by demonstrating its great potential as a literary text profoundly concerned with philosophy.

Mary Wollstonecraft Godwin Shelley (1797–1851) was the daughter of the Enlightenment feminist writer Mary Wollstonecraft (1759–1797) and the political philosopher, author and publisher William Godwin (1756–1836). In 1816, she married the Romantic poet Percy Bysshe Shelley (1792–1822). In the same year, she began to write her first and, at the same time, best-known novel *Frankenstein; or The Modern Prometheus* (published anonymously in 1818).[2] Apart from *Frankenstein*, Mary Shelley authored five novels in addition to short stories, biographies and travel books.[3] She also penned essays and reviews, and edited the first collected edition of her husband's poems after the poet's early death in Italy in the summer of 1822.[4] In spite of the broad spectrum of her authorship, Mary Shelley was for a long time one of the least acknowledged authors of her age, and it is only in the last few decades that an interest in her life and works has awakened.[5]

Mary Shelley's third novel *The Last Man*,[6] the topic of the present chapter, is a complex and puzzling work.[7] The novel presents a pessimistic vision of Europe of the late twenty-first century, which is plagued by constant wars and a pandemic that almost results in the extinction of humanity. The story is told by Lionel Verney, the lone survivor of the plague. The novel can be seen as a criticism of and protest against war and conquest, which characterized many of the European powers, not least Great Britain, in the nineteenth century. The work also contains several parts that bear witness to its author's scepticism about modern city life, which is described as shallow and pleasure-seeking, and which leads, among other things, to 'disappointment, weariness and solitude'.[8]

The secondary literature generally recognizes that the two main characters of the story, Adrian and Raymond are based respectively on Mary Shelley's husband and the poet Lord George Gordon Byron (1788–1824), who was a close friend of the Shelleys. However, the new claim that I wish to argue for is that Mary Shelley herself is actually the first-person narrator of the work. Moreover, the novel deals with a number of existential questions inasmuch as it bears clear witness to the pain and sorrow that Mary Shelley felt after losing her husband. Indeed, I wish to argue in the present chapter that *The Last Man* is *primarily* about the pain, despair and loneliness that its author felt in the years when she wrote this work. But what makes this work especially worth examining is the fact that while Mary Shelley writes about the suffering of the characters of her novel, this is portrayed in a way that evokes some of the basic philosophical questions about the meaning of human life, death and suffering. And it is precisely these recurring reflections about human existence that make this novel so interesting for our purpose, since by examining the text we can better understand how literature deals with questions of value, meaning and general ethical issues and even what advantages it might have over philosophy in this regard.

In what follows, I will first give a brief overview of Mary Shelley's life and the context in which her text was written. This is followed by the main part of my chapter, which is divided into four large subsections. The first three of these will help to establish the autobiographical nature of the novel, while the last subsection deals with the more general philosophical questions that the work raises. From this analysis it will be clear that important elements in the text have a biographical origin, and that the pain and suffering depicted in the novel are in fact a reflection of Shelley's own personal struggle. In addition, it will be shown that the novel can be considered as an early example of the existentialist novel as we know it from the twentieth century.

Mary Shelley's life and the context of *The Last Man*

The first two decades of the nineteenth century were turbulent times in the history of Europe. The French Revolution and the decade-long Napoleonic Wars affected almost every country on the continent. They brought about profound changes in European societies which paved the way to modernity, but they also brought with them great suffering and chaos. England, although spared from revolution, was not saved from the Napoleonic Wars and from countless economic difficulties and social tensions. But the Regency era (as this period of British history is often called) was not only characterized by severe economic difficulties and widespread poverty among the common people – it was also a time of cultural blossoming. It was, for example, the period in which authors such as Jane Austen, William Blake, John Keats and William Wordsworth published their literary works.

It was into this historical and cultural background which Mary Shelley was born. Since her parents, Mary Wollstonecraft and William Godwin, were among the most famous thinkers of the time, Mary Shelley grew up in an educated and highly intellectual environment. Although she received a formal education only for a short period of time, she was taught by both her father and other private tutors, and she also enjoyed the use of William Godwin's extensive library. At the same time, Mary Shelley suffered a great deal as a child and young person. Her mother died of puerperal fever shortly after Mary's birth. Four years later, her father married anew, and her relationship with her stepmother was characterized by conflict. Her feeling of loneliness was deepened by the fact that she had to grow up with the absence of a loving mother.

Not yet seventeen years old, Mary Shelley fell in love with her future husband Percy Bysshe Shelley, who was a regular guest in her father's house. At the time, Shelley was already married to Harriet Westbrook, who was expecting their first child. Shelley left her in order to run away with Mary. From this time, that is, from the summer of 1814 until Shelley's death only eight years later, Mary Shelley had a highly instable and uncertain existence, and her life was shaped by a series of personal tragedies and disappointments. She suffered five miscarriages and lost two other children. The Shelleys had only one son who reached adulthood, Percy Florence Shelley (1819–1889). The couple lived in permanent financial difficulties and changed their dwellings frequently. They also travelled extensively, primarily in France and Italy, and lived in the latter country for long periods of time.

Mary's relationship to her father became troubled when she decided to run away with Shelley; indeed, Godwin forced her to choose between him and Shelley. Godwin's radical political views regarding marriage had their limits when it came to his own daughter, and it took some years before father and daughter were reconciled. Finally, Mary's marriage with Shelley had more ups and downs than was good for either of them. The repeated tragedies of losing one child after another in the course of only a few years took their toll on Mary's mental health, and she was plagued by recurring bouts of depression and emotional instability. This was not made easier by the fact that Shelley was decidedly not the most faithful of husbands. He frequently had relationships with other women, among others, Mary Shelley's own stepsister, Claire Clairmont, who joined them when they left England for Continental Europe in the summer of 1814 and who, over the years, repeatedly lived together with the Shelleys.

During the fatal year of 1822, Mary and Percy Bysshe Shelley were living in Italy. They initially stayed in Naples and Rome before moving to the northwest, to an isolated estate, the Villa Magni at San Terenzo, on the Lerici Coast. Here they lived together with Claire Clairmont and the English couple, Jane and Edward Williams. In June of the same year, Mary Shelley almost died during a miscarriage, an event which was followed by a deep depression and emotional estrangement from her husband, who is thought to have been having an affair with Jane Williams at the time. These were the general circumstances when Percy Shelley and Edward Williams decided to sail to Livorno in order to visit Byron who lived in Pisa at this time. They left on 1 July and planned to return on the 8 July; however, on the way back, their boat was caught in a storm. They suffered shipwreck, and both of them drowned.

Mary Shelley was left behind alone with their son Percy and with no financial resources to speak of. A year later, in the summer of 1823, she decided to return to London, where she had to face countless severe difficulties including her bouts of depression and struggles with her father-in-law, Sir Timothy Shelley, who wanted nothing to do with her and was unwilling to help her financially. He was also against the idea of publishing Shelley's poems. In spite of this, Mary Shelley managed to publish the *Posthumous Poems of Percy Bysshe Shelley* in June 1824, but as soon as Sir Timothy learned of this, he succeeded in forcing the publisher to stop selling the work.

It was around this time that Mary Shelley started to work on her novel *The Last Man*. In a journal entry, written on 15 May 1824, Mary Shelley writes as follows:

> This, then, is my English life; and thus I am to drag on existence; confined in my small room, friendless. Each day I string me to the task. I endeavour to read and write, my ideas stagnate and my understanding refuses to follow the words I read; day after day passes while torrents fall from the dark clouds, and my mind is as gloomy as this odious sky. Without human friends I must attach myself to natural objects; but though I talk of the country, what difference shall I find in this miserable climate … The Last Man! Yes, I may well describe that solitary being's feelings: I feel

> myself as the last relic of a beloved race, my companions extinct before me.[9]

This passage shows the profound loneliness and emptiness that Mary Shelley felt upon returning from Italy to England in the summer of 1823. She had been living with Shelley in Italy for years when the latter suffered the fatal boat accident. Life was extremely difficult for Mary Shelley upon her return to England, and tasks that used to be important to her such as reading and writing seemed to have become meaningless. Here she clearly feels as if she would be the last man on earth doomed to live an existence without anybody else around to talk to.

If this wasn't enough, the news that Byron had died of a fever in April 1824 while fighting for Greece in the Greek War of Independence (1821–9) also reached her during this time. In a journal entry, dated the day after the previously quoted entry, she writes:

> Albé [i.e. Byron] – the dear, capricious, fascinating Albé – has left this desert world! God grant I may die young! A new race is springing about me. At the age of twenty-six I am in the condition of an aged person. All my old friends are gone, I have no wish to form new. I cling to the few remaining; but they slide away, and my heart fails when I think by how few ties I hold to the world. 'Life is the desert and the solitude – how populous the grave' – and that region – to the dearer and best beloved beings which it has torn from me, now adds that resplendent spirit whose departure leaves the dull earth dark as midnight.[10]

This is written in the tone of many of the key passages in *The Last Man*, which again strengthen the autobiographical interpretation. This passage clearly reflects the anguish that Mary Shelley felt during this time. Although still young, by this time she had lost almost everyone whom she loved. Hence, it is no wonder that she felt isolated in the world without those people around her with whom she was also deeply connected intellectually and spiritually. Thus, the creation of a novel in which characters based on her loved ones are set against the backdrop of deadly war and contagion appears to function as a means by which the author may process her own grief and despair.

The novel *The Last Man*

The prophetess: The Sibyl at Cumae

The novel, which is divided into three parts, begins with a brief Introduction. In this subsection, I would like to deal at length with this introductory part of the work since it helps to establish the autobiographical nature of the work. The narrator, who I argue represents Mary Shelley herself, tells the story of a visit to Naples. She writes about an excursion across the Gulf of Naples to the city of Baiae, which is famous for its ancient historical sites. It is recounted, with an allusion to Virgil, 'We visited the so-called Elysian Fields and Avernus; and wandered through various temples, baths, and classic spots; at length we entered the gloomy cavern of the Cumaean Sibyl'.[11] They wander around the cavern, and while doing so, they find a hidden passage that leads to other rooms. In the end, they find *the* cave where the famous prophetess Sibyl gave her prophecies: 'My friend, who had taken up some of the leaves strewed about, exclaimed, "This *is* the Sibyl's cave; these are Sibylline leaves."'[12]

Later on, the narrator reports that during their stay in Naples they frequently visited the cave and that she has started to decipher the texts, which were written on the leaves that they had found and had taken with them: 'I have been employed in deciphering these sacred remains. Their meaning, wondrous and eloquent, has often repaid my toil, soothing me in sorrow, and exciting my imagination to daring flights, through the immensity of nature and the mind of man. For a while my labours were not solitary; but that time is gone.'[13] Then she quotes a few lines from sonnet 322 of the famous Renaissance poet Francesco Petrarch (1304–1374) in Italian, which in English reads: 'From my tender beginnings a very different outcome I hoped to show you; and what hard fate was so envious of us, O my noble treasure?' And finally: 'I present the public with my latest discoveries in the slight Sibylline pages.'[14]

The quoted passages might seem somewhat cryptic at first sight, but upon a closer look, their relevance becomes more apparent. First, the narrator reports that the visit at Baiae takes place on 8 December 1818. According to a journal note, the Shelleys in fact visited this place, and their visit took place on exactly the day that is mentioned by the narrator.[15] Thus, although the story of the Introduction is a fictitious one, this strongly suggests that it is Mary Shelley's voice that we hear and that the 'friend', with whom the narrator visits the cave, is none other than her husband.

Second, as is well-known, the Sibyl of Cumae was, in Roman mythology, a prophetess, who lived in a cave situated below Apollo's temple. She plays an important role in Virgil's *Aeneid*. Aeneas, the famous Trojan warrior, flees Troy when the Greeks sack the city in the final battle of the Trojan War. He wanders through the Mediterranean with his family and a group of refugees. His goal is to fulfil his destiny, which is to found a new civilization, but for a long time he doesn't know where this should be. Eventually, he comes to Cumae, Italy. In Book VI of *The Aeneid*, we read: 'But pious / Aeneas seeks the peaks where high Apollo / is king and, in a deep, enormous grotto, / the awful Sibyl has her secret home.'[16] The prophetess is able to hear the god Apollo and convey his prophecies. So Aeneas visits the temple, and while offering a sacrifice to Apollo, he hears the voice of the Sibyl, who gives him her prophecy. Aeneas asks the Sibyl not to write her prophecy on leaves, as she usually does, but just to recite it to him. He talks to the Sibyl as follows: 'Only do not entrust / your verses to the leaves, lest they fly off / in disarray, the play of rapid winds: / chant them yourself, I pray.'[17] The Sibyl's prophecy helps Aeneas to understand that the new civilization that he is destined to found is that of Rome.[18]

Finally, by quoting the mentioned lines from Petrarch's sonnet, Mary Shelley's reference is undoubtedly to her beloved Shelley,[19] which again emphasizes the autobiographical character of the novel's Introduction. On the basis of the previously analysed parts of the text together with the stated intention of the narrator to 'present the public' what she has found written on the leaves, we might say that it is not only the Introduction of the novel but the story itself, which is autobiographically motivated. Especially the reference to the prophetess Sibyl is a clear indication that the story told in the novel is to be understood as a prophecy about the future – a future, which is written by the prophetess on leaves, which was then found, as depicted in the text, and which the narrator then decides to publish.

The 'futuristic' setting of the novel also contains ambiguity. Are we to read it as being set in the twenty-first century, as is stated in the text – or is it rather Mary Shelley's own near future? There are some indications in the text that speak for the latter. The author does not make, for example, any great effort to create the impression that we are actually in the distant future. Most of the descriptions about the environment fit in fact much better into Mary Shelley's own nineteenth-century milieu than into an imagined world so far away in time. There are, for instance, virtually no references to the use of any kind of developed technology, apart from the one scene where Adrian travels by means of a 'sailing balloon'.[20] The emphasis is always on the experienced reality of the characters, what they think and how they feel. There is nothing unfamiliar about the environment they live in, and the novel does not contain anything that we might expect from science fiction. We might thus say that the prophecy of the Sibyl that she writes on the leaves and that the narrator shares with the world is actually not about the twenty-first century but rather about Mary Shelley's own future. This was a future that brought Shelley's tragic death and that left Mary Shelley alone and destined her to live the rest of her life in solitude. That she nonetheless chose to place her story in such a distant future might have been because this way she could create a narrative space that allowed her to tell her *own* story without immediately giving the impression that she is talking about herself.

It is worth quoting from one of Mary Shelley's letters on this point. The letter was written to Maria Gisborne, a friend of the Shelleys, on 15 August 1822, that is, only a few weeks after Shelley's death. Mary Shelley reports in the letter about the day when Shelley sailed out. She writes:

> I was then just better, had begun to crawl from my bedroom to the terrace, but bad spirits succeeded to ill health, and this departure of Shelley's seemed to add insufferably to my misery. I could not endure that he should go. I called him back two or three times, and told him that if I did not see him soon I would go to Pisa with the child. I cried bitterly when he went away … In my letters to him I entreated him to return; 'the feeling that some misfortune would happen', I said, 'haunted me'. I feared for the child, for the idea of danger connected with him never struck me.[21]

This quotation speaks clearly about the premonition that tormented Mary Shelley while her husband was away. Previously, both of them had gone through difficult times. Mary Shelley had a miscarriage that almost cost her her life, and her recovery from it was slow. Shelley's health was also poor, and he fought with recurring nightmares. And then, a few days later when Shelley was supposed to return, the fatal accident occurred. It is easy to imagine that receiving the news of Shelley's death and the circumstances of his departure, Mary Shelley was left with the feeling that it was her frightening prophecy that had come true. In the letter she talks about her anxiety that something bad would happen, but she feared for her child and not for Shelley. Premonitions, like the predictions of the Sibyl and other prophetesses of the ancient world, are ambiguous feelings that are often difficult to interpret correctly. These circumstances can thus explain Mary Shelley's choice of the use of the prophetess Sibyl. She might have felt that her destiny had been written long before, and she could do nothing about it.

The motto she chose for her novel can also be seen in this context. She quotes from Milton's *Paradise Lost*:

> Let no man seek
> Henceforth to be foretold what shall befall
> Him or his Children.
>
> Milton[22]

This might seem to stand in opposition to the story itself, inasmuch as it is presented as something that is predicted to happen. But I would like to suggest that this is another hint that the novel is in reality Mary Shelley's own story. In my view it is an expression of her tormented soul after having lost Shelley. On the one hand, she was devastated by losing her husband, but, on the other hand, she also suffered because she felt she had known that something bad was about to happen, but was unable to prevent it. This must have been an overwhelming feeling, perhaps even accompanied by a degree of guilt.

Finally, towards the end of the Introduction, there is one last passage worth mentioning:

> My labours have cheered long hours of solitude, and taken me out of a world, which has averted its once benignant face from me, to one glowing with imagination and power. Will my reader ask how I could find solace from the narration of misery and

> woeful change? ... I confess, that I have not been unmoved by the development of the tale; and that I have been depressed, nay, agonized, at some parts of the recital, which I have faithfully transcribed from my materials. Yet such is human nature, that the excitement of mind was dear to me, and the imagination, painter of tempest and earthquake, or, worse, the stormy and ruin-fraught passions of man, softened my real sorrows and endless regrets, by clothing these fictitious ones in that ideality, which takes the mortal sting from pain.[23]

These lines suggest that writing the book served as a comfort for the narrator, that is, Mary Shelley, since, as she writes, working with her imagination diverted her from her pain and made her suffering easier to endure. Upon returning to England after her husband's death, Mary Shelley must have felt utterly miserable. Therefore, the claim seems to be plausible that choosing a story about a catastrophe that leaves only one person alive might have indeed served her as a means of soothing her pain and helping her come to terms with what had happened.

The survivor: The storyteller

In this second subsection, I would like to explore the narrative structure of the novel, which will further help to establish the autobiographical nature of the work. The story of the novel is told in the first-person singular by Lionel Verney, the lone survivor of the pandemic, who is thus 'the last man'. As mentioned earlier, Mary Shelley regarded herself as a kind of 'last man', who was destined to live alone in the world without confidants or friends. In Part 3 of the book, when the plague had already spread throughout the world, Lionel loses everyone dear to him: first, his wife Idris dies, and then also Clara, the orphaned daughter of his sister Perdita and Lord Raymond, whom he loved very much. The plague might thus be regarded as a metaphor representing all the tragedies and catastrophes that Mary was forced to endure and that took away almost everyone who was important to her. Even the name of Lionel's beloved niece, Clara, has a direct autobiographical connection since the Shelleys lost two daughters in early infancy, both of whom were named Clara. A letter gives witness to how devastated Mary Shelley was during the time that followed Shelley's death. She writes from Pisa to her friend, the previously mentioned Maria Gisborne, on 10 September 1822:

> And so here I am! I continue to exist – to see one day succeed the other; to dread night, but more to dread morning, and hail another cheerless day. My Boy, too, is alas! no consolation. When I think how he loved him, the plans he had for his education, his sweet and childish voice strikes me to the heart. ... I have but one hope for which I live, to render myself worthy to join him, – and such a feeling sustains one during moments of enthusiasm, but darkness and misery soon overwhelm the mind when all near objects bring agony alone with them. People used to call me lucky in my star; you see now how true such a prophecy is! I was fortunate in having fearlessly placed my destiny in the hands of one who, a superior being among men, a bright 'planetary' spirit enshrined in an earthly temple, raised me to the height of happiness. So far am I now happy, that I would not change my situation as his widow with that of the most prosperous woman in the world; and surely the time will at length come when I shall be at peace, and my brain and heart no longer be alive with unutterable anguish.[24]

This passage bears clear witness to Mary Shelley's suffering and pain. Not even her only surviving child, Percy Florence, meant a consolation to her. It proves also how much she loved Shelley, and how much she longed to join him somewhere in the beyond.

Taking into consideration these circumstances, the similarities between Lionel's fate and Mary Shelley's own life seem to be apparent. Lionel is a survivor just like she herself, and he also loses everyone whom he loved and is destined to continue to live alone. Thus, Lionel might have served for the author as a figure, into whom she could project herself. Furthermore, the choice of a male figure, who tells his story in first-person singular, made it possible that Mary could write about herself, about Shelley and about their relationship, without immediately leading the reader to the conclusion that she is telling her own story.

But Lionel's character can only be understood, if one sees him in relation to Adrian, who is one of the main characters, or probably even *the* main character, of the novel. Adrian is the Earl of Windsor and the son of the last British king who was forced to abdicate in 2073.[25] There is a general agreement in the secondary literature that Adrian's character is based on Shelley.[26] He is described in the novel as 'imbued with the spirit of high philosophy' and as a person who 'hardly appeared of this world; his slight frame was overinformed by the soul that dwelt within; he was all mind'.[27] This is very much in accordance with how Shelley was perceived by his contemporaries.[28]

In the first part of the novel there are several passages that describe Lionel's love for, devotion to and admiration of Adrian. One telling passage is the following:

> We both [i.e. both Lionel and his sister Perdita] agreed in *loving* Adrian: although she [i.e. Perdita] not having yet escaped from childhood could not appreciate as I did the extent of his merits, or feel the same sympathy in his pursuits and opinions. I was *for ever* with him. There was a sensibility and *sweetness* in his disposition, that gave a *tender* and unearthly tone to our converse. Then he was gay as a lark carolling from its skiey tower, soaring in thought as an eagle, innocent as *mild-eyed dove*.[29]

This passage describes how Lionel feels towards Adrian shortly after they met for the first time. Reading these lines, one could easily get the impression that they depict a romantic relationship and not merely a friendship. These lines are littered with amorous vocabulary, and one could easily assume that one is hearing the narrator talking about his beloved, reinforcing the idea that by writing about Lionel and his relationship to Adrian, Mary Shelley writes in reality about herself and her feelings for Shelley.

To support this statement, one could also mention the part of the novel where Adrian becomes very ill and is sent to Scotland, where Lionel visits him. In order to arrive as quickly as possible at his sick friend's side, Lionel travels by means of a 'sailing balloon'.[30] He describes as follows his arrival in Scotland in the next morning:

> The rising sun first tinged the pine tops; and my mind, rendered through my mountain education deeply susceptible of the graces of nature, and now on the eve of again beholding my beloved and perhaps dying friend, was strangely influenced by the sight of those distant beams: surely they were ominous, and as such

> I regarded them, good omens for Adrian, on *whose life my happiness depended.*[31]

This passage, which also gives an excellent impression of the stunning Romantic style and the richness of Mary Shelley's language, is another proof of Lionel's love for Adrian. These sentiments again seem to fit more to a loving wife worried for her sick husband than that to a friend. Thanks to Lionel's devoted care of his sick friend, Adrian regains his health: 'The faint rose again blushed on his cheek; his brow and lips lost ashy paleness of threatened dissolution; such was the dear reward of my unremitting attention.'[32] This episode's biographical similarity with Shelley's life is clear. We know that he was often sick from his early twenties until the end of his life.[33] And, as we have seen earlier, Mary Shelley regarded her husband indeed as someone on whose life her happiness depended.

Concluding, we might say that, apart from placing her story in the distant future, by choosing a male protagonist, Mary Shelley created a distance, which gave her more freedom than would have been the case if she would have chosen the form of a genuine autobiography. Her motivation for creating this distance might well have been her desire to avoid conflict with her father-in-law, which would be certain, had she chosen to write a traditional autobiography. Moreover, since depicting Lionel's poignant love for Adrian, whose figure is so reminiscent of Shelley, we might read the text as Mary Shelley's way of coping with the trauma and grief of losing her husband.

The dreamer: The poet

The topic of this third subsection is the political-philosophical content of the work, which will contextualize the autobiographical elements of this novel. While Percy Bysshe Shelley is primarily known as a Romantic poet, he also wrote political and philosophical works. Among these writings one finds, for example, the unfinished *A Philosophical View of Reform*, on which he began to work in the fall of 1819.[34] As mentioned earlier, the 1810's were turbulent years in Europe due mainly to the Napoleonic Wars. However, Great Britain was not only involved in a war on the Continent but also fought against the United States in the War of 1812, which ended officially only in 1815. The British involvement in two wars at the same time led to economic depression. The conditions of the working class in Britain had been shockingly bad even beforehand. The labourers had long working hours, they had to work under often extremely dangerous conditions, they were poorly paid, and they had to come to terms with the high food prices caused by the economic recession.

It is no wonder that common people became desperate and protested by vandalizing factories and organizing rallies. They not only demanded the improvement of the general economic situation but also asked for political reforms. They requested a reform of the voting system, where the right to be elected to Parliament was not tied to land or wealth. This series of rallies culminated in a meeting held on St. Peter's Fields in Manchester in August 1819, which was intended as a large protest of the common people. The cavalry brutally dispersed the meeting by an armed attack on the crowd, although the protest was peaceful, and there were many women and children among the participants. When Shelley began writing his work towards the end of 1819, he thought that revolution was about to break out.[35] To people who wished to reform the political system in Great Britain, like Shelley, this event was a symbol of the tyranny of the Tory government.

In his work *A Philosophical View of Reform*, Shelley pleads for political and governmental reforms. He regards the British form of government despotic and refers to the American Revolution as a good example of a 'just and successful revolt'.[36] At this time, the Shelleys were living in Pisa, in part, because of the repressive nature of the political system in England.[37] Also in this respect, Adrian's character in *The Last Man* shows obvious similarities with Shelley and his political views. Adrian is very much occupied with how he might contribute to 'the improving of mankind',[38] and he spends all his time making detailed plans for a reform:

> In solitude, and through many wanderings afar from the haunts of men, he matured his views for the reform of the English government, and the improvement of the people …. His enthusiasm for good which did not exist; his contempt for the sacredness of authority; his ardour and imprudence were all at the antipodes of the usual routine of life; the worldly feared him; the young and the inexperienced did not understand the lofty

> severity of his moral views, and disliked him as a being different from themselves.[39]

This passage illustrates how close Adrian's political views were to those of Shelley. As will be recalled, in the novel the last British king abdicates in 2073, and the empire becomes a republic. The political fights in Parliament occupy considerable space in Part 1 of the novel, and Adrian's political vision is clearly based on Shelley's ideas of political reform. This is another argument for the claim that writing her novel was, for Mary Shelley, important primarily because of existential reasons. By giving such a large space to political visions very similar to those of her husband, she could also in this regard pay tribute to Shelley.

As mentioned earlier, Mary's father William Godwin was a well-known political thinker of the time, famous for his radical and anarchist views. According to him, the only thing that a human being really needs is complete freedom from all political and social restrictions. Once people attain this freedom, they will be able to live in harmony with the world, which he regarded as the natural state of human beings.[40] Shelley, as a regular guest in Godwin's house in his young years, was highly influenced by Godwin's political views. But as one commentator underlines, Shelley's own political views had two sides. On the one hand, he tried to articulate a universal political philosophy, which is based on ideas and not on material interests, and these ideas could be libertarian and anarchistic. On the other hand, he didn't believe that changes require violence. At the same time, he acknowledged that the economic misery of the common people and the general political oppression might justify a political conflict of pure material interest.[41]

Hence, it is no surprise that living in an environment where discussions about political issues took place every day, Mary Shelley herself was interested in these issues. But her own political views were on the more moderate side of the political spectrum, for which there might have been different reasons. One can mention, for example, the fact that she came of age at a time when the cruel consequences of the French Revolution, such as the tyranny of the Jacobian rule (The Reign of Terror) and the long years of war during the Napoleonic era, were highly visible.[42]

In *The Last Man*, Mary Shelley adapts her husband's ideas for political reform presumably with the goal of paying tribute to

Shelley as a political thinker. Here, the emphasis is very much on the person himself, and Adrian, that is, Shelley, is portrayed as a dreamer filled with visions of improving humankind. However, Shelley's more radical and anarchistic views are absent in the novel. The transition from monarchy to republic, for example, takes place in Great Britain without cruelty, and this is portrayed as something positive.

However, the Greek Revolution against the Ottoman Empire is depicted negatively since it leads to a war that never ends and that, in addition to the plague, contributes to the decline and ruin of humanity. Part 2 of the novel deals in detail with this war, which has fatal consequences for Lionel's family since his sister Perdita loses her beloved husband, Lord Raymond, and Perdita herself dies subsequently too. As mentioned, Lord Raymond's character closely resembles Byron, while Perdita reminds the reader of Mary Shelley's sister Claire Clairmont. Byron and Claire Clairmont indeed had an affair, from which a daughter was born, and Byron, as is well-known, died in the Greek War of Independence in 1824. Hence, these episodes are also filled with autobiographical references, but the point I want to make here is about the political-philosophical aspect of the novel, namely, that revolution and war are depicted as horrible things that only lead to destruction and suffering. *The Last Man* effectively serves as a political plea against war, encompassing a profound and impactful portrayal of the destruction and endless suffering that are its inevitable consequences.

With regard to political philosophy, *The Last Man* is very much in line with *Frankenstein*. By choosing as the subtitle to the latter *The Modern Prometheus*, Mary Shelley refers to the famous Greek mythological figure who, according to the legend, stole fire from Zeus in order to give it to humans. Because of this, his figure is mostly associated with progress against the forces of nature. But Mary Shelley's story is about a doctor Victor Frankenstein who, in his endless belief in his own technological and medical knowledge, creates a monster. Consequently, calling a person like Frankenstein, who uses his knowledge and inadvertently causes suffering, the modern Prometheus is without doubt a negative view of human achievements of the time. As we have seen, similarly negative is the view of certain aspects of human progress depicted in *The Last Man*. Thus, both works express Mary Shelley's critique of modern civilization that takes its origin in the unconditional belief of the Enlightenment in rationality and human progress.

The Last Man as an early existentialist novel

After having established my understanding of the autobiographical nature of this novel, I would like to examine in this last subsection how exactly *The Last Man* deals with general existential and philosophical questions. In Part 3 of the novel there are only a few people left who survive the plague in England. They decide to leave Britain and go to France. Thereafter they travel to Switzerland and end up finally in Italy. By this time, everybody has died but three people, Adrian, Lionel and Lionel's niece Clara. They decide to sail from Venice to Greece. However, on the way to Athens, they get caught in a sudden and violent storm and suffer shipwreck. Only Lionel survives, and, thus he remains 'the last man'.

There is a striking similarity between Adrian's and Shelley's death, that is, that both of them die by drowning at sea in a storm. The description of the boat accident fills an entire chapter towards the end of the novel and is in many ways the most dramatic part of the story. Lionel reports in great detail about how they depart from Italy, how they looked forward to arriving in Athens, but he also tells that he was, at the same time, concerned and afraid that something bad would happen. He writes: 'A sudden fear stung me while I gazed [up to the sky].'[43] His worst premonitions came true since a storm arose, which became stronger and stronger, and they are carried by it towards the shore. Night falls, and the storm is at its highest, when Lionel suddenly finds himself in the water. He swims towards the shore and hopes that he will find the two others there as well, but then he realizes that he is the lone survivor.

The description of the storm and the death of Adrian is filled with intensity. When Lionel suddenly realizes that he is alone, his words convey the depth of human suffering. He writes:

> The day passed thus; each moment contained eternity; although when hour after hour had gone by, I wondered at the quick flight of time. Yet even now I had not drunk the bitter potion of the dregs; I was not persuaded of my loss; I did not feel in every pulsation, in every nerve, in every thought, that I remained alone of my race, – that I was the LAST MAN.[44]

It is difficult to imagine a situation where a human being can experience a deeper abandonment, despair and suffering than being left alone in the world, after having survived a shipwreck, where one has lost the two last people one most loved. A scene like this provokes some fundamental existential questions such as what the meaning of life is, how to deal with death and suffering and how to transform the desperation into something that makes it possible to continue to live on in spite of everything that has happened.

The very last chapter tries to answer these questions. After the shipwreck, Lionel wanders through Italy for a while and finally decides to go to Rome. He is completely alone in the big city, but he opts to stay for a while. And slowly, he starts to find some consolation in spending time in Rome, which he regards as 'the capital of the world, the crown of man's achievement'.[45] He visits the famous sites of the city, and starts to read the works of the classics such as Horace, Virgil and Cicero, and begins to write as well. But he asks himself the question again and again:

> Yet how could I resign myself? Without love, without sympathy, without communion with any, how could I meet the morning sun, and with it trace its oft repeated journey to the evening shades? Why did I continue to live – why not throw off the weary weight of time, and with my own hand, let out the fluttering prisoner from my agonized breast?[46]

The narrator poses the well-known question of Camus from *The Myth of Sisyphus*. If one can perceive no meaning in the world, what prevents one from committing suicide? The narrator thus engages in a philosophical reflection on the meaning and value of human existence that foreshadows the existentialist authors. Again, it's difficult to imagine a situation where a human being can feel deeper despair than this scene, that is, when one considers ending one's life because one cannot imagine continuing to live the way one should. However, Lionel decides: 'But this I would not do.'[47] Rather, choosing to surrender to his fate, he writes: 'I had, from the moment I had reasoned on the subject, instituted myself the subject to fate, and servant of necessity, the visible laws of the invisible God.'[48] Thus, Lionel's way of consoling himself and enduring his lone existence is to accept the will of an invisible power and to occupy himself with intellectual work.

It is often thought that twentieth-century existentialism arose out of the trauma of the World Wars and the Holocaust. These experiences confronted Europe and the rest of the world with a deep crisis of meaning. The French existentialists, such as Sartre, de Beauvoir and Camus, all struggled to try to establish some kind of ethics or meaning in a world abandoned by God. Central motifs of their novels include despair, isolation, loneliness, alienation and meaninglessness. Mary Shelley's writing fits nicely with this picture. She too lived in an age of wars and political turmoil. With the loss of her husband and children, she too was confronted with the question of the meaning or purpose of life. It can only be imagined that she must have done a lot of soul-searching and repeatedly asked how it was possible that her husband, who was such a light of the human spirit, could have died so young and in such a meaningless way. What was the meaning of her having lost so many children in childbirth and infancy? Given all of this, it makes perfect sense that she wrote what we today would regard as an existential novel as she fought her own personal battle with the feelings of isolation, loneliness and meaninglessness.

Conclusions: Philosophical reflections and *The Last Man*

Mary Shelley's novel *The Last Man* was not the only 'last man' story of the time. On the contrary, the 1810's and 1820's witnessed a fascination with apocalyptic visions. One can mention here Byron's poem 'Darkness', written in 1816, the Scottish poet Thomas Campbell's poem 'The Last Man' (1823) and an anonymously published poem again with the title 'The Last Man' from 1826.[49] This fascination with the idea of an extinguished humanity can be in part explained by the consequences of the 1815 eruption of Mount Tambora in the Dutch East Indies (today Indonesia), which caused a disastrous change in the global climate in the following year. The year 1816 was the 'year without summer' with cold summer temperatures and almost no sunshine. It was also the summer, when the Shelleys met Byron at the Lake Geneva, where Mary Shelley began to write her *Frankenstein*.

The descriptions of the devastation and suffering caused by the wars and the plague are important elements of the novel, but, as we have seen earlier, it is always the suffering of individual human beings, especially that of the last man, that is in the foreground rather than a vision of the extinction of humanity as such. As we have seen as well, the suffering and anguish portrayed in the novel are to a large extent based on Mary Shelley's life. Here, at the end of this article, I would like to quote a passage from the very last chapter of the novel, where Lionel, now completely alone in the world, laments as follows:

> If regret and sorrow came athwart me, as well it might in our solitary and uncertain state, the clear tones of Adrian's voice, and his fervent look, dissipated the gloom; or I was cheered unaware by the mild content and sweet resignation Clara's cloudless brow and deep blue eyes expressed. They were all to me – the suns of my benighted soul – repose in my weariness – slumber in my sleepless woe. Ill, most ill, with disjointed words, bare and weak, have I expressed the feeling with which I clung to them.[50]

It is significant that Lionel doesn't say this to Idris, his wife in the story, or his own children, who mean everything to him, but rather these words are spoken as he is feeling the loss of Adrian and his niece Clara. This is again evidence that Lionel's character served a special purpose for Mary Shelley. She could project her own anguish about having lost her husband and daughters (both named Clara) onto this figure. Thus, the biographical references are unmistakable.

We have been following two strands of argument: (1) that *The Last Man* is in large part autobiographical, and (2) that it can be regarded as an existentialist novel. These two strands of my thesis now come together in the end. Existentialism is known for its rejection of abstract thinking and for its focus on the individual subject and the immediate lived experience. The French existentialists in particular were insistent that their movement had a direct value for the lives of people in contrast to academic philosophy, which was only for other specialists. This point of dogma in the movement presumably arose from the personal experiences of the existentialist writers during the Second World War and later the Cold War. In their eyes there was no fundamental distinction between philosophy and life. The two were intimately and necessarily bound together. *The Last Man* by Mary Shelley fits with this description perfectly. It is a profound reflection and meditation on human nature and the human condition that is based to a great extent on the personal life experiences of the author herself. Like the existentialists, Mary Shelley had no interest or desire in separating her experiences and feelings from the universal philosophical questions. My autobiographical interpretation of the novel is thus not just a trivial curiosum, but rather it paves the way for us to understand her as a serious philosophical thinker in her own right.

11

'The salamander of the human soul': The melodrama of scepticism in Dostoevsky and Tarkovsky

Stephen Mulhall

George Steiner's early exercise in what he pointedly called 'the old criticism', *Tolstoy or Dostoevsky: An Essay in Contrast* assigns a central role in its characterization of Dostoevsky's achievement to the concept of 'melodrama' (more precisely, to a confluence of the Gothic and the melodramatic).[1] In part, this is designed to demonstrate an important continuity between Dostoevsky's body of work and an absolutely central strand of the literary and theatrical culture of his time. In this respect, it acknowledges something about the nineteenth-century Western European art for which Peter Brooks's more recent book, *The Melodramatic Imagination: Balzac, Henry James, Melodrama and the Mode of Excess* is intended to supply an explanation, or at least an interpretation.[2] In this essay, I propose to use Stanley Cavell's critical engagement with Brooks's interpretative schema, and the alternative interpretation of melodrama in film, psychoanalysis and philosophy upon which it draws, to develop a reading of Dostoevsky that brings out points of contrast (and so of comparison) with the cinematic achievement of Tarkovsky that might otherwise be overlooked.

The melodramatic imagination: Steiner, Brooks, Cavell

On Steiner's account, acknowledging Dostoevsky's indebtedness to the melodramatic is a precondition for appreciating that his inheritance of those generic conventions reconfigured them in such a way as to interpenetrate with or recuperate a dramatic genre to which the melodramatic is usually contrasted: that of tragedy. In Dostoevsky's hands – so Steiner argues – the contemporary city's Gothic representation articulated a vision of human experience in which the merely melodramatic became tragic. By contrast, Brooks (while acknowledging the Gothic inflection of the nineteenth-century melodrama) silently resists Steiner's perception of its porosity to tragedy, whether in general or in its Dostoevskean incarnation. Although Dostoevsky is as absent from the body of his book as his name is from its subtitle, Brooks explicitly apologizes for not awarding him a starring role – describing him in his preface as someone whose absence 'may most be felt', given his ability 'to put melodramatic representations to most effective use'.[3] But the nature of these representations – figures of polarized and hyperbolic good and evil, lurid and grandiose events, masked relationships and disguised identities, the drive towards ever more concentrated and totally expressive gestures and statements – is understood in terms of a mode of the melodramatic that is essentially antithetical to the tragic.

> The origins of melodrama can be accurately located within the context of the French Revolution and its aftermath. This is the epistemological moment which it illustrates and to which it contributes: the moment that symbolically, and really, marks the final liquidation of the traditional Sacred and its representative institutions (Church and Monarch), the shattering of the myth of Christendom, the dissolution of an organic and hierarchically cohesive society, and the invalidation of the literary forms – tragedy, comedy of manners – that depended on such a society. Melodrama ... represent[s] ... a response to the loss of the tragic vision ... In the course of this process, tragedy ... became impossible.[4]

What kind of response, then, does melodrama offer to this liquidation, this loss; and what does the melodramatic mode consequently offer to artists?

> Such writers as Balzac and James need melodrama because their deep subject ... has come to be what we have called the 'moral occult': the domain of spiritual forces and imperatives that is not clearly visible in reality, but which they believe to be operative there, and which demands to be uncovered, registered, articulated. In the absence of a true Sacred ... they continue to believe that what is most important in a man's life is his ethical drama and the ethical implications of his psychic drama. Yet here they are dealing in quantities and entities that have only an uncertain ontology and ... an uncertain visibility: they are not necessarily seen in the same manner, if at all, by an audience, since the social cohesion of ... a greater community of belief no longer obtains. ... [S]uch writers must locate, express, demonstrate, prove the very terms in which they are dealing. They must wrest them forth from behind the facades of life, show their meaning and their operation. Precisely to the extent that they feel themselves dealing in concepts and issues that have no certain status or justification, they have recourse to the demonstrative, heightened representations of melodrama.
>
> [T]he melodramatic mode [i]s a central fact of the modern sensibility ... in that modern art has typically felt itself to be constructed on, and over, the void, postulating meanings and symbolic systems which have no certain justification because they are backed by no theology and no universally accepted moral code ... [T]hese are ... versions of a reaction to the vertiginous feeling of standing over the abyss created when the necessary centre of things has been evacuated and dispersed ... [T]here is a desperate effort to renew contact with the scattered ethical and psychic fragments of the Sacred through the representation of fallen reality, insisting that behind reality, hidden by it yet indicated within it, there is a realm where large moral forces are operative, where large choices of ways of being must be made.
>
> The melodramatists refuse to allow that the world has been completely drained of transcendence; and they locate that transcendence in the struggle of the children of light with the children of darkness, in the play of ethical mind.[5]

It's not hard to feel that this is a highly melodramatic mode of articulating the centrality of the melodramatic in the nineteenth-century European art. According to this account, the historically dateable death of God and King not only symbolically but really disperses and annihilates the sacred centre of all things; the French Revolution thereby engenders an absolute break between modernity and the premodern, transforming reality into an impenetrable veil behind which large moral forces are concealed, and from which they must be conjured by the hyperbolic, incantatory speech and gestures of desperate creatures warding off an abyss of meaninglessness.

Is Brooks unaware of this consonance between the polarized, Manichean, hyperbolic form and content of his account, or is he rather creating it? Either way, would this help us to determine whether he takes himself to be analysing one central mode in which modernity represents itself to itself, or rather analysing one central feature of what it is to be modern? On the one hand, he says that 'melodrama becomes the principal mode for uncovering, demonstrating and making operative the essential moral universe in a post-sacred era',[6] which seems to presuppose that the modern moral universe just *is* melodramatic; on the other, he says that it 'expresses the anxiety brought by a frightening new world in which the traditional patterns of moral order no longer provide the necessary social glue',[7] which rather suggests that the melodramatic is a mode of response to modernity that requires diagnosis and even therapeutic treatment (and for which a precondition might be to inhabit and articulate its excesses).

Cavell's inclination is to think that Brooks would understand his own participation in the melodramatic mode he aims to analyse as no more than a further indication of its ontological fundamentality to the modern era.[8] And although he shares Brooks's conviction of a connection between modernity and melodrama, he interprets that connection differently – in part, perhaps, because he perceives it in the first instance as a dimension of modern philosophy. This thread runs from Descartes' hyperbolic articulation of sceptical doubt (which variously invokes the reason-dethroning possibility of others as automata disguised beneath cloaks, and of oneself as possessed of a body made of glass, not to mention an evil demon) as threatening the evaporation of external reality altogether; through Nietzsche's madman, who seeks God by the light of the very Enlightenment that induced his absence; and on into the later work of Wittgenstein, who repeatedly invokes melodramatic scenarios (in which one imagines oneself turning into stone, or affirming the reality of one's pain by emphatically striking oneself on the chest, or obsessively wondering whether the picture of a pot emitting steam really contains boiling water). What motivates Cavell's very different interpretation of this melodramatic dimension is revealed by a lesson he draws from Wittgenstein's interpretation of his own melodramatic outbreaks, and one that he draws from the resolutely unmelodramatic critical settlement of Kant.

On Cavell's reading of Wittgenstein, what Brooks takes as a datum – the tendency of melodrama towards excessive or hyperbolic expressiveness – is in fact a response to a prior sense of the emptiness of our expressions of ourselves, of our pervasive failure or inability to mean, whether because we take language to be necessarily inadequate to that task, or because we take ourselves to be always already expressing ourselves, to be necessarily giving ourselves away in every word and deed. Such fantasies of suffocation and exposure are twinned, equal and opposite, modes of our interpretation of our modern selves as absolutely voiceless. Accordingly, Cavell sees the staged or enacted theatricality of Wittgenstein and Nietzsche, like that of Balzac and James, as participating in that fantasy as part of an attempt to comprehend and overcome what drives us to cultivate it or abandon ourselves to it.

> If we sense that a certain theatricality is the sign of an inability to mean, to get our meaning across, then such [theatrical] writing comes across to us by understanding this desperation, figuring our hidden screams, and then understanding us despite ourselves, despite our inexpressiveness, the poverty and pathos of all expression.[9]

When Cavell asks why we experience ourselves as voiceless, he turns to Kant. First, he points out that Brooks's conception of the moral occult inverts Kant's critical conception of the relation between religion and morality. Brooks's sense of morality's recession behind the veil of reality as caused by the destruction of the Sacred presupposes morality's dependence on the Sacred; whereas Kant is concerned precisely to demonstrate that morality (and its ideal of equal participation in a kingdom of ends) in fact provides the ground of the religious. And he specifies that the consequence of reversing this dependency is to plunge into one of the various forms of madness that he calls 'transcendental illusions' – among which he numbers scepticism, fanaticism and magic (or the occult).

> Kant's idea of spiritual derangement is, roughly, that we are each put into the position of attempting to provide a transcendence in our, as it were, private experience, a link with the beyond that only membership in a realm of law can sanely provide. It is like searching for the power of a word when the conditions of language have been lost. We might say that the word would have to become absolutely expressive, as with a metaphysical voice.[10]

From Cavell's perspective, then, whereas Brooks pictures modern melodrama as the response to a historical event (the loss of conviction in a transcendent basis for the distinction between good and evil), to which melodrama is a self-evidently excessive response, the relevant event is that of melodrama itself (it is the regicide, and not alone a consequence of it). This is why he interprets Nietzsche's parable of the madman as letting us in 'at the obstetrical scene of melodrama, born crying into the world with an inexpressible tale'.[11] For according to that parable, the madman's melodramatic account of God's death at our hands is produced by his interlocutors' earlier dismissal of his initiating impulse to seek God in the public square (i.e. to seek a sane connection with the divine in the community's shared form of life) as making a drama out of a banality of the modern scene. It is his sense of being rendered mute by their denial of him that engenders his hyperbolic response; and this is a parabolic expression of Nietzsche's sense that melodramatic excess is itself a response – an equal and opposite response to a prior sense that there is nothing to be said (because anyone to whom one might convey this information already knows it). In this way, a perception of the pointlessness of speech engenders a counter-perception of the need for absolute expressivity, and both function as ways of occluding what moral sanity actually requires: concrete individual contributions to an unending process of collective self-articulation whose specific outcomes make manifest what melodrama constructs as a hidden essence – authentically moral judgement.

Unknown women: Cavell and Coetzee

The key themes I have isolated in the Cavellian counter-reading of the melodramatic – voicelessness, isolation, madness, proving one's existence and that of our world in the face of hyperbolic scepticism (moral and otherwise) – also shape his use of it when identifying a genre of film that he labels 'Melodramas of the Unknown Woman', and presents as the complement of another genre that he labels 'Comedies of Remarriage'.

In the comedies, the drive of the narrative is not to get the central pair together but rather to get them *back* together: marriage is not the hoped-for culmination of a tale of young lovers striving to overcome obstacles to their union, but an attained relationship currently subject to the threat of divorce, so that a willingness to be married here appears as requiring an unending willingness to remarry. Central to these relationships is the woman's demand for an education of some kind from the man (deriving from her sense that her life asks for some transformation, a re-creation that is also a re-creation of the human), and the man's willingness to undergo an investigation of his authority to provide it; his authority is demonstrated and her transfiguration effected by means of their ability to sustain a meet and happy conversation, a mutually appreciative witty responsiveness. The melodramas, by contrast, concern women who could neither manage nor relish such relationships with men, and so must achieve genuine existence (or fail to) apart from marriage; they lack a common language with the (always inadequate and often villainous) men of their world, so that their words are pervaded with an isolating irony, often rising to arias of divorce from all around them, to which those around them react with bewildered hostility.

This melodramatic vision of the crippling loneliness of such (mis-) marriages entails that the route to re-creation or recovery canvassed by these women involves a systematic negation of the existing world's claims upon them, in the name of a higher, unattained state of society in which alone genuine individuality is attainable for them, and apart from which that society's claims upon them are shown to lack any real authority. In this way, the self's non-self-identity and that of its society appear as internally related; and in one exemplary case (that of Bette Davis playing Charlotte Vale in

Now Voyager), the general task of finding a way to accept their difference from and sameness with themselves appears in more specific terms – namely, Charlotte's willingness to acknowledge some given name or description as rightly applied or not, or more precisely as a willingness to question whether even rightly applied names or descriptions could in principle capture who she is.

J. M. Coetzee's character Elizabeth Costello resembles Cavell's cinematic women (Charlotte, Paula (Ingrid Bergman) in *Gaslight*, Lisa (Joan Fontaine) in *Letter from an Unknown Woman* and Stella (Barbara Stanwyck) in *Stella Dallas*), while further specifying what they exemplify in ways that are pertinent to our current concerns. In Coetzee's Tanner Lectures, Costello (a famous Australian novelist) delivers the Gates Lecture at Appleton College – an opportunity she uses to address the moral status of non-human animals, and in particular the ways in which we currently organize the production of meat for food.[12] Costello is immensely isolated from the world around her, to the point of madness; and just as pretty much every word its inhabitants utter during her stay at Appleton College irritates or bruises her, so she perfects the negation of conversation that her exchanges with them represent by ensuring that every wounding word she utters gives expression to her own woundedness: 'I am ... an animal exhibiting, yet not exhibiting ... a wound, which I cover up under my clothes but touch on in every word I speak.'[13]

Her speech consequently takes the form of passionately judging her world: she finds it wanting, in need of radical, pervasive transformation that is no more than a step away (that is, not blocked by material or moral necessities, but essentially available, neighbouring us); but because its currently attained state is such as to render her voiceless (her horrified perception of its present dispensation inarticulable in the terms provided by our dominant conception of rationality), any claim she stakes in the name of its unattained but attainable state, and so of her own unrealized but realizable capacity to exist otherwise (to transcend her current haunting of her own life), inevitably takes on the accents of insanity.

What to her is a condition of absolute expressiveness is for that very reason also one of absolute inexpressiveness: because everything she says is touched by her woundedness, nothing she says can truly touch her hearers. From their viewpoint, her sense of victimization by what she knows can only appear hyperbolic, inordinate, melodramatic – an apparently excessive response to apparently banal facts or circumstances; what she thinks she knows remains utterly unknown to her interlocutors, and since the trauma of that knowledge constitutes her as the animal she is, she too remains to that extent unknown.

The most obvious difference between Costello and her sisters from the melodramas is that there is no specific man in her life whose failure to acknowledge her, and thereby to hold open the possibility of her finding her voice within their current state of society, incites her rejection of its terms and conditions more generally. On the other hand, Costello's fame as a writer is founded on her novel *The House on Eccles Street*, in which she gives Molly Bloom a voice in such a way as to reveal the limitations of Joyce's original attempts to realize an authentic femininity. So one can regard Costello's general way with words as inflected by that origin, hence as always amounting to a recovery of the woman's voice from its male counterfeits and confinements. Her Gates Lecture would then appear as an aria of vengeful divorce, comparable in its tone and range to that delivered by Paula to her husband; the difference is that Costello speaks (or sings or screams) prophetically to her captive audience from out of a yet-to-be-realized world in which literature has at last divorced itself from philosophy, having transcended its oppressive subordination to that discipline's ideas of what reason and knowledge and experience and passionate speech might be.

Pronouncing the end of this currently forced or cursed marriage between philosophy and literature (or art more generally) is evidently related to the project of emancipating the female voice (in philosophy, in literature, in western culture). The fact that the male voice of philosophy is, in Coetzee's staging, primarily embodied in Costello's daughter-in-law does not so much conflict with this suspicion as inflect it, by suggesting that women are no less capable of subjecting themselves to coercively masculine tones of speech and thought than men are capable of disclosing feminine registers of the human voice within their own expressions. Such a suggestion fits with Cavell's more general understanding of how Freud's account of human subjectivity should be understood: and it supports his more specific claim that the women of the melodramas participate in what Freud regards as the hysteric's distinctive capacity for conversion – 'a psychophysical aptitude for transposing very large sums of excitation into the somatic innervation': that is, a capacity for modifying the body as such, rather than allowing the excitation to transpose into consciousness or to discharge itself in practice.

Elizabeth Costello cannot be said to have difficulties transposing her excessive agitation into consciousness or discharging it into her linguistic practice; but the mode of its transposition into words could certainly be thought of as modifying the body of our language as such (call it 'semantic innervation'). For just like Cavell's unknown women, Coetzee's Costello aims to reconfigure the entire circle of our moral concepts. Where they seek to create the conditions in which they might reclaim a voice in their own history and so a distinctively female voice in the conversation of humankind, Costello seeks to create the conditions in which animals might speak to and through specifically human animals on behalf of the fellowship of animate being. As Emerson almost said, around every circle of embodied knowledge, another circle always waits to be drawn; the human animal's vulnerability to experience is inherently (although not of course inveterately) inordinate – always capable of exceeding its known bounds or limits.

In this respect, Elizabeth and her cinematic sisters draw attention to a phenomenon of the moral life of language users that is largely passed over or even positively repressed in philosophy. For each finds that – as Emerson would put it – every word another speaks might either cheer or chagrin us, not so much because they use those words to make assertions that are true or false in some particular respect, as because they make up an inhabitable discursive universe (one whose inhabitants can render themselves intelligible to one another, and thereby enable each other's achievement of genuine individuality) or fail entirely to do so. For them, the offer of marriage (and the possibility of its refusal, whether on each new day of its continuation or before it can even begin) discloses a world as such (a field of existential and expressive possibilities), and asks whether it elicits our assent or our aversion (in the name of some other available or at least conceivable world, some unattained but attainable city of words).

In this respect, Cavell's work on unknown women aligns itself with his treatment of two other mythological locales – adolescence and midlife crises. On his conception, adolescence is an epistemologically and politically significant rite of passage:

> When the world's legitimacy comes to rest upon consent – when the public world is something that each individual has at some moment to agree to join – then adolescence is invented as the time for preparing for that agreement and is ended by it ... The world posed before it, beckoning it, is a field of possibilities ... [I]nstead of opening secrets to you, it informs you that it has none, that what you see is all there is to it.
>
> You wish to be presented with a world you can want, to which you give yourself. [But] the world as a whole [may] present itself ... as uninhabitable; [it may elicit] disgust [or] repugnance. [14]

In the same way, Cavell identifies the phenomenology of a midlife crisis as figured in the opening lines of Dante's *Divine Comedy*: 'At the mid-point of the path through life, I found myself lost in a wood so dark, the way ahead was blotted out.' Dante's narrator's condition is not best understood as confronting a specific obstacle on his way, or a particular limitation in his character; it is one of general bewilderment, of an absolute loss of orientation, an inability to conceive of himself as having a path to follow at all. And Cavell's treatment of literary and cinematic treatments of marriage identifies an analogous condition: one which incarnates the possibility and necessity of bringing a world as such under judgement.

Dialogical theology

As we saw, Nietzsche's madman ends by claiming that 'lightning and thunder require time, the light of the stars requires time, deeds require time ... before they can be seen and heard'. But time is not just the condition for narrative (for intelligible sequences of human activity in a coherent world); it is also the condition for genuine conversation, for a sane mode of speech in the sense to which Kant aspires, one in which individuals explore their commonalities and distances, and so extend their understandings of one another and of themselves. The meet and happy intercourse of the remarriage comedies would exemplify such conversations, and the baulked, ironized and impotent exchanges of the melodramas would embody its negation. And here the sources I have thus far laid out make contact with one other thinker, whose engagement with Dostoevsky is much more direct.

Rowan Williams's commentary on Dostoevsky's religious understanding of the world is anchored in the following vision:

> The only [moral and spiritual] advance ... is in time, in the history of struggle and self-purification. The radical and destructive temptation is to halt time itself, [whether] by refusing certain sorts of future as morally unthinkable ... [or by regarding such possible futures as merely deferred, and hence inevitable].
>
> [These are among] the strategies we devise to take ourselves out of time – out of *narrative,* it is tempting to say. To settle for the truth in the sense of that ensemble of finished propositions we can securely defend is one of the ways of removing ourselves from the narrative continuum of our lives; to opt for Christ in the face of this is to accept that we shall not arrive within history at a stage where there are no choices and no commitments to be made. The truth of defensible propositions, a truth demanding assent as if belief were *caused* by facts, generates a diminished view of what is human; it educates us in ignoring aspects of human narrative that we disapprove of or find impenetrable.[15]

For Williams's Dostoevsky, denying the narrative form of human existence amounts to denying the historicality and temporality of the self, and so its freedom – its freedom to shape its identity over time. This leads Williams to say more than once that the devil is 'the enemy of narrative', because 'he is out to stop history'.[16] And even when Dostoevsky's Devil portrays himself (in his conversation with Ivan Karamazov) as the force that ensures the continuation of events, and so of history, he isn't exactly disproving Williams's claim. For what he thereby declares is an unwillingness to assent prematurely to the universal hosanna that Ivan rules out of court in principle – a desire to defer the moment at which a divine apotheosis of history and time is actually attained. But on Williams's reading, Dostoevsky himself aspires to a position which neither assumes nor denies any such preordained triumph of Christ – because both alternatives amount to a kind of moral closure, in which the future is utterly clear, as if entirely in the possession of the present, and hence history is hollowed out, no longer viewable as the arena for individual struggle and self-definition, but merely a medium in which to mark time. A theologically adequate conception of temporality and historicality would be one in which the future is always open, 'with the possibility of future choices, future events',[17] in which silence, insanity or suicide are not inevitable, but not because timeless, ecstatic acceptance of God's will is inevitable instead.

What we really have, therefore, is a contrast between diabolical and divine modes of narrative – between the Devil's world in which 'humanity is given roles to play, songs to sing, even emotions to enjoy, in which rebellion is catered for in advance', a world which 'will have in its relation to its rulers the kind of transparency that might be expected in a fictional character's relation to an author',[18] and the world of Christ, in which contingency repeatedly escapes control in just the way that Dostoevsky's characters repeatedly appear to escape their author's control and understanding, with neither their coherence nor their narrative trajectory reflective of any easy harmonic resolutions, any sense that their author possesses their future.

The Christian narrative option leads naturally to a fundamentally dialogic understanding of character and so of personal identity, insofar as one central mode in which one closes oneself off to contingency and alteration is by closing oneself off from others. To enter into conversation is to enter into openness not simply because it acknowledges others as part of a world that exists and is at work outside our control, but more specifically insofar as it opens us to the possibility of being surprised by something another may say – whether about us or about whatever it is that concerns us in our conversation. Even if what surprises us is something we take to be a misunderstanding of what we said and did, we can either reject it as such and return to our starting points, or take responsibility for the mis-recognition and explore the options for expressing ourselves that we did not take, and thus the unnoticed element in ourselves that we have ignored – areas of ourselves that have been hidden or alien or simply not worked through. And what applies to us applies to the other: acknowledging that I misspeak myself prompts me to allow time for the probing of another's misspeaking, as opposed to assuming that the words I am confronted with represent utterly self-sufficient and internally coherent closure.

As Williams notes, this view of the nature of conversation has implications for its narrative representation:

> Inconsistency is the energy of the novel, not because of any supposed exaltation of the arbitrary ... but because it is this which animates the process of dialogue. If I am hidden from myself, it is not because there is a buried identity which sustained introspection ... can exhume, but because my identity is in the future, unfolding itself as it is formed in speech, and thus in encounter.[19]

Generating such animation requires a very particular kind of relation between author and character:

> The author does not *contend* with his or her characters, and so does not appear as *a* character in any simple sense. In whatever it is that moves the interaction and discourse of the characters towards life and definition rather than death, we can see the authorial energy that makes a narrative of the whole rather than an assemblage of disconnected reporting. But that energy ... cannot be coercive, must act only through the provision of the time in which response can be made and exchanged. In a word, the author takes responsibility for the time in which the narrative unfolds, setting out the landscape in which each is given the possibility of speaking and hearing. The moment of response in the continuing dialogue is itself the gift of a future; that is the mode in which the authorial initiative is present within the text itself.[20]

And this relation reflects the relation between God and his creatures:

> Christ ... is a presence within the historical narrative that perfectly and unconditionally gives time and space to others in the way the creator does, so that there is the possibility for every character to find his destiny in relation specifically to him. He is the 'last word', not as the force which provides the final episode in a sequence or closes down the otherness of other characters, but as the presence with whom ultimately every speaker may discover an exchange that is steadily and unfailingly life-giving and free of anxiety. Christ is, within history, the possibility for us of a future without fear of the other, an assurance that within other and more conflicted dialogues there is still the potential for life.[21]

In other words, while the Christian faith regards one particular human narrative as basic, it does not lend itself to being narrated in a way that would foreclose the possibilities of failure or cost (by, e.g. underwriting a providential narrative of history, or positing an inevitable realization of some ideal state of individual and collective life). Christianity rather exemplifies the conviction that there is something that makes it worthwhile continuing the narration, and thus the processes of self-defining which narrative works with, because divine purpose cannot be extinguished even if it can be defeated in any one measurable time span. This, one might say, is the narrative equivalent of negative theology; and what makes a narrative religious in this sense is not that it opts for a certain kind of closure but rather that it avoids any kind of closure – even one which offers this thesis about how the Incarnation might ground a theory of the novel, what one might call a theology of narrative. For Dostoevsky's narrative universe also contains the Devil's theory of the novel as perpetual restlessness, just one damn thing after another.

Dostoevsky and Tarkovsky's unknown women

We're now finally in a position to interweave the various concepts and perspectives I've been articulating so as to bring out the aspects of Dostoevsky's work that I was most struck by when I re-read it for the purposes of this volume. *Devils* (otherwise known as *The Possessed* or *Demons*) is my proof-text: and what leapt out to me, in the light of Brooks's, Cavell's and Williams's work, was that what Williams calls its 'typology of diabolical victories'[22] could be seen to be organized around the phenomenon of unknownness and its distinctive modes of negating conversation.[23] When Williams enumerates that typology, he is – like most commentators – primarily preoccupied with the men of the novel: with Nikolai Stavrogin and Peter Verkhovensky in the first instance, and then with the other prominent male figures that make up their secret revolutionary circle. But this occludes the large number of women who play significant roles in the narrative: in particular, it gives little salience either to Varvara Stavrogina (the patron of Peter's father, Stepan), or to the three women who orbit around Stavrogin – Marya Lebydakina (the lame and mentally ill woman who is revealed to be Stavrogin's wife), Lizaveta Tushina (who is briefly Stavrogin's lover) and Darya Shatova (who maintains a mysteriously intimate relation to Stavrogin).

Williams's willingness to let these four women recede into the background of his analysis amounts to transposing and redoubling their unknownness: just as the society of their 'undistinguished little town' offers no space for them to exercise their talents or otherwise acknowledge the individuality of their existence, so his critical commentary passes over the nature of their condition and the particular mode of its manifestation. As Cavell's conception would lead us to expect, a crucial dimension of the melodramatic mode of Dostoevsky's art here is constituted by their modes of speech – by the theatricality of its aspiration to absolute or hysterical expressiveness (in the case of Varvara and Liza), which appears as a refusal of (and so as a response to) their society's inclination to deprive them of a voice in their own narrative history (a muteness exemplified in the case of Marya and Dasha).

In many ways the narrative of *Devils* pivots around the two peculiar modes of marriage in which the four are involved: Varvara's relationship with Stepan Verkhovensky, and what one might call the mystery of Stavrogin's marital status (legally married to Marya, carnally betrothed to Liza and spiritually bonded with Dasha). Varvara has spent her widowhood sponsoring Stepan, in the first instance because of his claim to embody an emancipatory confluence of art and politics: he represents to her an indirect way of claiming a voice in contemporary society which speaks in favour of its revolutionary transformation, and for the possibility of an unattained but attainable state of that society within which Varvara might speak for herself. In the terms of Cavell's cinematic mythology, she seeks an education from him, and he entirely fails to show himself worthy of supplying it: more precisely, the voice he gives her – with its patchwork of cliché and citation, and its unending failure to reach a conclusion, to resolve itself into concrete judgement and action – only reinforces her absence from society, and in particular from the kinds of intercourse that might genuinely help to realize an emancipatory revolution of its current terms and conditions.

Stavrogin is both more and less than Stepan in this respect. More, in that he appears to take speech seriously: he does not say a great deal, and often fails to speak when others expect or demand it of him, but whatever he does say (usually with passionate sincerity), he means. It is precisely this reserve, this withdrawal from the ceaseless currents of idle talk that makes up the everyday life of the town, that seems to constitute his attractiveness to his three wives. It's as if they are desperate to interpret his silence as a sign that he shares their refusal of their society's present options for self-expression and self-understanding; as if his unknownness promises a capacity to acknowledge their own, and so a prospect of not only sharing a condition that currently isolates them, but of judging the world that imposes it, and working to overcome it (if only within their relationship). Peter Verkhovensky's obsessive, incessant attempts to discover what Stavrogin really thinks and feels – his ferocious incarnation of what Cavell calls the man's desire to know what the woman knows (about herself) – strongly suggest that this is also how Stavrogin presents himself to men: as a man who appears to embody that distinctively feminine register of the human voice.

Two pivotal scenes or sites in the novel reveal the emptiness of this appearance (at once different from Stepan's hollowness and equal to it). The first occurs the morning after Liza has spent the night with Stavrogin, after the catastrophic festival. The mood is one of black disappointment, with a strong sexual flavour but one which plainly stands for a more pervasive failure. The theme of their conversation is time: they talk of their differing relations to the calendar, and then when Liza makes it clear that their time together is almost over, Stavrogin expresses bewilderment at the idea that they can't stay together, if necessary by running away together. But Liza points out that Stavrogin's other actions have made it impossible for them to live together in any substantial sense – to share a life in time, a life in which their relationship might become real by its diurnal reiteration in the eyes of their community, as opposed to the purest fantasy. Stavrogin's bewilderment shows that he simply has no conception that his already being married to Marya might have any bearing on his relationship with Liza. When Liza is present, Marya might as well not exist; and Liza sees that the same will be true of her should Marya be present. Stavrogin speaks and acts as if these two aspects of his life have no bearing on each other because to do otherwise would be to acknowledge the necessity to choose, and so to make a commitment over time that might be tested by external contingency and inner shifts of feeling.

This sense of utter internal disconnection or atomization is confirmed by Stavrogin's final letter to Dasha, in which he describes himself as incapable of relating intention to action, or of choosing between intentions, or of investing in any idea or value as opposed to toying with it – all in a letter which oscillates repeatedly between urging Dasha to run away with him and warning her against doing so. He has removed himself from what Williams call the narrative continuum of a life; and this letter epitomizes his consequent tendency to gaslight the people, but particularly the women, in his life – to become the Gregory to Ingrid Bergman's Paula in the eponymous film melodrama, by using words in such a way as to detach their addressee from reality and consign them to madness. In one respect, however, he differs from Gregory, although in a way that confirms Cavell's sense of something deathly in such villainous males. For he no sooner despatches this letter, in which he declares that he will leave the town with or without her, than he returns to his family home and commits suicide.

As Stavrogin puts it in that letter: 'One can argue endlessly about everything, but the only thing to emanate from me is negation without magnanimity, without power. Not even negation has come from me.'[24] Negation is itself an act or power or judgement, a refusal, and so a refusal of something: Stavrogin cannot even attain that capacity – he is an absolute absence, a mere appearance of selfhood, an interlocutor without a perspective from which to speak and be spoken to. He is the diabolic negation of the capacity of Cavell's unknown women to negate conversation; for the latter is always a mode of judging their discursive world with a view to creating a possible future in which that refusal might itself be refused. His eventual self-murder precisely matches the death he has dealt out to Marya and Liza, and that would have awaited Dasha, had she gone to the gloomy, boring, isolated Swiss village to which he invited her – had she chosen, as he puts it, 'to bury her life with mine'.[25]

Tarkovsky has repeatedly declared his admiration of and indebtedness to Dostoevsky: he says, for example, in *Sculpting in Time*[26] that 'those traditions in Russian culture that have their beginnings in the work of Dostoevsky ... are of great significance to me'.[27] As the title of that book suggests, he also shares what Williams sees as Dostoevsky's perception of the redemptive possibilities inherent in the open-ended temporality of human existence. In *Sculpting in Time*, he puts it this way: 'Time ... is the flame in which there lives the salamander of the human soul.'[28] Just as the salamander was thought at once to be created by fire and to possess immunity from its destructive power, so humans are both dependent on time and capable of neutralizing or neutering it, and so of negating or denying themselves.

Against that background, it makes sense to ask whether the issues we have identified in *Devils* can also be seen in Tarkovsky's films: and *Mirror* immediately suggests itself. It begins with a long scene in which a female speech therapist helps a young man to overcome a deeply debilitating stutter – to find his voice, or at least one register of that voice. And the film then interweaves its portraits of two women whose relationships with men fail to satisfy them. The first is Aleksei's mother, whose husband apparently abandons the family, leaving her to bring up her children in an isolated rural setting during wartime. She says very little indeed – in large part because her potential interlocutors are few, consisting either of children or neighbours, and the only neighbour we see in any detail is a woman whose ways of speaking and acting utterly fail to establish common conversational ground. The second woman is Aleksei's wife, Natalia: we meet her after their relationship has broken down, mostly as the two bicker over their faults while dividing the labour of parenting their child, Ignat.

Tarkovsky makes two crucial decisions that complicate and purify his achievement. He casts the same actor (Margarita Terekhova) as Aleksei's mother and as Aleksei's wife; and he never allows the adult Aleksei to appear in front of the camera (rather implying an approximate identity between the camera's point of view and his). The second choice strongly suggests that the identity between mother and wife imputed by the first choice is a reflection of Aleksei's perspective: but that hardly fixes its significance. Should we think that he married Natalia because he saw his mother in her, or that his childhood memories of his abandoned mother have been inflected by his relationship with Natalia? Aleksei makes remarks that push us in both directions – first by saying (when we first see his wife, or rather Terekhova playing his wife) that he'd always claimed that Natalia looked like his mother; then by saying that Natalia's presence in his life had led to his mother taking on her appearance in his memories. Does this explain the failure of his own marriage ('I failed to establish a relationship of mutual acknowledgement with Natalia because my mother failed to do so with me: she fixed for me an image of women as essentially unknowable'), or is it just a further expression of that failure ('Natalia has declared herself unknowable by and to me, and thereby her judgement of me as insufficient to satisfy her, so I now see my mother's remoteness as an aspect of her own judgement of my father')?

Here, however, we have to remember that both remarks occur in one of Aleksei's mutually lacerating conversations with Natalia, so neither needs to be taken as a sincere expression of his views, as opposed (say) as part of an attempt to defend himself or to wound her. In that same conversation, Natalia describes their marriage as one in which they could never talk like normal human beings; and she traces this negation of meet and happy conversation to Aleksei's assumption that his mere presence will automatically make those near to him happy, and to his ability only to demand. Aleksei in turn presents these putative deficiencies of his character as a consequence of being brought up by women (by one woman in particular), and advises Natalia to marry (again) in order to ensure that the same fate doesn't befall Ignat.

Set aside for a moment the depth of their mutual desire to wound, and assume that they're well placed to maximize the injury inflicted by directing it at acknowledged weak points. How might a child acquire the idea that to relate to a woman is to demand something of her – at root, to demand that she be made happy by his mere existence? Most likely because his mother responded to him as if he were making just such a demand on her, a response which presupposes that she isn't in fact made happy by him, and that she denies this failure on her part (to respond as every mother might be expected to) by reinterpreting it as a refusal to accede to a sheer or pure demand made by her child. The child, knowing that she wasn't in fact made happy by his sheer existence, learns to think of his mere existence as embodying a demand, and goes on to make the same demand of Natalia, So when she refuses to be made happy by his mere presence in their marriage – when she expects him to show some willingness to participate in their conversation in a way that might actually earn a meet and happy response from her, and so acknowledge her as free to withhold it – he takes her to be judging the worth of his existence as such, rather than refusing the terms on which it is currently staked. And he worries that Ignat will find himself similarly forced to demand acknowledgement from her, and similarly condemned to suffer its absence.

What anchors this whole diagnostic structure is thus the child's interpretation of his mother's interpretation of him. But it is a child's interpretation; and simply to reiterate it as an adult is to fail to acknowledge that his mother was not reducible to her parental role; she was also a woman, and one abandoned by her husband. So when he recalls his mother as remote, uncommunicative and essentially self-contained, as if judging her world and finding it inadequate (including her children), he ought to be asking himself how far this was a response to a man's refusal to acknowledge her worth – to acknowledge her as a meet and happy conversation partner – rather than an unmediated response to her child. And insofar as he doesn't ask himself this question, he aligns himself with his father. So when he worries about what Ignat might learn from his mother, he fails to acknowledge his own responsibility for the absence of Ignat's father from Ignat's home, and for whatever impact that absence might have on the face Ignat's mother might find herself presenting to him.

When Philip Larkin notes that the misery man hands on to man deepens like a coastal shelf, he recommends not having children (as well as ending your own existence in time). But whatever misery Aleksei's parents have handed on to him and Natalia, Tarkovsky gives us reason to hope that Ignat might escape his patrimony. The sequence in which, after being left in his absent father's apartment by his mother, he encounters a mysterious woman (and her maid) is at once riveting and utterly resistant to interpretation. However, looked at from the angle I have been constructing, it has a mysteriously apt and undeniably emancipatory atmosphere. Poised in a space created as one parent departs before the other arrives, Ignat submits to the authority of a genuinely unknown woman, and reads out a letter by Pushkin which identifies Russia as itself attaining unknownness (in relation to Western Europe and to Christianity) while affirming his own wholehearted identification with it. By taking on (the feminine register of) that masculine voice, Ignat renders himself unknowable to his grandmother, who arrives at his door immediately after his recitation only to declare that she has the wrong address – quite as if denying that her grandson is hers. But to deny his relation to her is to free him from his genealogical inheritance: it is to show that and how a kind of receptivity to time's passage can disclose and realize its evanescence – the inevitable and beautiful evanescence of the slowly disappearing condensation mark left by the unknown woman's glass of tea, to which Tarkovsky's camera gravitates and with which it leaves us.

NOTES

Editor's introduction

1 Grace Whistler, *Camus' Literary Ethics: Between Form and Content* (London: Palgrave Macmillan, 2020).
2 David Whyte, 'Seeking Language Large Enough', *On Being with Krista Tippet* (7 April 2016), https://onbeing.org/programs/david-whyte-seeking-language-large-enough/ (accessed 12 April 2025).
3 Martha Craven Nussbaum, *Poetic Justice: The Literary Imagination and Public Life* (Boston: Beacon Press, 1995), 12.
4 Richard Posner, 'Against Ethical Criticism', *Philosophy and Literature* 21, no. 2 (1997): 5.

1 Reading as a way of seeing: Literature and the perception of place

1 Edward Said, *Culture and Imperialism* (London: Vintage, [1993] 1994), 80.
2 Ibid.
3 Jeff Malpas, 'Is There an Ethics of Place?' *Localities* 2 (2012): 22.
4 Ibid.
5 Ibid., 24.
6 For more on the concept of the 'sense of place', see Indranil Acharya and Ujjwal Kumar Panda, 'Sense of Place: Humanistic Geography, Literature, and Spatial Identity', in *Geographical Imaginations: Literature and the 'Spatial Turn'* (Oxford: Oxford University Press, 2022), 20–54.
7 Seamus Heaney, 'The Sense of Place', in *Preoccupations: Selected Prose 1968–1978* (London: Faber, 1984), Kindle, part II.
8 Jamaica Kincaid, *A Small Place* (New York: Farrar, Straus and Giroux, 1988).

9 Virginia Woolf, *Mrs Dalloway* (Hertfordshire: Wordsworth Classics), 3–4.
10 Jeff Malpas, *Place and Experience: A Philosophical Topography* (Oxon: Routledge, 2018), 34.
11 Much has been written about *Mrs Dalloway* and London. See, for instance, Miroslav Beker, 'London as a Principle of Structure in *Mrs. Dalloway*', *Modern Fiction Studies* 18, no. 3 (1972): 375–85. My concern in this essay is not just with the function and portrayal of London in Woolf's novel, but – to reiterate – with the ways in which the novel's manner of wedding London and human experience is an example that showcases literature's capacity of capturing the intricacies and impressions of place which, in turn, could encourage a more ethical relationship with it.
12 Woolf, *Mrs Dalloway*, 7.
13 Ibid., 18.
14 Ibid.
15 Ibid., 52.
16 Alexandra Burlina, whose translation of Shklovsky's well-known essay I am using here, stresses that 'in terms of effect *enstrangement* [which should not be confused with *estrangement*] is close to Shklovsky's neologism [*ostranenie*], which is itself enstranging. Unfortunately, this choice of word … did not catch on.' See Berlina's introduction in Victor Shklovsky, 'Art, Device', trans. Alexandra Berlina, *Poetics Today* 36, no. 3 (2015): 152–4.
17 Shklovsky, 'Art, Device', 162.
18 Ibid.
19 Jacques Rancière has demonstrated how modern literary writing, as exemplified in the novel, is based on a 'regime of expressivity' and not on one of causal representation, that is, on the power of words to *express*, thanks to language, the *poeticity* of objects. For 'poetry [after Vico] is no longer the activity that produces poems; it is the quality of poetic objects'. Any object, as a result, is doubled, being both 'a set of properties' and 'the manifestation of an essence', that of the power of language that 'produced it'. That is to say, poeticity manifests the object and conceals the power of language that made that object visible; it expresses rather than represents the object. See Jacques Rancière, *Mute Speech: Literature, Critical Theory, and Politics*, trans. James Swenson (New York: Columbia University Press, [1998] 2011), 59–60.
20 Tahir Wattar, *The Earthquake*, trans. William Granara (London: Saqi Books, [1974] 2000), 166.
21 Ibid., 25.
22 Ibid.

23 Ibid., 26.
24 Ibid.
25 Ibid., 29.
26 Frantz Fanon, *The Wretched of the Earth*, trans. Richard Philcox (New York: Grove Press, [1963] 2004), 128.
27 Ibid.
28 Wattar, *The Earthquake*, 33.
29 Ibid., 33–4.
30 Ibid., 50–1.
31 Ibid., 51.
32 Ibid., 109.
33 Ibid., 114.
34 Ibid., 135.
35 Ibid.
36 Mourid Barghouti, *I Saw Ramallah*, trans. Ahdaf Soueif (London: Bloomsbury, [1997] 2004), 87.
37 Ibid., 6.
38 Ibid., 23.
39 Ibid., 88.
40 Ibid., 140.
41 Ibid., 38.
42 Ibid., 41.
43 Ibid., 66.
44 Ibid.
45 Ibid., 63.
46 Ibid., 31.
47 Ibid.
48 Rancière explains: 'Politics revolves around what is seen and what can be said about it, around who has the ability to see and the talent to speak, around the properties of spaces and the possibilities of time.' Jacques Rancière, *The Politics of Aesthetics: The Distribution of the Sensible*, trans. Gabriel Rockhill (London: Continuum, [2000] 2004), 13. Rancière, perhaps, was not thinking of occupation, but the occupation here does illuminate and illustrate his argument about aesthetics and politics, about the relationship between the visible and the sayable.
49 Barghouti, *I Saw Ramallah*, 141.
50 Ibid., 69.
51 Ibid.
52 For instance: 'Ein al-Deir is not a place, it is a time. Evidence of the last rain that we see on our shoes even though our eyes tell us it has dried ... Ein al-Deir is specifically the time of Mourid as a child', and 'Ammi Ibrahim, a peasant and hunter'; Ibid., 87.

53 Ibid., 143.
54 Ibid., 144.
55 John Berger, *Landscapes: John Berger on Art* (London: Verso, 2016), 62.
56 Abdelfattah Kilito, *The Clash of Images*, trans. Robyn Creswell (New York: New Directions Books, [1996] 2010), 94.
57 Ibid., 95.
58 Ibid., 97.
59 Ibid., 97–8.
60 Ibid., 98.
61 Ibid., 99.
62 Ibid., 100.
63 Ibid., 102.
64 Andrey Tarkovsky, *Sculpting in Time*, trans. Kitty Hunter-Blair (Austin: University of Texas Press, [1985] 1989), 66.
65 Ibid.
66 Ibid.
67 Ibid., 67.

2 'My non-alibi in being': Bakhtinian ethics and the literary dynamics of subjectivity

Note: In view of the complex publication history of Bakhtin's works, the dates given in parenthesis indicate the approximate time of the writing and the (often much later) time of the text's first publication in Russian. The precise periodization of the various texts is still in progress.

1 See Daphna Erdinast-Vulcan, 'Bakhtin's Homesickness: A Late Reply to Julia Kristeva', *Textual Practice* 9, no. 2 (1995): 223–42. Daphna Erdinast-Vulcan, 'Borderlines and Contraband: Bakhtin and the Question of the Subject', *Poetics Today* 18, no. 2 (1997): 251–69. Daphna Erdinast-Vulcan, '"The I That Tells Itself": A Bakhtinian Perspective on Narrative Identity', *Narrative* 16, no. 1 (2008): 1–15. Daphna Erdinast-Vulcan, 'Borderline Subjectivity: The Futurity of the Present in Bakhtin's Work', *Partial Answers* 8, no. 1 (2010): 169–83. Daphna Erdinast-Vulcan, *Between Philosophy and Literature: Bakhtin and the Question of the Subject* (Stanford: Stanford University Press, 2013). Daphna Erdinast-Vulcan, 'Between Representation and Performance: A Bakhtinian Perspective on Literature and Ethics', in *Values of Literature*, ed. Hanna

Meretoja, Pirjo Lyytikäinen, Saija Isomaa and Kristina Malmio (Amsterdam: Rodopi, 2015), 63–77. Daphna Erdinast-Vulcan, 'Heterobiography: A Bakhtinian Approach to Autobiographical Writing', *Life-Writing* 15, no. 3 (2018): 413–30. Rpt. in *Philosophy and Life Writing*, ed. Christopher Cowley and D. L. Mahieu (Milton Park: Routledge), 108–25. Daphna Erdinast-Vulcan, '"New Philosophical Wonder": Bakhtin, Shklovsky, and the Re-enchantment of the World', in *Understanding Bakhtin, Understanding Modernism*, ed. Philippe Birgy (London: Bloomsbury, 2024), 149–61.

2 I am grateful to the Israel Science Foundation (ISF) for the generous support of my engagement with this ongoing project.

3 Mikhail M. Bakhtin, *Toward a Philosophy of the Act*, trans. and with notes by Vadim Liapunov, ed. Michael Holquist and Vadim Liapunov (Austin: University of Texas Press, [1921–2/1986] 1993).

4 Ibid., 8–9.

5 Ibid., 6.

6 Ibid., 38.

7 Ibid., 42; see also 40.

8 For a full discussion of this concept, see Erdinast-Vulcan, *Between Philosophy and Literature: Bakhtin and the Question of the Subject*, 129 and *passim*.

9 Julia Kristeva, 'The Ruin of a Poetics', in *Russian Formalism*, ed. Stephen Bann and John E. Bowle (Edinburgh: Scottish University Press, [1970] 1973), 102–19. Julia Kristeva, 'From One Identity to an Other', in *Desire in Language: A Semiotic Approach to Literature and Art*, trans. Thomas Gora, Alice Jardine and Leon S. Roudiez, ed. Leon S. Roudiez (New York: Columbia University Press, [1969] 1980), 124–47. Julia Kristeva, 'Word, Dialogue and Novel', in *Desire in Language: A Semiotic Approach to Literature and Art*, trans. Thomas Gora, Alice Jardine and Leon S. Roudiez, ed. Leon S. Roudiez (New York: Columbia University Press, [1969] 1980), 64–91.

10 Mikhail M. Bakhtin, 'Author and Hero in Aesthetic Activity', in *Art and Answerability: Early Philosophical Essays by M. M. Bakhtin*, trans. Vadim Liapunov, ed. Michael Holquist and Vadim Liapunov (Austin: University of Texas Press, [1922–4/1977–8] 1990), 4–256.

11 Ibid., 91.

12 Ibid., 142–3.

13 Ibid., 35–6.

14 Ibid., 82–3.

15 Ibid., 14.

16 Ibid., 59; italics in the original.

17 Ibid., 188–9.

18 Alasdair MacIntyre, *After Virtue: A Study in Moral Theory*, 2nd edition (London: Duckworth, 1980).
19 Paul Ricoeur, 'Life: A Story in Search of a Narrator', trans. J. N. Kraay and A. J. Scholten, in *Facts and Values*, ed. M. C. Doeser and J. N. Kraay (Dordrechet: Martinus Nijhoff Publishers, 1986), 121–32. Paul Ricoeur, *Oneself as Another*, trans. K. Blamey (Chicago: The University of Chicago Press, 1992).
20 For an extensive discussion of Bakhtin's position with regard to the 'narrative identity thesis', see Erdinast-Vulcan, 'The I that Tells Itself'.
21 Bakhtin, 'Author and Hero in Aesthetic Activity', 100.
22 Ibid., 119.
23 Ibid., 109.
24 Ibid., 14.
25 Ibid., 118.
26 Ibid., 17; see also 20.
27 Mikhail M. Bakhtin, *Problems in Dostoevsky's Poetics*, trans. and ed. Caryl Emerson, intr. Wayne C. Booth (Minneapolis: University of Minnesota Press, [1929] 1984), 49.
28 Ibid., 53.
29 Ibid., 63.
30 Ibid., 53.
31 For a full discussion of the Bakhtinian shift from representation to performance, see Erdinast-Vulcan, 'Between Representation and Performance'.
32 Bakhtin, *Problems in Dostoevsky's Poetics*, 59.
33 Ibid., 287.
34 Ibid., 59.
35 Ibid., 287–8; italics in the original.
36 Bakhtin, 'Author and Hero in Aesthetic Activity', 142–3.
37 Ibid., 83; see also 118.
38 Ibid., 126.
39 Ibid., 119.
40 Ibid., 14.
41 Ibid., 100.
42 This distinction between the 'aesthetic' and the 'ethical' mode of being was already made by Bakhtin, albeit in a muted and fragmented form, in *Toward a Philosophy of the Act*, where Bakhtin already notes the irreducible difference between aesthetic seeing (based on what he would later call 'outsideness'), and the 'world that is correlated with me' (his concept of 'I-for-myself') which is 'fundamentally and essentially incapable of becoming part of an aesthetic architectonic' (74–5). In the same fragment, Bakhtin writes of the 'temptation of aestheticism', that is, the temptation to act out

a conception of oneself through the eyes of the other, which must be resisted by the intensely situated, participative, and answerable subject (18).

43 Bakhtin, 'Author and Hero in Aesthetic Activity', 112.

44 Ibid., 145.

45 Ibid., 117.

46 Ibid.

47 Ibid., 109.

48 Viktor Shklovsky, 'Art as Technique', in *Russian Formalist Poetics: Four Essays*, trans. and intr. Lee T. Lemon and Marion J. Reis (Lincoln: University of Nebraska Press, [1917] 1965), 3–24.

49 For a full discussion of the affinities between Shklovsky and Bakhtin, see Erdinast-Vulcan, 'New Philosophical Wonder'.

50 See Bakhtin, *Problems in Dostoevsky's Poetics*, 287–8.

51 Joseph Conrad, *Heart of Darkness* (London: The Dent Uniform Edition, [1899] 1923).

52 Chinua Achebe, 'An Image of Africa: Racism in Conrad's "Heart of Darkness"', *The Massachussetts Review* 18, no. 4 (winter 1977). Rpt. *The Massachusetts Review* 57, no. 1 (Spring 2016): 14–27.

53 Conrad, *Heart of Darkness*, 48.

54 Ibid., 49–50.

55 Ibid., 51.

56 Ibid., 50–1.

3 Cows on the highroad: Making ethical literary criticism real

1 I attempted a summary of these in John Krapp, *An Aesthetics of Morality: Pedagogic Voice and Moral Dialogue in Mann, Camus, Conrad, and Dostoevsky* (Columbia: University of South Carolina Press, 2002), 2.

2 The early wave of texts by Wayne Booth, *The Company We Keep: An Ethics of Fiction* (Berkeley: University of California Press, 1988); Christopher Clausen, *The Moral Imagination: Essays on Literature and Ethics* (Iowa City: University of Iowa Press, 1986); John Gardner, *On Moral Fiction* (New York: Basic Books, 1977); J. Hillis Miller, *The Ethics of Reading* (New York: Columbia University Press, 1986); Martha Craven Nussbaum, *The Fragility of Goodness: Luck and Ethics in Greek Tragedy and Philosophy* (Cambridge: Cambridge University Press, 1986); Martha Craven Nussbaum, *Love's Knowledge: Essays on Philosophy and Literature* (Oxford: Oxford

University Press, 1990); Frank Palmer, *Literature and Moral Understanding* (Oxford: Clarendon Press, 1992); David Parker, *Ethics, Theory, and the Novel* (Cambridge: Cambridge University Press, 1994); James Phelan, ed., *Reading Narrative: Form, Ethics, Ideology* (Columbus: Ohio State University Press, 1989); Richard Rorty, *Contingency, Irony, and Solidarity* (Cambridge: Cambridge University Press, 1989); and Tobin Siebers, *Morals and Stories* (New York: Columbia University Press, 1992) that entered the post-structuralist moment and catalysed the 'ethical turn' with arguments to 'rehabilitate' ethical literary criticism remains seminal and continues to be cited by so much of the writing that followed to the present day. A look at the essays collected in James Harold, ed., *The Oxford Handbook of Ethics and Art* (Oxford: Oxford University Press, 2023) will provide a good sense of the quality and scope of the most contemporary scholarship in the field.

3 Another way of saying something similar is in Michael Eskin, 'On Literature and Ethics', *Poetics Today* 25, no. 4 (2004): 'Insofar as we take literature to be ethically significant in an exemplary way, we may want to start thinking about locating its ethical force not so much in its referential makeup and thematics – for reasons that I shall clarify – as in, among other things, what I would call, for lack of a better term, its discursive-transformational "capaciousness", that is, in its ability to absorb and transform virtually any kind of discourse, including the discourse of ethics' (575). The operational metaphors in Eskin's claim – transform, absorb, capaciousness – insofar as they all measure change, can only signify in time.

In the coming years, we are likely to see growing research into the *cognitive* basis for literature's ethically instructive dimension. Referencing Mark Johnson, *Moral Imagination: Implications of Cognitive Science for Ethics* (Chicago: University of Chicago Press, 1993) to discuss the way our minds make sense of things; John Rethorst, 'Moral Density: Why Teaching Art Is Teaching Ethics', *Philosophy and Literature* 43, no. 1 (2019) explains, 'Reason cannot, initially, connect dots. Connections and resulting recognition are made with what cognitive science calls prototype theory, in opposition to the more traditional and readily accepted category theory. While the latter operates deductively, prototype recognition is fundamentally imaginative. While category specifies that recognition of an object occurs because the parts of the object meet necessary and sufficient conditions for identification of it, prototype posits that we recognize something because it resembles objects in our experience. There are no preexisting conditions for the second dot' (157) and cites Nancy Sherman,

The Fabric of Character (Oxford: Clarendon Press, 1989) to move his argument forward: 'Something must be ready to initiate moral thinking: whatever makes us look to principles for guidance cannot itself be a principle. In any given circumstance, the "reading, or reaction, is informed by ethical considerations expressive of the agent's virtue. Perception is thus informed by the virtues .... Much of the work of virtue will rest in knowing how to construe the case"' (29). Literature can be that something due to its peculiar 'density', a term Rethorst borrows from Iris Murdoch, *Metaphysics as a Guide to Morals* (New York: Penguin Books, 1992), to then paraphrase the assertion of Nelson Goodman, *Languages of Art* (Indianapolis: Hackett Publishing Company, 1976) that 'a work of art contains an uncounted number of referents, so constructed that between any two points, there is room for a third. There is thus no limit or priority, or necessary distinction, among the referents ... Each element might add something, and it's hard to say which elements add how much, or which contributions are most important ... The number, variety, and density of referents is sufficient that paraphrase ... of the artwork is impossible. To do so would require that, from the density and profusion of referents, a finite number be extracted. To do that requires prioritizing. Abstraction and extraction by their nature omit something and, when the original has aesthetic dimensions, Goodman would say that there is no guarantee that this something left out is not critical to the meaning of the whole work. The omissions impoverish the experience of the original' (168–9). Rethorst concludes that prototype theory would be one way to map literature, via its density, onto the moral domain: 'A prototype is never necessarily finished or complete. Its only requirement is that it be something like its reference. Category has to be complete to make sense, while prototype evolves as we develop a better understanding of its reference. While certain aspects of a moral situation are of course more important than others, it may be hard to list aspects in order of relevance, or to find a rule that says this or that facet of the situation is not worthy of consideration. Nor can an observer be certain that paraphrase of the situation captures all its meaning. Thus *the aesthetic and the moral share density*, seminal to perception and conducive to the connection of metaphor' (169).

4 I do not attempt to differentiate among genres of 'literature' here because I contend that it little matters whether the conflict is expressed among characters, between reader and text, or via any other configuration of voices that may inform exegesis. What matters is the dialogue, whether explicit or implicit, interior or exterior, generated

by the act of reading. Dialogue between characters in a narrative text is only a more obvious, immediate site of ideological tension.

5 I might be able to assert what I, and perhaps a coterie of others, believe to be a compelling thematic assessment of Leo Tolstoy's major fiction that finds the cures for all of contemporary western culture's ills in his novels, but it would not likely resonate with readers unwilling to commit to working through the thousands of pages of his fiction on which my argument is based.

6 Mark Kingwell, 'The Ethics of Ethics and Literature', *World Literature Today* 88, no. 5 (2014) identifies this problem, if it may be so called, in an elegant reflection that includes an assessment I find in sympathy with my own: 'Moral instruction is thus much more like a conversation than it is like an algorithm' (26).

7 What Robert Eaglestone, 'One and the Same? Ethics, Aesthetics, and Truth', *Poetics Today* 25, no. 4 (2004) calls the 'mismatch between lived experience and text' (604) in his excellent delineation of what he names the 'neo-Aristotelian' and 'deconstructive' wings of ethical literary criticism, which he summarizes thus: 'Both of these "wings", while making important points, seem to rely on an idea that literature offers a certain sort of truth, a sort of positivist knowledge, which can offer – or be made to offer – axioms or propositions that correspond, even if not in a strict way, to some form of reality. However heuristically experienced and complex the path, the first "wing" seems very close to offering positivist assertions: a sort of "the moral of the story is ..." claim (perhaps, "be sympathetic"). The second "wing" seems to offer a negative version of the first, showing the impossibility of deriving a "moral from the text" and then leaving us with both the experience of undecidability and particularity and the responsibility for our ineluctable choices. (Perhaps this amounts to a paradoxical axiom that warns "do not trust axioms: each case is different.") In this sense, then, both "wings" of the debate assume certain ideas about the sort of truth and thus the sort of knowledge that the work of art can create. More than this, they also rely on the idea that ethics and literature represent two different fields that need to be joined' (605). Eaglestone is never dismissive of either approach to ethical literary criticism. His point is that neither adequately addresses the question his essay seeks to answer; to wit: how might we understand the Wittgensteinian proposition that 'ethics and aesthetics are one and the same' (595; Eaglestone is citing *Tractatus Logico-Philosophicus* 6.421).

8 I am hardly the only proponent of ethical literary criticism looking for its significance less in any thematic lesson literature may express than in the form of literature's ethically instructive value. Indeed,

I share this space with many ethical literary critics writing during and after the aforementioned 'ethical turn' in theory. Ross Collin, 'Models of Literature and Ethics', *The English Journal* 109, no. 6 (2020), offers a succinct taxonomy of 'models of literature and ethics' and identifies four: 'Transmission, Transaction, Clarification, and Cultural Identity and Difference' (47). On his definitions, I rather clearly fit into his transactional, clarificatory categories.

9 This cognitive need is a matter of some debate, but John Teehan, *In the Name of God: The Evolutionary Origins of Religious Ethics and Violence* (West Sussex: Wiley-Blackwell, 2010) asserts its evolutionary inevitably in his study of the psychological basis of religious violence, a phenomenon with direct relevance to my forthcoming discussion of *The Crucible*. The role literature might play in the dynamics of community was the focus of a special issue of *University of Toronto Quarterly* in summer 2007; Marlene Goldman, ed., 'Introduction: Literature, Imagination, Ethics', *University of Toronto Quarterly* 76, no. 3 (2007): 809–20 provides the overview to its content.

10 Stating this goal, I feel obliged to make special note of the truly exceptional role that Nussbaum, *The Fragility of Goodness, Love's Knowledge*, has played in the field. Her comprehensive scholarship on ethical literary criticism has not only advanced arguments for the ethical value of literature that have been persuasive on their own and helped to refine the scholarship of contemporary colleagues with whom she shares ideological sympathies; it also inspires critics and detractors whose work expands the discourse on literature's ethical significance. The trajectory of her career concretizes the ethically instructive value of dialogue even when no single moral position is privileged, no single lesson learned. There is likely no ethical literary critic more frequently cited. For one of the best article length overviews of Nussbaum's place in the field, of which I am at any rate aware, see the contribution to *Interdisciplinary Literary Studies*' special issue on 'Cultivating Humanity: The Literary and Moral Thought of Martha Nussbaum' of John Wrighton, 'Reading Responsibly Between Martha Nussbaum and Emmanuel Levinas: Towards a Textual Ethics for the Twenty-First Century', *Interdisciplinary Literary Studies* 19, no. 2 (2017): 149–70.

11 Jeffrey Burton Russell, *The Devil: Perceptions of Evil from Antiquity to Primitive Christianity* (Cornell: Cornell University Press, 1977), 123.

12 There will always be people who accept ambiguity as the inscrutable workings of the divine mind, or that God writes straight with crooked lines, or that what is uncertain to human beings is not

inexplicable to a higher source of knowledge. Others may deploy faith to eschew ambiguity outright in order to attain ideological certainty. Faith, however, closes off dialogue of the kind needed for the *production* of practical ethical knowledge in the temporal world. Contrarily, literature offers a site where ideological tension cannot be felicitously resolved through an act of interpretive faith, whatever that might look like, because stories typically move forward through moments of formal disruptions of varying magnitudes that only end when the story does. Literature constructed upon monistic concepts makes certainty that much harder to ascertain.

13 Plato, *The Trial and Death of Socrates*, trans. G. M. A Gruber (Indianapolis: Hackett Publishing Company, 2000), 7.

14 Perhaps this is why Socrates and Plato posit the Forms, Truth in its ideal, metaphysical state, as the final stop in their theory of knowledge. Maybe they believed the Forms could exist side by side with the unknowable authority of divine, monistic gods. Or maybe they needed something to replace these gods because they weren't quite ready to put the authority for their community's values into the mouths of mere mortals. Looking back at Socrates' execution, this certainly looks prescient.

15 Consistently exposing the inconsistencies of fate, Homer's *Iliad* and *Odyssey* critique the very value of honour for which the Myceneans go to war for ten years. Aeschlyus's *Oresteia* contends with the profound ambiguity and ambivalence burgeoning from the shift from the community's investment in the matriarchal, chthonic gods to the more patriarchal Olympians, recasting an impossible verdict on matricide as a straightforward either/or. Euripedes relentlessly displays the contradictions between ethical theory and practice, particularly intergenerationally and among genders, devolving on defining certainty where language will not permit it. Sarai laughs at the news she will bear a child at her age. At the moment Moses is presenting the Ten Commandments, whose first is the confirmation of monotheism, to the Ancient Hebrews, they are committing idolatry.

16 Vergil, *The Aeneid*, trans. Shadi Bartsch (New York: The Modern Library, 2021), xxx.

17 As a quick aside, we know this is true because only a few years later, during Augustus's rule, Jesus suffers state execution by crucifixion on this very charge.

18 Ibid., xxxi.

19 Ibid., 239.

20 In the early Egyptian *Story of Sinuhe* (*c.*1800 BCE), as he catalogues the new king's virtues, Sinuhe describes how 'Wide-striding he smites

the fleeing, / No retreat for him who turns his back;/Steadfast in time of attack, / He makes turn back and turns not his back' in Miriam Lichtheim, ed., *Ancient Egyptian Literature: A Book of Readings. Volume l: The Old and Middle Kingdoms* (Berkeley: University of California Press, 2006), 226. Whether read to mean that the king will not allow surrender and forces enemies to re-engage, or that he will attack them from behind, the message is clear: sometimes, you cannot let your enemies live. The Mycenean Greeks slaughtered the Trojan men and enslaved the women and children they let live. And, in perhaps one of the greatest examples of violence against an out-group in the ancient world in order to reiterate and clarify with certainty a community's values, the Hebrews in the *Book of Joshua* show very little mercy when called to war by God.

21 Vergil, *The Aeneid*, 1.456–7.

22 Ibid., 6.851–3.

23 I refer hereafter to Christianity as the broad term for theologies whose common denominator is acceptance of Jesus Christ as personal saviour. My hope is to avoid misrepresentating even as I perhaps oversimplify the designation.

24 Russell, *The Devil*, 251.

25 Ibid., 258; my emphasis.

26 Jeffrey Burton Russell, *Satan: The Early Christian Tradition* (Cornell: Cornell University Press, 1981), 32.

27 Peirce's emphasis on emotion is part of a nineteenth-century shift towards reassessing the long-acknowledged primacy of reason in epistemology. In *The Antichrist*, trans. Walter Kaufmann (New York: Viking Penguin Inc., 1954), Nietzsche asserts, 'What is good? Everything that heightens the feeling of power in man, the will to power, power itself. What is bad? Everything that is born of weakness. What is happiness? The feeling that power is *growing*, that resistance is overcome' (570) and calls into question over two thousand years of moral philosophy that aligned reason with virtue and happiness.

28 Charles Sanders Peirce, 'The Fixation of Belief', *Popular Science Monthly* 12 (1877): 3.

29 Russell, *Satan*, 100–1.

30 Arthur Miller, *The Crucible* (New York: Penguin Books, 1952), 115.

31 Miller, *The Crucible*, xv.

32 Irrespective of one's particular interpretation of the originary act, from the moment Lucifer defied God and ruptured the stasis of heaven, this breaking of community – between human and human, between human and God – has been the Devil's defining role in the western theological tradition since the beginning of Christianity.

33 Miller, *The Crucible*, xiii, xvii. For a sample of these principles in action drawn from primary source historical documents, see Frances Hill, *The Salem Witch Trials Reader* (Boston: Da Capo Press, 2000), 25–34.
34 Miller, *The Crucible*, xxiv.
35 Ibid., 68. Referencing American Christendom in the mid-twentieth century, Miller explains in one of the play's long notes at the introduction of a new, major character, in this instance, Hale: 'Like Reverand Hale and the others on this stage, we conceive the Devil as a necessary part of a respectable view of cosmology. Ours is a divided empire in which certain ideas and emotions and actions are of God, and their opposites are of Lucifer … The concept of unity, in which positive and negative are attributes of the same force, in which good and evil are relative, ever-changing, and always joined to the same phenomenon – such a concept is still reserved to the physical sciences and to the few who have grasped the history of ideas … it is recalled that until the Christian era the underworld was never regarded as a hostile area, that all gods were useful and essentially friendly to man despite occasional lapses' (31).
36 Miller, *The Crucible*, 61.
37 Ibid., 62.
38 Ibid., 64.
39 Ibid., 87.
40 Ibid., 10.
41 Ibid., 34.
42 Ibid., 35–6.
43 Ibid., 37; my emphasis.
44 Ibid., 43.
45 Ibid., 62.
46 Ibid., 61.
47 Ibid., 66.
48 Ibid.
49 Ibid.
50 Ibid.
51 Ibid., 79.
52 Ibid., 82.
53 Ibid., 91.
54 Ibid., 97.
55 Ibid., 100.
56 Ibid., 103.
57 Ibid., 110.
58 Ibid., 111.
59 Ibid., 120. A more subtle gesture of Danforth's authority is revealed when he attempts to ascertain whether Elizabeth might persuade

Proctor to confess to witchcraft. He begins, 'Pray be at your ease, we come not for your life. We – *uncertain how to plead, for he is not accustomed to it.* Mr. Hale, will you speak with the woman?' (121). Danforth is a man whose power has for decades been reflexively performed.

60 Ibid., 121.

61 Ibid., 122.

62 See, for example, W. Scott Poole, *Satan in America: The Devil We Know* (London: Rowman & Littlefield Publishers, 2009).

63 When Fyodor Dostoevsky was writing what would be his final novel, *The Brothers Karamazov*, he planned a conversation between two brothers on the existence and nature of God. Propelling their debate was a graphic catalogue of horrors and brutalities that human beings visit upon one another. Dostoevsky did not need to apply much creative imagination to contrive these acts: he simply reported stories he had read in the Russian newspapers. It would not take long to adduce a formidable collection of references to the devil in American politics with just a simple search on any web browser to supplement the two I recall here to start the conversation.

64 Nowhere did I find record of a neutral response.

4 Community, self, trust and shared reality in Alice Munro's 'Fits'

1 The story appeared as part of Munro's collection *The Progress of Love* (first published in 1982) and is set, as far as I can tell, in the present of its time of writing.

2 By saying constitutive I do not mean to suggest that these three, exclusive of others, form the foundation of morality, or some such thing. Only that all of them contribute centrally to what morality or ethics *is*, and are kinds of things we need to attend to when trying to make sense of a moral form of life. For an intriguing discussion where all three are reflectively represented is Judith Butler's *Giving an Account of Oneself* (2005). Translating between her discussion and the present one – especially concerning the last of the three – involves some complexities that I will not go into here.

3 Alice Munro, 'Fits', in *The Progress of Love* (London: Vintage, [1982] 2007), 108.

4 Ibid., 108–9.

5 Ibid., 116.

6 Ibid., 118.

7 Ibid., 109.
8 Ibid., 124.
9 Ibid., 126.
10 Ibid.
11 Stanley Cavell, *Disowning Knowledge in Seven Plays of Shakespeare* (Cambridge: Cambridge University Press, 1987). Stanley Cavell, *Must We Mean What We Say* (Cambridge: Cambridge University Press, 1976). Stanley Cavell, *The Claim of Reason: Wittgenstein, Skepticism, Morality, and Tragedy* (New York: Oxford University Press, 1979).
12 Iris Murdoch, *Existentialists and Mystics: Writings on Philosophy and Literature*, ed. P. Conradi (London: Chatto & Windus, 1997).
13 Cavell, *The Claim of Reason*, 337.
14 Munro, 'Fits', 130.
15 Ibid., 109.
16 Ibid., 110.
17 Susan Warwick, 'Alice Munro and the Shame of Murder', in *Ethics and Affects in the Fiction of Alice Munro*, ed. Ameila DeFalco and Lorraine York (Dordrecht: Springer, 2018), 134.
18 This is key to why murder stories are found interesting and engaging: as the ultimate breach of morality, murder, unsettles community; and the unsettled state – the temporary loss of normality – is conducive to a literary investigation of that very (lost) normality. It perhaps goes without saying that this is a feature of fiction and perhaps historiography rather than of real-life experience. Real murder is far too disruptive to serve as an intellectual laboratory of this kind for anyone even remotely involved.
19 For discussion of moral liminality in the relevant sense, see Cecilie Eriksen, 'Moral Borderlands: Moral Change and Ethical Normativity in Liminal Spaces', in *New Perspectives on Moral Change: Anthropologists and Philosophers Engage with Transformations of Life Worlds*, ed. Cecilie Eriksen and Nora Hämäläinen (New York: Berghahn, 2022) 143–58.
20 Munro, 'Fits', 131.
21 Veena Das, *Textures of the Ordinary: Doing Anthropology After Wittgenstein* (New York: Fordham University Press, 2020). See also Nora Hämäläinen, *The Making of the Good Person: Self-Help, Ethics and Philosophy* (London: Routledge, 2023); and Nora Hämäläinen, *Descriptive Ethics: What Does Moral Philosophy Know About Morality* (New York: Palgrave, 2016) for discussion of the moral philosophical relevance of banal everyday negotiations.
22 Murdoch, *Existentialists and Mystics*.
23 Cora Diamond, *The Realistic Spirit: Wittgenstein, Philosophy, and the Mind* (Cambridge, MA: MIT Press, 1991).

24 Martha C. Nussbaum, *Love's Knowledge: Essays on Philosophy and Literature* (New York: Oxford University Press, 1990).
25 For a concise discussion of this, see the interview with Brian Magee in Murdoch, *Existentialists and Mystics*.
26 This is to say: relevant and potentially interesting types of moral relations are not reducible to these. An analogous type of relation, not discussed here, is the relation of *us to them*. An observant reader of the short story may however find this relation in it as well: in the big city upper middle class represented by Robert, against the small town way of life.
27 See Hämäläinen, *Descriptive Ethics*.
28 See S. L. Goldberg, *Agents and Lives – Moral Thinking in Literature* (Cambridge: Cambridge University Press, 1993); Joshua Landy, 'A Nation of Madame Bovarys: On the Possibility and Desirability of Moral Improvement Through Fiction', *Art and Ethical Criticism*, ed. Garry Hagberg (London: Blackwell, 2008), 63–94; and Joshua Landy, *How to Do Things with Fictions* (New York: Oxford University Press, 2012). For a philosopher's critique among these lines, see Candace Vogler, 'The Moral of the Story', *Critical Inquiry* 34 (2007): 5–35, and for a classical rebuttal from a legal scholar (in conversation with Martha Nussbaum), see Richard Posner, 'Against Ethical Criticism', *Philosophy and Literature* 21, no. 1 (1997): 1–27.
29 Amanda Anderson, Rita Felski and Toril Moi, *Character – Three Inquiries in Literary Studies* (Chicago: University of Chicago Press, 2019), 3.
30 Ibid., 2–3.
31 Nussbaum, *Love's Knowledge*.
32 Erich Auerbach, *Mimesis: The Representation of Reality in Western Literature*, 50th Anniversary edition, trans. Willard R. Trask (Princeton: Princeton University Press, 2013), 12.
33 Ibid.
34 This reflection on Auerbach is spurred and inspired by reading my friend Caterina Stenius's essay on the topic of Hebrew interpretation of the Torah (Caterina Stenius, *Sanningen är alltid större: en essä på sju famnars djup* (Vasa: Scriptum, 2022)).
35 A great literary illustration of this is the way the rural characters of Sara Lidman's novels, set in nineteenth-century northern Sweden, live with the biblical narratives as if they had happened in a neighbouring parish. Lidman is also a relevant author for exploring the moral significances of casual, community-enhancing talk, but that will be the topic for a different paper.
36 Rita Felski, *Hooked: Art and Attachment* (Chicago: University of Chicago Press, 2020), xiii.

37 My warmest thanks to the participants of the online seminar of Nordic Ordinary Language Criticism (NOLC) coordinated by Ingeborg Löfgren, Uppsla University, for helpful comments on a previous version of this chapter.

5 'A match in a dark wilderness': Philosophy, literature and morality

1 E. M. Cioran, *A Short History of Decay*, trans. Richard Howard (New York: Arcade, 1998), 47.
2 Javier Marías, 'Exclusive Q&A with Spanish Author Javier Marias', *Flavorwire* (2009), https://www.flavorwire.com/48731/exclusive-qa-spanish-author-javier-marias (accessed 1 July 2023).
3 Elisabeth Schellekens, *Aesthetics and Morality* (London: Continuum, 2007), 53–6.
4 Martha Nussbaum, *Poetic Justice: The Literary Imagination and Public Life* (Boston: Beacon Press, 1995), 130.
5 Ibid., 10.
6 Frank Palmer, *Literature and Moral Understanding* (Oxford: Clarendon Press, 1992), 215.
7 Jenefer Robinson, 'L'éducation sentimentale', in *Art and Its Messages*, ed. Stephen Davies (Pennsylvania: Pennsylvania State University Press, 1997), 34–48.
8 Noël Carroll, 'Art, Narrative and Moral Understanding', in *Aesthetics and Ethics: Essays at the Intersection*, ed. Jerrold Levinson (Cambridge: Cambridge University Press, 2001), 150.
9 Cf. Richard Posner's comments on Wayne Booth and Martha Nussbaum, both of whom seek to extract moral lessons from literature (Richard A. Posner, 'Against Ethical Criticism', *Philosophy and Literature* 21, no. 1 (1997): 3): 'Nussbaum thinks moral philosophy incomplete without literature. She does not deny the importance of aesthetic values, but she is prepared to trade them off against the moral, so that the morality of the work affects its final evaluation of a work as literature. Booth, the professional literary critic, being more systematic and wide-ranging in his ethical criticism, is also more censorious. He discusses works that do not meet his high standards for ethical literature as well as ones that do. Nussbaum confines herself to the latter.'
10 Ibid., 9.
11 Friedrich Nietzsche, *Morgenröte*, in *Sämtliche Werke: Kritische Studienausgabe*, 15 vols, Band 3, 2nd edition, ed. G. Colli and

M. Montinari (Berlin: Deutscher Taschenbuch Verlag, [1881] 1988), §240.

12 Cf. Morris Beckstein in his review of Nussbaum's *Poetic Justice*: 'Are novels really this virtuous and high-minded [as Nussbaum claims]? They can also seduce us in illicit and unexpected ways. There are novels in which we identify with the rich and successful, not the "disadvantaged"; novels that turn people into butts of satire, even hatred; novels manipulating our fantasies rather than enlarging our sympathies' (Morris Beckstein, 'Moral Fiction', *New York Times*, https://www.nytimes.com/1996/04/07/books/moral-fiction.html (accessed 3 July 2023).

13 Christopher Ricks, *Keats and Embarrassment* (Oxford: Oxford University Press, 1976), 95.

14 Ludwig Wittgenstein, *Culture and Value*, trans. Peter Winch, ed. G. H. von Wright (Oxford: Blackwell, 1992), 4e.

15 Blaise Pascal, *Pensées* (Paris: LGF, [1670] 2000), §25.

16 Jane Adamson, 'Against Tidiness: Literature and/versus Moral Philosophy', in *Renegotiating Ethics in Literature, Philosophy, and Theory*, ed. Jane Adamson et al. (Cambridge: Cambridge University Press, 1998), 88.

17 Ibid., 85.

18 Virginia Woolf, *The Waves*, ed. with intro. and notes by Gillian Beer (Oxford: Oxford University Press, [1931] 2008), 155.

19 Ibid., 213.

20 Ibid., 210.

21 Ibid., 222, 223.

22 Charles Altieri, *The Particulars of Rapture: an Aesthetics of the Affects* (Ithaca: Cornell University Press, 2003), 23.

23 Altieri discusses very interestingly Nussbaum's moralized criticisms of Proust in the context of Baron Charlus. See Altieri, *The Particulars of Rapture*, 173.

24 Charles Altieri, 'What Differences Can Contemporary Poetry Make in Our Moral Thinking?', in *Renegotiating Ethics in Literature, Philosophy, and Theory*, eds. Jane Adamson et al. (Cambridge: Cambridge University Press, 1998), 117.

25 Gabriel Josipovici, 'Josipovici, Gabriel (David) 1940', *Encyclopedia.com* (n.d.), https://www.encyclopedia.com/arts/educational-magazines/josipovici-gabriel-david-1940 (accessed 1 July 2023).

26 Cf. Posner (Posner, 'Against Ethical Criticism', 3): 'Some ethical critics want a work of literature to have a tidy moral, as in Aesop's fables, while others think the moral value of literature lies in a more diffuse influence on thinking and action. Booth and Nussbaum liken the reading of imaginative literature to friendship and emphasize that the

effect of a friendship on one's character and outlook is complex and uncertain, yet surely not unimportant. But they do not want to stop with this observation. They want to extract, albeit by consideration of the form as well as the paraphrasable content of the work, a moral lesson.'

27 Theodor Adorno, 'The Essay as Form', in *Notes to Literature*, vol. I, trans. Shierry Weber Nicholsen (New York: Columbia University Press, 1991), 3–16.
28 Gabriel Josipovici, 'Reading Kafka Today', in *The Teller and the Tale: Essays on Literature and Culture 1990–2015* (Manchester: Carcanet, 2016), 81.
29 T. S. Eliot, *The Use of Poetry and the Use of Criticism: Studies in the Relation of Criticism to Poetry in England* (Cambridge, MA: Harvard University Press, [1933] 1986), 144.

6 Ways of flourishing: Literature and moral philosophy

1 See M. Jay, *Immanent Critiques: The Frankfurt School Under Pressure* (New York: Verso, 2003).
2 Hannah Arendt, *The Human Condition* (Chicago: University of Chicago Press, 1970).
3 Flourishing often requires external goods, since it is not easy to perform noble actions without resources. This raises a question that Aristotle sidesteps: if the human good is flourishing, then it would seem to be a good thing if as many people as possible could be said to flourish. And yet the scarcity of external goods would seem to make this difficult, if not impossible to achieve.
4 Aristotle, *Nicomachean Ethics*, trans. Roger Crisp (Cambridge: Cambridge University Press, 2000), 1095a.
5 Ibid., 1098a.
6 On this point, Lear (J. Lear, *Imagining the End: Mourning and Ethical Life* (Cambridge, MA: The Belnkap Press of Harvard University Press, 2022), 58–61) signals the importance of repetition in Aristotle.
7 John Rawls, *A Theory of Justice* (Cambridge, MA: Harvard University Press, 1971), 325.
8 Derek Parfit, 'Overpopulation and the Quality of Life', *Applied Ethics* 162, ed. Peter Singer (New York: Oxford University Press, 1986), 162; emphasis is mine.

9 See Stanley Cavell, *Conditions Handsome and Unhandsome: The Constitution of Emersonian Perfectionism* (Chicago: University of Chicago Press, 1990).
10 Stanley Cavell, *In Quest of the Ordinary: Lines of Skepticism and Romanticism* (Chicago: University of Chicago Press, 1989), xii.
11 S. Bates, 'Stanley Cavell and Ethics', in *Stanley Cavell* 42, ed. Richard Eldridge (Cambridge: Cambridge University Press), 42.
12 Friedrich Nietzsche, *The Birth of Tragedy*, trans. Walter Kaufmann (New York: Vintage Books, 1967), 59.
13 Lear, *Imagining the End*, 75.
14 Richard Rorty, *Contingency, Irony, and Solidarity* (Cambridge: Cambridge University Press, 1989), xv.
15 This view is established in Richard Rorty, *Philosophy and the Mirror of Nature* (Princeton: Princeton University Press, 1979).
16 See Hilary Putnam, *Ethics Without Ontology* (Cambridge, MA: Harvard University Press, 2004).
17 Friedrich Nietzsche, *The Anti-Christ*, trans. H. L. Mencken (New York: Knopf, 1930), 42.
18 Ibid.
19 Friedrich Nietzsche, *Beyond Good and Evil*, trans. Walter Kaufmann (New York: Random House, 1966), 80.
20 L. Ferry, *What is the Good Life?* trans. Lydia Cochrane (Chicago: University of Chicago Press, 2005), 93.
21 Ibid.
22 Ibid.
23 Anthony J. Cascardi, 'Does Literature Make Us Better Human Beings?: Literature and the Moral Imagination', in *The Cambridge Companion to Literature and Philosophy*, ed. Lanier Anderson and Karen Zumhagen-Yekplé (Cambridge: Cambridge University Press, 2024).
24 I am paraphrasing C. Altieri, 'Valuing Stevens's Acts of Imagination', *Wallace Stevens Journal* 41, no. 2 (2017): 162.
25 S. Philips, *The Poetics of the Everyday: Creative Repetition in Modern American Verse* (New York: Columbia University Press, 2010), 111.
26 Ibid., 469.
27 Mikhail M. Bakhtin, *The Dialogic Imagination* (Austin: University of Texas Press, 1981), 282.
28 Ibid., 279.
29 Ibid., 333.
30 Ibid., 34.
31 Ibid., 37.

32 M. Cervantes, *Don Quixote*, trans. Edith Grossman (New York: Vintage, 2005), 195.
33 Ibid., vol. I, 44.
34 René Descartes, *Meditations on First Philosophy*, trans. John Cottington (Cambridge: Cambridge University Press, 1996), 21.
35 A. Smith, *The Theory of the Moral Sentiments* (Edinburgh: Alexander Kincaid and J. Bell, 1759), vol. I, 1.
36 David Hume, *A Treatise on Human Understanding* (New York: Dover, 2003), 225.
37 Ibid., 423.
38 Smith, *The Theory of the Moral Sentiments*, 2–3.
39 See M. Conde, 'Does Fiction Actually Make Us More Empathetic?: On 5 Works That Explore the Connection Between Art and Understanding', *Literary Hub* (2016), https://lithub.com/does-fiction-actually-make-us-more-empathetic/.
40 Ludwig Wittgenstein, *Philosophical Investigations*, trans. G. E. M. Anscombe, P. M. S. Hacker and Joachim Schulte (London: Blackwell, 2009), 108.

7 The ethics of narrative art: Philosophy in schools, compassion and learning from stories

1 This chapter was first published under an open access creative commons licensing agreement as Laura D'Olimpio and Andrew Peterson, 'The Ethics of Narrative Art: Philosophy in Schools, Compassion and Learning from Stories', *Journal of Philosophy in Schools*, 5 no. 1 (2018): 92–110. DOI: 10.21913/jps.v5i1.1487.
2 Martha C. Nussbaum, 'Finely Aware and Richly Responsible: Literature and the Moral Imagination', in *Literature and the Question of Philosophy*, ed. Anthony J. Cascardi (Baltimore: John Hopkins University Press, 1987), 170.
3 See, for example, N. Carroll, 'Art and Ethical Criticism: An Overview of Recent Directions of Research', *Ethics* 110, no. 2 (2000): 350–87; A. Mejia, and S. E. Montoya, 'On the Meeting of the Moral and the Aesthetic in Literary Education', *Journal of Philosophy of Education* 51, no. 2 (2017): 370–86; Laura D'Olimpio, 'When Good Art Is Bad: Educating the Critical Viewer', *Theory and Research in Education* 18, no. 2 (2020): 137–50; Laura D'Olimpio, *Media and Moral Education: A Philosophy of Critical Engagement* (London: Routledge, 2018).

4 See Carroll, 'Art and Ethical Criticism', on moderate moralism and Gaut's ethicism.
5 Martha C. Nussbaum, 'Exactly and Responsibly: A Defence of Ethical Criticism', *Philosophy and Literature* 22 (1998): 343–65.
6 Alasdair MacIntyre, *After Virtue: A Study in Moral Theory*, 2nd edition (Indianapolis: University of Notre Dame Press, [1981] 1984).
7 Ibid., 216.
8 M. Lipman, A. M. Sharp, and F. S. Oscanyan, *Philosophy in the Classroom* (Upper Montclair: Institute for the Advancement of Philosophy for Children, Montclair State College, 1977), 23.
9 Iris Murdoch, quoted in B. Magee, 'Philosophy and Literature: Dialogue with Iris Murdoch', in *Men of Ideas*, ed. B. Magee (London: British Broadcasting Corporation, 1978), 278.
10 Iris Murdoch, *Existentialists and Mystics: Writings on Philosophy and Literature*, ed. P. J. Conradi (London: Penguin, 1998), 27–8.
11 Martha C. Nussbaum, *Upheavals of Thought: The intelligence of Emotions* (Cambridge: Cambridge University Press, 2001), 244.
12 Ibid., 301.
13 L. Blum, 'Compassion', in *The Virtues: Contemporary Essays on Moral Character*, ed. R. B. Kruschwitz and R. C. Roberts (Belmont: Wadsworth, 1987), 232.
14 For a fuller discussion of these elements of compassion, see Andrew Peterson, *Compassion and Education: Cultivating Compassionate Children, Schools and Communities* (London: Palgrave Macmillan, 2017).
15 Aristotle, *The Nichomachean Ethics* (Oxford: Oxford University Press, 2009), 30.
16 Nussbaum, *Upheavals of Thought*, 328.
17 Martha C. Nussbaum, *Love's Knowledge: Essays on Philosophy and Literature* (Oxford: Oxford University Press, 1992), 152.
18 Henry James, *The Golden Bowl* (London: Methuen & Company, 1905).
19 For a more detailed and nuanced philosophical discussion of how readers engage with narrative works, see Mejia and Montoya, 'On the Meeting of the Moral and the Aesthetic in Literary Education'; Gregory Currie, 'The Paradox of Caring', *Emotion and the Arts*, ed. M. Hjort and S. Laver (Oxford: Oxford University Press, 1997), 63–92; and N. Kreitman, 'Fantasy, Fiction and Feelings', *Metaphilosophy* 37, no. 5 (2006): 605–22.
20 Nussbaum, *Upheavals of Thought*.
21 Ibid., 317.
22 Martha C. Nussbaum, *Poetic Justice: The Literary Imagination and Public Life* (Boston: Beacon Press, 1995), xvi.

23 There are too many examples to cite here, but – and, for example – the current version of the National Australian Curriculum includes a focus on care and compassion, as well as empathy, for instance, as identified under the general capability entitled 'ethical understanding'. Empathy also features strongly within the International Baccalaureate curriculum. Initiatives such as the Social and Emotional Aspects of Learning programme in England provide practical instances of such a focus.

24 Peterson, *Compassion and Education.*

25 P. Cam, 'Philosophy for Children, Values Education and the Inquiring Society', *Educational Philosophy and Theory* 46, no. 11 (2014): 1204.

26 S. Millett and A. Tapper, 'Benefits of Collaborative Philosophical Inquiry in Schools', *Educational Philosophy and Theory* 44, no. 5 (2012): 546–67; K. Topping and S. Trickey, 'Collaborative Philosophical Enquiry for School Children: Cognitive Effects at 10–12 Years', *British Journal of Educational Psychology* 77 (2007): 271–88; K. Topping and S. Trickey, 'Collaborative Philosophical Inquiry for Schoolchildren: Cognitive Gains at 2-Year Follow-Up', *British Journal of Educational Psychology* 77 (2007): 787–96; S. Trickey and K. Topping, 'Collaborative Philosophical Enquiry for School Children: Socio-Emotional Effects at 11–12 Years', *School Psychology International* 27, no. 5 (2006): 599–614; EEF, *Philosophy for Children: Evaluation Report and Executive Summary*, evals. S. Gorard, N. Siddiqui and B. H (2015). See, Education Endowment Foundation; F. Fair, L. Haas, C. Gardosik, D. Johnson, D. Price and O. Leipnik, 'Socrates in the Schools from Scotland to Texas: Replicating a Study on the Effects of a Philosophy for Children Program', *Journal of Philosophy in Schools* 2, no. 1 (2015): 18–37; F. Fair, L. Haas, C. Gardosik, D. Johnson, D. Price and O. Leipnik, 'Socrates in the Schools: Gains at a Three-Year Follow-Up', *Journal of Philosophy in Schools* 2, no. 2 (2015): 5–16; S. Gorard, N. Siddiqui and B. H. See, 'Can "Philosophy for Children" Improve Primary School Attainment?', *Journal of Philosophy of Education* 51, no. 1 (2017): 5–22.

27 Charles Dickens, *A Tale of Two Cities* (London: Chapman & Hall, 1859).

28 Richard A. Posner, 'Against Ethical Criticism', *Philosophy and Literature* 21, no.1 (1997): 4–5.

29 Nussbaum, 'Exactly and Responsibly', 352.

30 Mark Twain, *Adventures of Huckleberry Finn* (London: Chatto & Windus, 1884).

31 R. W. Hepburn, 'Art, Truth and the Education of Subjectivity', *Journal of Philosophy of Education* 24 (1990): 185–98.
32 Nussbaum, 'Exactly and Responsibly', 358.
33 Nussbaum, *Upheavals of Thought*, 433.
34 K. Bohlin, *Teaching Character Education Through Literature: Awakening the Moral Imagination in Secondary Classrooms* (London: Routledge, 2005), 15.
35 Ibid., 49.
36 Ibid., 18.
37 Ibid., 25.
38 M. Lipman, *Harry Stottlemeier's Discovery*, (Upper Montclair: Institute for the Advancement of Philosophy for Children, Montclair State College, 1974).
39 Lipman, Sharp and Oscanyan, *Philosophy in the Classroom*, 11.
40 Ibid.
41 L. Splitter, 'Identity, Citizenship and Moral Education', *Educational Philosophy and Theory* 43, no. 5 (2011): 497.
42 Ibid., 497–8.
43 D'Olimpio makes a similar argument about the virtue of trust in Laura D'Olimpio, 'Trust as a Virtue in Education', *Educational Philosophy and Theory*, Special Issue: *Trust and Schooling*. https://doi.org/10.1080/00131857.2016.1194737.
44 Splitter, 'Identity, Citizenship and Moral Education', 498.
45 Aristotle, *The Nichomachean Ethics*.

8 The literary evolution of the philosophical metaphor of *theatrum mundi*

* Elements of this essay deepen and augment fragments that appeared in Sophie Bastien, 'La métaphore théâtrale pour penser la vie', in *Que peut la métaphore? Histoire, savoir et poétique*, ed. Sylvain David, Janusz Przychodzen and François-Émmanuël Boucher (Paris: L'Harmattan, 2009), 97–113.
1 Pierre Fontanier, *Les Figures du discours*, ed. Gérard Genette (Paris: Flammarion, [1830] 1977), 103.
2 All Old Testament quotes are drawn from *The English Standard Version Bible with Apocrypha* (Oxford: Oxford University Press, 2009).

3 Homer, *The Odyssey*, trans. T. E. Lawrence (London: Macmillan Collector's Library, [2004] 2016), Book 10, 189.
4 Louis Van Delft, *Les Spectateurs de la vie. Généalogie du regard moraliste* (Quebec: Presses de l'Université Laval, 2005), 44.
5 Lynda Christian, *Theatrum Mundi: The History of an Idea* (New York: Garland Publishing, 1987), 1–4.
6 Plato, *The Republic*, III, 392a–94c.
7 Aristotle, *Poetics*, chap. II, 1448a.
8 Ibid., chap. IV, 1448b.
9 Roselyne Dupont-Roc and Jean Lallot, 'Notes', in Aristote, *La Poétique* (Paris: Seuil, 1980), 145 (note 4 of chap. I).
10 Fontanier, *Les Figures du discours*, 103.
11 Plato, *The Laws*, trans. Thomas L. Pangle (Chicago: Chicago University Press, 1988), Book VII, 817b, 208.
12 Ibid., Book I, 644d, 24–5.
13 Cicero, *Laelius on Friendship. Cato on Old Age*, trans. W. A. Falconer (North Haven: Aquila Press, 2021), §65, 70, 82 (88, 92, 100).
14 Epictetus, *Handbook*, in *Discourses, Fragments, Handbook*, trans. Robin Hard (Oxford: Oxford University Press, 2014), §17, 291.
15 Lucretius, *On the Nature of the Universe*, trans. Ronald Melville (Oxford University Press, [1997] 2008), Book 6, 50–69, 180–1.
16 Epictetus, *Handbook*, §17, 291–2.
17 Marcus Aurelius, *Meditations*, trans. Martin Hammond (New York: Penguin Classics, 2006), Book 6, §42, 54 and Book 12, §36, 122.
18 Ibid., Book 3, §8 and Book 12, §35.
19 Éric Bordas, *Les Chemins de la métaphore* (Paris: Presses universitaires de France, 2003), 24.
20 Suetonius, *The Lives of the Caesars*, trans. J. C. Rolfe (Boston: Loeb Classical Library, 1914), II, 99, 281.
21 Seneca, *Letters on Ethics*, trans. Margaret Graver and A. A. Long (Chicago University Press, 2015), Letter 80, §7–8 and Letter 10, 262–3.
22 Erasmus, *The Praise of Folly*, trans. Clarence H. Miller (New Haven: Yale University Press, [1979] 2003), 108.
23 Michel de Montaigne, *The Essays*, trans. Charles Cotton (Project Gutenberg, 2001), Book III, chap. 9, https://www.gutenberg.org/files/3600/3600-h/3600-h.htm#link2HCH0102.
24 Erasmus, *The Praise of Folly*, 120.
25 Ibid., 110–11.
26 Ibid., 101.
27 Niccolo Machiavelli, *The Prince*, ed. Oliver Francis (London: Macmillan Collector's Library, [2004] 2019), chap. 18, 89.

28 William Shakespeare, *The Complete Works*, ed. Stanley Wells and Gary Taylor (Oxford: Oxford University Press, [1986] 2005), *The Tempest*, IV.1.148–51, 153–6, 1238.
29 Ibid., *As You Like It*, II.7.137–42, 666.
30 Ibid., *The Merchant of Venice*, I.1.77–8, 455.
31 Ibid., *The Tragedy of Macbeth*, V.5.23–7, 992.
32 Ibid., *The Tragedy of King Lear*: The Folio Text, IV.5.179, 1178.
33 Ibid., *The Tragedy of King Richard the Second*, III.2.33, 353.
34 Ibid., *The Tragedy of King Richard the Third*, II.1.83, 196.
35 Ibid., *The Tragedy of Macbeth*, II.3.8–11, 977.
36 *Ibid.*, I.5.52, 974.
37 Ibid., *The Tragedy of Coriolanus*, V.3.185–6, 1119.
38 Ibid., *The History of King Lear*, 15.35–6, 930.
39 Georges Forestier, *Le Théâtre dans le théâtre: sur la scène française du XVIIe siècle* (Genève: Droz, [1981] 1996), 42.
40 See Manfred Schmeling, *Métathéâtre et intertexte: aspects du théâtre dans le théâtre* (Paris: Lettres modernes, 1982), 98.
41 René Descartes, *The Philosophical Writings*, trans. John Cottingham, Robert Stoothoff and Dugald Murdoch (Cambridge University Press, 1985), Vol. I, 2.
42 See Fernand Hallyn, *Descartes. Dissimulation et ironie* (Genève: Droz, 2006).
43 Descartes, *The Philosophical Writings*.
44 Descartes, *Discourse on Method*, trans. John Veitch (Project Gutenberg, 1995), Part III, https://www.gutenberg.org/files/59/59-h/59-h.htm.
45 François de La Rochefoucauld, *Reflections, or Sentences and Moral Maxims*, trans. J. W. Willis Bund and J. Hain Friswell (Project Gutenberg, 2005), maxim 119, https://www.gutenberg.org/files/9105/9105-h/9105-h.htm.
46 Jean de La Bruyère, *The Characters*, trans. Henri Van Laun (Project Gutenberg, 2014), VIII: 'Of the Court', §99, https://www.gutenberg.org/files/46633/46633-h/46633-h.htm#Page_183.
47 Jacques-Bénigne Bossuet, 'Sermon on Death', trans. Christopher O. Blum (Scribd, 2014), First point, https://www.scribd.com/document/233006855/Bossuet-Sermon-on-Death#.
48 Bernard De Fontenelle, *Conversations on the Plurality of Worlds*, trans. Elizabeth Gunning ((London: Hurst, 1803, 9) Project Gutenberg, 2021), 'First Evening', https://www.gutenberg.org/cache/epub/66559/pg66559-images.html#FIRST_EVENING.
49 Charles de Montesquieu, *Considerations on the Causes of the Greatness of the Romans and Their Decline*, trans. David Lowenthal (Cambridge, MA: Hackett, [1965] 1999), 95.

50 Edward Gibbon, *The History of the Decline and Fall of the Roman Empire*, vol. I, ed. David Womersley (London: Penguin, [1994] 2005), 168.
51 I translate 'Sur le théâtre du monde'. Ariane Chebel d'Appollonia, *Histoire politique des intellectuels en France (1944–1954)*, tome I: *Des lendemains qui déchantent* (Bruxelles: Éditions Complexe, 1991), 37–54.
52 I translate 'le spectacle d'une science qui se consacre au meurtre organisé'. Ibid., 38.
53 Roger-Gérard Schwatzenberg, *L'État spectacle. Le star-system en politique* ((Flammarion, 1977) Paris: Plon, 2009), 12 and 14.
54 Christian, *Theatrum Mundi*, 195.
55 Forestier, *Le Théâtre dans le théâtre*, 344.
56 Anne Larue, 'Le théâtre du monde: du jeu de l'acteur aux lieux du cosmos', *L'Information littéraire* 46, no. 1 (1994): 20.
57 Martin Esslin, *The Theatre of the Absurd* (New York: Vintage, [1961] 2004), 23.
58 Albert Camus, *The Myth of Sisyphus*, trans. Justin O'Brien (New York: Vintage, [1955] 1983), 6.
59 Ibid., 12.
60 Marie-Louise Audin, 'Le paradigme du théâtre dans *Le Mythe de Sisyphe*', in *Albert Camus et le théâtre*, ed. Jacqueline Lévi-Valensi (Paris: Imec, 1992), 120.
61 Camus, *The Myth of Sisyphus*, 94.
62 Ibid., 24–5.
63 Howard D. Pearce, 'A Phenomenological Approach to the *Theatrum Mundi* Metaphor', *Publications of the MLA* 95, no. 1 (1980): 48.
64 Camus, *The Myth of Sisyphus*, 117.
65 Jean-Paul Sartre, 'Being and Nothingness', in *An Essay in Phenomenological Ontology*, trans. Sarah Richmond (New York: Washington Square Press, 2018), 110–13.
66 Samuel Beckett, *Proust* (New York: Grove Press, [1931] 1966), 46.
67 Arthur Adamov, *Je… Ils…* ((previously published under the title *L'Aveu*. Paris: Sagittaire, 1946) Paris: Gallimard, 1969), 32.
68 Kostas Axelos, *Le Jeu du monde* (Paris: (Minuit, 1969) Encre marine, 2018).
69 Gilles Deleuze, 'La méthode de dramatisation', *Bulletin de la Société française de philosophie* 62 (1967): 89–118; *Différence et répétition* (Paris: PUF, 1968).
70 Jacques Henriot, *Sous couleur de jouer. La métaphore ludique* ((Paris: Corti, 1989) Lyon: ENS éditions, 2023).
71 Jean Duvignaud, *Le Jeu du jeu* (Paris: Balland, 1980); Erving Goffman, *The Presentation of Self in Everyday Life* (New York: Anchor, 1959).

72 Jean-François Côté, Jean-François Morissette and Jonathan Roberge, eds., *Théâtralité et société. Positions de la sociologie, Cahiers de recherche sociologique* 51 (2011).
73 Jean Gillibert, *Ça n'est plus ça: notes cliniques et métapsychologiques sur l'autre théâtre de l'Être* (Lyon: Césura, 1987).
74 Luigi Pirandello, *Six Characters in Search of an Author*, trans. Anthony Mortimer (Oxford: Oxford University Press, [1921] 2014).
75 Ruby Cohn, *Currents in Contemporary Drama* (Bloomington: Indiana University Press, 1969), 232.
76 Eric Bentley, *The Life of the Drama* ((New York: Atheneum, 1964) Milwaukee: Applause Books, 2000), 150.
77 Jean Molino, 'Anthropologie et métaphore', *Langages* 54 (1979): 115.
78 Van Delft, *Les Spectateurs de la vie*, 37.
79 Larue, 'Le théâtre du monde', 10.
80 Van Delft, *Les Spectateurs de la vie*, 44.
81 Pearce, 'A Phenomenological Approach to the *Theatrum Mundi* Metaphor', 44.
82 Van Delft, *Les Spectateurs de la vie*, 37.

9 The dream of reason: Giannina Braschi's ethics of in-betweenness

1 Giannina Braschi, *Yo-Yo Boing!* (Ithaca: Latin American Literary Review Press, 1998), English translation Giannina Braschi, *Yo-Yo Boing!* trans. Tess O'Dwyer (Seattle: AmazonCrossing, 2011); hereafter *YYB*.
2 Braschi, *YYB* (2011), 85.
3 Ibid., 86.
4 Francisco de Goya, *Los Caprichos* (New York: Dover Publications, 2022), 43. The word, 'marabillas' is a now-redundant form of the contemporary Spanish 'maravillas'.
5 Alexander Nehamas, 'The Sleep of Reason Produces Monsters', *Representations* 74, no. 1 (2001): 38.
6 Ibid.
7 Ibid., 52.
8 Ibid., 124.
9 In Rolando Pérez, 'My Dinner with Giannina', in *Poets, Philosophers, Lovers: On the Writings of Giannina Braschi*, ed. Frederick Luis Aldama and Tess O'Dwyer (Pittsburgh: University of Pittsburgh Press, 2020), 177–8.

10 In Amy Sheeran and Amanda M. Smith, 'A Graphic Revolution: Talking Poetry & Politics with Giannina Braschi', *Chiricú Journal: Latina/o Literatures, Arts, and Cultures* 2, no. 2 (2018): 141, https://doi.org/10.2979/chiricu.2.2.10.
11 Giannina Braschi, 'What to Read Now: Mixed-Genre Literature', *World Literature Today* (September 2012), https://www.worldliteratu retoday.org/2012/september/what-read-now-mixed-genre-literature-giannina-braschi (accessed 6 November 2024).
12 In Pérez, 'My Dinner with Giannina', 168.
13 Braschi, *YYB* (2011), 156.
14 Ibid., 196.
15 Ibid., 198.
16 John 'Rio' Riofrio, 'Rompiendo esquemas: Catastrophic Bravery in *United States of Banana*', in *Poets, Philosophers, Lovers: On the Writings of Giannina Braschi*, ed. Frederick Luis Aldama and Tess O'Dwyer (Pittsburgh: University of Pittsburgh Press, 2020), 36.
17 Madalena Gonzalez, 'The Uncommon Wealth of Art: Poetic Progress as Resistance to the Commodification of Culture in *United States of Banana*', in *Poets, Philosophers, Lovers: On the Writings of Giannina Braschi*, ed. Frederick Luis Aldama and Tess O'Dwyer (Pittsburgh: University of Pittsburgh Press, 2020), 30.
18 Braschi, *YYB* (2011), 229.
19 Gonzalez, 'The Uncommon Wealth of Art', 29.
20 Martha Craven Nussbaum, 'Exactly and Responsibly: A Defense of Ethical Criticism', *Philosophy and Literature* 22 (1998): 354.
21 Krista Ratcliffe, *Rhetorical Listening: Identification, Gender, Whiteness* (Carbondale: Southern Illinois University Press, 2005), 1.
22 Giannina Braschi, *Empire of Dreams*, trans. Tess O'Dwyer (Seattle: AmazonCrossing, 2011); hereafter *ED*.
23 Braschi, *ED*, 36.
24 Harold Bloom, *The Western Canon* (San Diego: Harcourt Brace, 1994), 29.
25 Nehamas, 'The Sleep of Reason Produces Monsters', 51.
26 Ibid., 38.
27 Frederick Luis Aldama, 'Introduction', in *Poets, Philosophers, Lovers: On the Writings of Giannina Braschi*, ed. Frederick Luis Aldama and Tess O'Dwyer (Pittsburgh: University of Pittsburgh Press, 2020), 11–13.
28 In Sheeran and Smith, 'A Graphic Revolution', 137.
29 Braschi, *YYB* (2011), 182; italicization in the original.
30 Ibid., 154.
31 Ibid., 170.
32 Dorian Lugo Bertran, 'Leaping Off the Page: Giannina Braschi's Intermedialities', in *Poets, Philosophers, Lovers: On the Writings*

of *Giannina Braschi*, ed. Frederick Luis Aldama and Tess O'Dwyer (Pittsburgh: University of Pittsburgh Press, 2020), 127.

33 Braschi, *YYB* (2011), 162; italicization in the original.

34 In Cristina Garrigós, 'Chicken with the Head off: Una conversación con Giannina Braschi', *Voices of America/Voces de America*, ed. Laura Alonso Gallo (Valencia: Aduana Vieja, 2004), 155.

35 Gonzalez, 'The Uncommon Wealth of Art', 30.

36 Giannina Braschi, *United States of Banana*, trans. Tess O'Dwyer (Seattle: AmazonCrossing, 2011), 40; hereafter *USB*.

37 Braschi, *USB*, 123.

38 Ibid., 235–6.

39 Gonzalez, 'The Uncommon Wealth of Art', 24–7.

40 Arnaldo Manuel Cruz-Malavé, "'Under the Skirt of Liberty': Giannina Braschi Rewrites Empire', *American Quarterly* 66, no. 3 (2014): 815.

41 Braschi, *YYB* (2011), 220.

42 Ibid., 158.

43 Ibid., 221.

44 Ibid., 188.

45 Leonard Bernstein, Arthur Laurents, Stephen Sondheim and Jerome Robbins, *West Side Story: A Musical* (London: Heinemann Educational, 1972), 53.

46 Aldama, 'Introduction', 5.

47 Daniela Daniele, 'Gamifying World Literature: Giannina Braschi's *United States of Banana*', in *Poets, Philosophers, Lovers: On the Writings of Giannina Braschi*, ed. Frederick Luis Aldama and Tess O'Dwyer (Pittsburgh: University of Pittsburgh Press, 2020), 116–17.

48 Ellen Jones, '"I Want My Closet Back": Queering and Unqueering Language in Giannina Braschi's *Yo-Yo Boing!*', *Textual Practice* 34, no. 2 (2018): 286.

49 Braschi, *YYB* (2011), 173.

50 Ibid., 158.

51 Maritza Stanchich, 'Bilingual Big Bang: Giannina Braschi's Trilogy Levels the Spanish-English Playing Field', in *Poets, Philosophers, Lovers: On the Writings of Giannina Braschi*, ed. Frederick Luis Aldama and Tess O'Dwyer (Pittsburgh: University of Pittsburgh Press, 2020), 70.

52 Jones, 'I Want My Closet Back', 295.

53 Braschi, *YYB* (2011), 157.

54 Braschi, *ED*, 41.

55 Braschi, *YYB* (2011), 167.

56 Anne Ashbaugh, 'Exile and Burial of Ontological Sameness: A Dialogue Between Zarathustra and Giannina', in *Poets, Philosophers, Lovers: On the Writings of Giannina Braschi*, ed. Frederick Luis

Aldama and Tess O'Dwyer (Pittsburgh: University of Pittsburgh Press, 2020), 44.

57 Gilles Deleuze, *The Logic of Sense*, ed. Constantin V. Boundas, trans. Mark Lester and Charles Stivale (London: Bloomsbury, 2013), 54.

58 Ibid., 55.

59 Ibid., 56; emphasis in the original.

60 Ibid., 55.

61 As Jones points out (Jones, 'I Want My Closet Back').

62 Braschi, *YYB* (1998), 167.

63 Braschi, *YYB* (2011), 162.

64 Braschi, *YYB* (1998), 135.

65 Braschi, *YYB* (2011), 130.

66 Ibid., 162.

67 Giannina Braschi, *Putinoika* (McAllen: FlowerSong Press, 2024).

68 Ibid., 29.

69 Ibid., 23–4.

70 Deleuze, *The Logic of Sense*, 90.

71 Ibid., 96.

72 Braschi, *Putinoika*, 14.

73 Ibid., 17.

74 Francisco José Ramos, 'The Holy Trinity: Money, Power, and Success in *United States of Banana*', in *Poets, Philosophers, Lovers: On the Writings of Giannina Braschi*, ed. Frederick Luis Aldama and Tess O'Dwyer (Pittsburgh: University of Pittsburgh Press, 2020), 161.

75 Deleuze, *The Logic of Sense*, 139; emphasis in the original.

76 Ibid., 146.

77 Ilan Stavans, 'Foreword', in *Poets, Philosophers, Lovers: On the Writings of Giannina Braschi*, ed. Frederick Luis Aldama and Tess O'Dwyer (Pittsburgh: University of Pittsburgh Press, 2020), xi–xii.

10 The sorrow of the lone one: Existential despair in Mary Shelley's *The Last Man*

1 This point has been argued in some detail in Jon Stewart, *The Unity of Content and Form in Philosophical Writing: The Perils of Conformity* (London: Bloomsbury, 2013).

2 Mary Shelley, *Frankenstein: or; The Modern Prometheus* (London: Lackington, 1818), (revised edition with new preface: London: Colburn and Bentley, 1831; reprint edition by

M. K. Joseph, Oxford: Oxford University Press, 1980). As for Mary Shelley's other works, see, for example, the novels *Valperga; or, The Life and Adventures of Castruccio, Prince of Lucca* (London: Whittaker, 1823); *Falkner: A Novel* (London: Saunders and Otley, 1837); and *Matilda*, written between 1819 and 1820 but published first in 1959, ed. Elizabeth Nitchie (Chapel Hill, NC: North Carolina Press, 1959).

3 See, for example, Mary Shelley and Percy Bysshe Shelley, *History of a Six Weeks' Tour Through a Part of France, Switzerland, Germany and Holland: With Letters Descriptive of a Sail Round the Lake of Geneva, and of the Glaciers of Chamouni* (London: Hookham and Ollier, 1817).

4 *Posthumous Poems of Percy Bysshe Shelley*, ed. and published by Mary W. Shelley (London: Hunt, 1824).

5 As for newer biographies, see, for example (in chronological order), Miranda Seymour, *Mary Shelley* (London: Simon & Schuster, 2018 (New York: Grove Press, 2000)); Charlotte Gordon, *Romantic Outlaws: The Extraordinary Lives of Mary Wollstonecraft and Her Daughter Mary Shelley* (London: Penguin Random House, 2015); and Fiona Sampson, *In Search of Mary Shelley* (New York: Pegasus Books, 2018). As for biographies of a bit antiquated date, see, for example, Mrs Julian Marshall, ed., *The Life and Letters of Mary Wollstonecraft Shelley*, vols 1–2 (London: Richard Bentley and Son, 1889) and Muriel Spark, *Child of Light: A Biography of Mary Shelley* (London: Tower Bridge Publications, 1951). As for the secondary literature about Mary Shelley, see, for example, Lucy Morrison and Staci Stone, *A Mary Shelley Encyclopedia* (Westport, CT: Greenwood Press, 2003); Betty T. Bennett and Stuart Curran, eds, *Mary Shelley in Her Times* (Baltimore, MD: The John Hopkins University Press, 2000); *The Cambridge Companion to Mary Shelley*, ed. Esther Schor (Cambridge: Cambridge University Press, 2003); and John Beer, *Romantic Consciousness: Blake to Mary Shelley* (Basingstoke: Palgrave Macmillan, 2003), 168–78.

6 Mary Shelley, *The Last Man* (London: Henry Colburn, 1826).

7 As for the secondary literature about *The Last Man*, see, for example, Jane Aaron, 'The Return of the Repressed: Reading Mary Shelley's *The Last Man*', in *Feminist Criticism: Theory and Practice*, ed. Susan Sellers (New York: Harvester Wheatsheaf, 1991), 9–22; Kari E. Lokke, 'The Last Man', in *The Cambridge Companion to Mary Shelley*, 116–34; and Young-Ok An, '"Read Your Fall": The Signs of Plague in *The Last Man*', *Studies in Romanticism* 44, no. 4 (2005): 581–604.

8 Mary Shelley, *The Last Man*, ed. Morton D. Paley (Oxford: Oxford University Press, 2008), 39. In the following, all references are made to this edition of the work.
9 Julian Marshall, *The Life and Letters of Mary Wollstonecraft*, (London: Richard Bentley & Son, 1889), vol. 2, 112.
10 Marshall, *The Life and Letters of Mary Wollstonecraft*, vol. 2, 113–14.
11 Shelley, *The Last Man*, 3.
12 Ibid., 5; italics in the original.
13 Ibid., 6.
14 Quoted from ibid., 471.
15 Marshall, *The Life and Letters of Mary Wollstonecraft*, vol. 1, 232. Cf. also Shelley, *The Last Man*, xx.
16 Virgil, *The Aeneid*, trans. Allen Mandelbaum (New York: Bantam Books, 1981), Book VI, lines 11–14.
17 *The Aeneid*, Book VI, lines 105–9.
18 More on the Sibyl of Cumae, see, for example, Kathleen N. Daly, *Greek and Roman Mythology A to Z*, revised by Marian Rengel (New York: Facts on File Publishing 2004), 34 and Luke Roman and Monica Roman, *Encyclopedia of Greek and Roman Mythology* (New York: Facts on File Publishing 2010), 13–14, 18–19.
19 Cf. Shelley, *The Last Man*, 471.
20 Ibid., 70.
21 Marshall, *The Life and Letters of Mary Wollstonecraft*, vol. 2, 14.
22 Shelley, *The Last Man*, 1. See also ibid., 471.
23 Ibid., 7.
24 Marshall, *The Life and Letters of Mary Wollstonecraft*, vol. 2, 23–4.
25 Shelley, *The Last Man*, 20.
26 See, for example, Shelley, *The Last Man*, ix; Morrison and Stone, *A Mary Shelley Encyclopedia*, 5; and Lokke, 'The Last Man', 117 and ff.
27 Shelley, *The Last Man*, 27.
28 See, for example, John Worthen, *The Life of Percy Bysshe Shelley*, Chichester: Wiley Blackwell, 2019, 19.
29 Shelley, *The Last Man*, 31; italics are mine.
30 Ibid., 70.
31 Ibid., 71.
32 Ibid., 74.
33 Worthen, *The Life of Percy Bysshe Shelley*, xx. See also Marshall, *The Life and Letters of Mary Wollstonecraft*, vol. 2, 264.
34 See *Percy Bysshe Shelley: Selected Poems and Prose*, ed. Jack Donovan and Cian Duffy (London: Penguin, 2016), 636–78. Cf. also, ibid., 868. For secondary literature on this topic, see, for

example, Michal Henry Scrivener, *Radical Shelley: The Philosophical Anarchism and Utopian Thought of Percy Bysshe Shelley* (Princeton, NJ: Princeton University Press, 1982), 210–18.

35 Cf. Scrivener, *Radical Shelley*, 210.

36 *Percy Bysshe Shelley: Selected Poems and Prose*, 640.

37 Cf. Scrivener, *Radical Shelley*, 211.

38 Shelley, *The Last Man*, 42.

39 Ibid., 44.

40 See William Godwin, *An Enquiry Concerning Political Justice*, vols 1–2 (London: Robinson, 1793).

41 Scrivener, *Radical Shelley*, xi–xii.

42 Cf. Lee Sterrenburg, 'Mary Shelley's Monster: Politics and Psyche in Frankenstein', in *The Endurance of Frankenstein: Essays on Mary Shelley's Novel*, ed. George Levine and U. C. Knoepflmacher (Berkeley, CA: University of California Press, 1979), 143–71; see 143.

43 Shelley, *The Last Man*, 441.

44 Ibid., 446.

45 Ibid., 460.

46 Ibid., 463.

47 Ibid., 464.

48 Ibid.

49 As for the latter poem, see Anonymous, 'The Last Man', *Blackwood's Edinburgh Magazine* 19 (March 1826): 284–6.

50 Shelley, *The Last Man*, 452.

11 'The salamander of the human soul': The melodrama of scepticism in Dostoevsky and Tarkovsky

1 George Steiner, *Tolstoy or Dostoevsky: An Essay in Contrast* (London: Faber, 1959).

2 Peter Brooks, *The Melodramatic Imagination: Balzac, Henry James, Melodrama and the Mode of Excess* (New Haven: Yale University Press, 1976).

3 Brooks, *The Melodramatic Imagination*, xvii.

4 Ibid., 15, 16.

5 Ibid., 20–2.

6 Ibid., 15.

7 Ibid., 20.

8 The disagreement is developed in the introduction to Stanley Cavell, *Contesting Tears* (Chicago: University of Chicago Press, 1996).
9 Cavell, *Contesting Tears*, 40.
10 Ibid., 42.
11 Ibid., 44.
12 J. M. Coetzee, *The Lives of Animals* (Princeton: Princeton University Press, 1999).
13 Ibid., 26.
14 Stanley Cavell, *Themes Out of School* (San Francisco: North Point Press, 1984), 99–100.
15 Rowan Williams, *Dostoevsky: Language, Faith and Fiction* (Waco, TX: Baylor University Press, 2008), 43–4.
16 Ibid., 93.
17 Ibid., 107.
18 Ibid., 78.
19 Ibid., 136.
20 Ibid., 138.
21 Ibid., 139.
22 Ibid., 85.
23 Fyodor Dostoevsky, *Devils*, trans. M. R. Katz (Oxford: Oxford University Press, 1992).
24 Ibid., 754.
25 Ibid., 753.
26 Andrei Tarkovsky, *Sculpting in Time*, trans. K. Hunter-Blair (London: Bodley Head, 1986).
27 Ibid., 193.
28 Ibid., 57.

FURTHER READING

Anthony J. Cascardi, ed. *The Cambridge Introduction to Literature and Philosophy* (Cambridge: Cambridge University Press, 2014).

Anthony J. Cascardi, ed. *Literature and the Question of Philosophy* (Baltimore: John Hopkins University Press, 1987).

Laura D'Olimpio, Panos Paris, and Aiden Thompson, eds. *Educating Character Through the Arts* (London: Routledge, 2022).

Daphna Erdinast-Vulcan, *Between Philosophy and Literature: Bakhtin and the Question of the Subject* (Stanford: Stanford University Press, 2013).

Gary Hagberg, ed. *Fictional Characters, Real Problems: The Search for Ethical Content in Literature* (Oxford: Oxford University Press, 2016).

Nora Hämäläinen, *Literature and Moral Theory* (London: Bloomsbury, 2015).

Christopher Hamilton, 'Art and Moral Education', in *Art and Morality*, ed. J. L. Bermúdez and S. Gardner (London: Routledge, 2003) 37–55.

John Krapp, *An Aesthetics of Morality: Pedagogic Voice and Moral Dialogue in Mann, Camus, Conrad and Dostoevsky* (Columbia: South Carolina University Press, 2002).

Stephen Mulhall, 'Ethics in the Light of Wittgenstein', *Philosophical Papers* 31, no. 3 (2002): 293–321.

Martha Nussbaum, *Love's Knowledge: Essays on Philosophy and Literature* (Oxford: Oxford University Press, 1990).

Richard Posner, 'Against Ethical Criticism', *Philosophy and Literature* 21, no. 2 (1997): 1–27.

Jon Stewart, *The Unity of Content and Form in Philosophical Writing* (London: Bloomsbury, 2013).

Galen Strawson, 'Against Narrativity', *Ratio* 17, no. 4 (2004): 428–52.

INDEX

Achebe, Chinua 34, 47–9
Adamov, Arthur 174
Adamson, Jane 110, 112
Adorno, Theodor 119–20
Aesop 36
Aldama, Frederick Luis 186
Altieri, Charles 114–15, 131
Anderson, Amanda 93
Angelopoulos, Theodoros 1
Aquinas, Saint Thomas 139
Arendt, Hannah 125
Aristotle 94, 126–7, 139–42, 159–60, 162, 165
Auden, W. H. 115
Audin, Marie-Louise 173
Auerbach, Erich 95–6
Augustine, Saint 139, 163
Aurelius, Marcus 161–2
Austen, Jane 39, 197
Axeloz, Kostas 174

Bakhtin, Mikhail 33–49, 132–3
Balzac, Honoré de 172, 217, 219, 221
Barghouti, Mourid 11, 13, 23–8, 31
Bartsch, Shadi 57–60
Beauvoir, Simone de 214
Beckett, Samuel 174
Bentley, Eric 175
Berger, John 28
Bergman, Ingrid 224, 234
Bernhard, Thomas 100, 103
Blake, William 197
Blum, Lawrence 142
Bohlin, Karen 149–50
Bordas, Éric 161
Bossuet, Jacques-Bénigne 171
Braschi, Giannina 179–94
Brooks, Peter 217–18, 220–2, 231
Bruyère, Jean de la 170
Buber, Martin 91
Büchner, Georg 115
Byron, Lord George Gordon 196, 199–200, 211, 214

Caesar, Julius 57
Calderón, Pedro 169
Campbell, Thomas 214
Camus, Albert 100, 173–4, 180, 213–14
Carroll, Lewis 192
Carroll, Noël 100–1, 103, 115, 139
Casseri, Giulio 165
Cavell, Stanley 82, 91–5, 120, 128, 135, 217–18, 220–7, 231–4
Cervantes, Miguel de 133
Christian, Lynda 159, 172
Cicero 161–2, 213
Cioran, Emil 97–8
Clairmont, Claire 198–9, 211
Coetzee, J. M. 223–6
Cohn, Ruby 175
Conrad, Joseph 12, 34, 47–9, 115, 124

Dante 172, 227
d'Appollonia, Ariane Chebel 172

Das, Veena 91
Davis, Bette 223
Defoe, Daniel 133
Deleuze, Gilles 174, 191–4
Descartes, René 130, 134–5, 169–70, 175, 220
Diamond, Cora 91–2
Dickens, Charles 124, 135, 147
Diogenes 160
Dostoevsky, Fyodor 41–3, 46, 135, 217–18, 227–9, 231–2, 234
Duvignaud, Jean 174

Eisenstein, Sergei 31
Eliot, George 112–13, 115
Eliot, T. S. 121
Emerson, Ralph Waldo 128, 226
Epictetus 161
Erasmus 163–4, 167

Fanon, Franz 20–1
Faulkner, William 98
Felski, Rita 93, 96
Ferry, Luc 130–1
Fontaine, Jean de la 171
Fontaine, Joan 224
Fontanier, Pierre 157, 160
Fontenelle, Bernard de 171
Forestier, Georges 168, 173
Forster, E. M. 124
Foucault, Michel 91
Freud, Sigmund 225

Galileo 170
Gibbon, Edward 171
Gillibert, Jean 175
Gisborne, Maria 203, 206
Godwin, William 195, 197–8, 210
Goffman, Erving 174
Goya, Francisco de 179–82

Heaney, Seamus 13
Hegel, Georg Wilhelm Friedrich 106
Henriot, Jacques 174
Heraclitus 140
Homer 55, 57–8, 95–6, 126, 159
Hopkins, Gerard Manley 115
Horace 160, 162, 213
Hume, David 130, 134
Huysmans, Joris-Karl 100

James, Henry 94, 143, 217, 219, 221
James, William 109
Jansen, Cornelius 170
Johnson, Samuel 102
Josipovici, Gabriel 117–18, 120–1
Joyce, James 179, 225
Juvenal 160

Kafka, Franz 115, 120
Kant, Immanuel 34, 98, 126, 221–2, 227
Keats, John 104, 197
Kilito, Abdelfattah 12, 14, 28–31
Kincaid, Jamaica 14
Kipling, Rudyard 12
Kleist, Heinrich von 99
Kristeva, Julia 35, 49

Larkin, Philip 115, 237
Larue, Anne 173, 176
Lawrence, D. H. 124
Leavis, F. R. 102
Levinas, Emmanuel 47, 91
Lévi-Strauss, Claude 174
Lichtenberg, Georg Christoph 113
Lipman, Matthew 140, 150–1
Lispector, Clarice 100
Lorca, García 135
Lucian 160–2
Lucretius 161

Machiavelli, Niccolò 164, 167, 172
MacIntyre, Alasdair 39, 139
Mahfouz, Najib 22
Malpas, Jeff 13, 16
Marías, Javier 98, 105, 107, 110, 117
Marx, Karl 123
Merchan, Juan 71
Miller, Arthur 52–3, 64, 70, 73
Milton, John 204
Moi, Toril 93
Molino, Jean 176
Montaigne, Michel de 119, 163, 166
Montesquieu, Charles de 171
Mozart, Wolfgang Amadeus 131
Munro, Alice 77–96, 180
Murdoch, Iris 82, 91–2, 94, 110, 116, 140–1, 180

Nehamas, Alexander 179–82, 185
Nietzsche, Friedrich 101, 103–4, 128, 130–1, 183, 220–2, 227
Nussbaum, Martha 1, 5, 92, 100–1, 104, 115, 139, 141–5, 148–9, 153, 185

Octavian (Caesar Augustus) 57, 59–60, 162
Ortelius 164
Orwell, George 124
Oscanyan, Frederick S. 151

Palmer, Frank 100, 103–4, 115
Parfit, Derek 128
Parmenides 140
Pascal, Blaise 109
Paul, Saint 163
Pearce, Howard 174, 177
Peirce, Charles Sanders 62–3, 72–3
Peterson, Andrew 146
Petrarch, Francesco 201–2
Petronius 160, 162, 166
Pirandello, Luigi 175
Plato 104, 139–40, 159–60, 165, 184, 190
Posner, Richard 2, 102, 148
Proust, Marcel 113–14
Pushkin, Alexander 237

Rancière, Jacques 26
Ricks, Christoper 104–5, 116
Ricoeur, Paul 39
Robinson, Jenefer 100, 115
Rochefoucauld, François de la 170
Rorty, Richard 129
Russell, Jeffrey Burton 55, 61–3
Ryle, Gilbert 148

Sagan, Carl 70
Said, Edward 12
Salisbury, John of 163, 166
Sartre, Jean-Paul 174, 214
Schellekens, Elisabeth 99
Schubert, Franz 131
Schumann, Robert 131
Schwatzenberg, Roger-Gérard 172
Seneca 161–3, 167
Shakespeare, William 82, 95, 100, 103–4, 113–15, 135, 165–8, 174
Sharp, Ann Margaret 151
Shelley, Mary 180, 195–216
Shelley, Percy Bysshe 196, 198–9, 208
Shelley, Percy Florence 198, 206
Shelley, Timothy 199
Shklovsky, Victor 18, 46
Smith, Adam 130, 134
Socrates 56, 58, 131
Sophocles 149, 193
Splitter, Laurance 152
Stanwyck, Barbara 224
Stavans, Ilan 194
Steiner, George 217–18
Stevens, Wallace 131–2
Suetonius 162

Svevo, Italo 115

Tarkovsky, Andrei 31–2, 217, 234–8
Terekhova, Maria 235
Tolstoy, Leo 113–14, 217
Trilling, Lionel 102
Trump, Donald 71–3

Van Delft, Louis 159, 176–7
Vega, Lope de 169
Vergil, Virgil 56–60, 201–2, 213

Wagner, Richard 131
Warwick, Susan 84
Wattar, Tahir 11, 13, 18–23
Westbroo, Harriet 198
Wharton, Edith 100
Whyte, David 1
Williams, Edward 199
Williams, Jane 199
Williams, Rowan 228–9, 231–2, 234
Wittgenstein, Ludwig 93–4, 108, 130, 135, 221
Wollstonecraft, Mary 195, 197
Woodrow, Steven 71
Woolf, Virginia 11, 13–18, 111, 116
Wordsworth, William 197

Zwinger, Theodor 164